Office XP For Dummies®

Cheat Sheet

KT-230-703

Microsoft Word Standard and Formatting toolbars

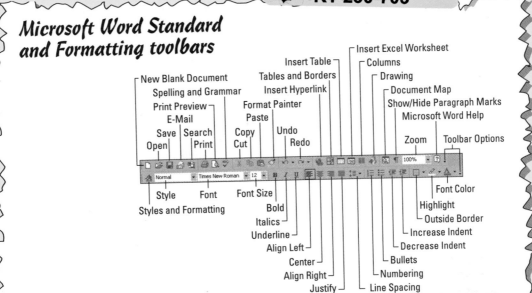

New Blank Document
Spelling and Grammar
Print Preview
E-Mail
Save
Open
Search
Print
Copy
Cut
Undo
Redo
Format Painter
Paste
Insert Hyperlink
Insert Table
Tables and Borders
Insert Excel Worksheet
Columns
Drawing
Document Map
Show/Hide Paragraph Marks
Microsoft Word Help
Zoom
Toolbar Options

Style
Styles and Formatting
Font
Font Size
Bold
Italics
Underline
Align Left
Center
Align Right
Justify
Line Spacing
Numbering
Bullets
Decrease Indent
Increase Indent
Outside Border
Highlight
Font Color

Microsoft Excel Standard and Formatting toolbars

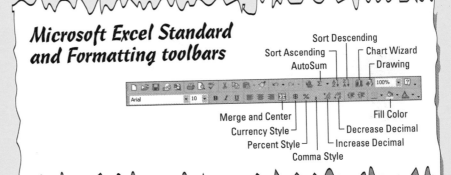

Sort Descending
Sort Ascending
AutoSum
Chart Wizard
Drawing
Merge and Center
Currency Style
Percent Style
Comma Style
Increase Decimal
Decrease Decimal
Fill Color

Microsoft PowerPoint Standard and Formatting toolbars

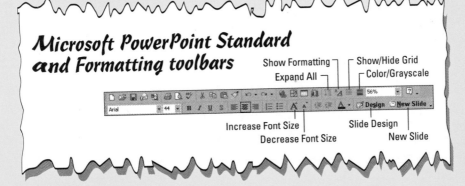

Show Formatting
Expand All
Show/Hide Grid
Color/Grayscale
Increase Font Size
Decrease Font Size
Slide Design
New Slide

For Dummies: Bestselling Book Series for Beginners

Office XP For Dummies®

Cheat Sheet

Microsoft Office XP Mouse Button Functions

Mouse Button Used	Action	Purpose
Left mouse button	Click	Moves the cursor, highlights an object, pulls down a menu, or chooses a menu command
Left mouse button	Double-click	Highlights a word or edits an embedded object
Left mouse button	Triple-click	Highlights a paragraph
Left mouse button	Drag	Moves an object, resizes an object, highlights text, or highlights multiple objects
Wheel mouse button	Click	Automatically scrolls a document
Right mouse button	Click	Displays a shortcut pop-up menu

Microsoft Office XP Shortcut Keys

Function	Keystroke
Copy	Ctrl+C
Cut	Ctrl+X
Find	Ctrl+F
Go To	Ctrl+G
Help	F1
Hyperlink	Ctrl+K
New	Ctrl+N
Open	Ctrl+O
Paste	Ctrl+V
Print	Ctrl+P
Redo	Ctrl+Y
Replace	Ctrl+H
Save	Ctrl+S
Select All	Ctrl+A
Spell Check	F7
Undo	Ctrl+Z

Online Resources for Microsoft Office XP

Microsoft Internet Sites	URL Addresses
World Wide Web site	http://www.microsoft.com
FTP site	ftp://ftp.microsoft.com

Microsoft Newsgroups

microsoft.public.access

microsoft.public.excel

microsoft.public.frontpage

microsoft.public.office

microsoft.public.outlook.general

microsoft.public.powerpoint

microsoft.public.word

For Dummies: Bestselling Book Series for Beginners

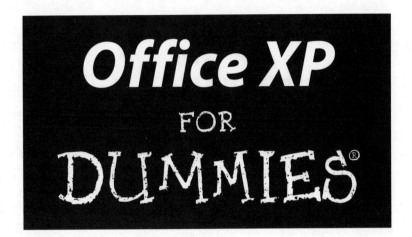

Office XP FOR DUMMIES®

by Wallace Wang

Wiley Publishing, Inc.

Office XP For Dummies®

Published by
Wiley Publishing, Inc.
909 Third Avenue
New York, NY 10022
www.wiley.com

Copyright © 2001 Wiley Publishing, Inc., Indianapolis, Indiana

Published simultaneously in Canada

For general information on our other products and services or to obtain technical support, please contact our Customer Care Department within the U.S. at 800-762-2974, outside the U.S. at 317-572-3993, or fax 317-572-4002.

Wiley also publishes its books in a variety of electronic formats. Some content that appears in print may not be available in electronic books.

Library of Congress Cataloging-in-Publication Data:

Library of Congress Control Number: 2001086300

ISBN: 0-7645-0830-X

Manufactured in the United States of America

10 9 8 7 6 5

1B/SY/QY/QS/IN

About the Author

The author is a carbon-based life-form who currently divides his time between writing computer books and performing stand-up comedy. At the time of this writing, he's trying to decide how to inject humor into this paragraph while being politically correct (to avoid offending people who are quick to anger at the mention of any idea that contradicts their way of thinking, even if it happens to be the truth).

So rather than digress into specifics, the author will continue referring to himself in the third person as a literary device to distance himself from his actual writing. By using this tactic, he hopes to placate the easily offended (although people who are easily offended are often, in the author's opinion, not worth talking to in the first place). Hey — just kidding around, okay? Sheesh.

Still, the About the Author page should contain at least some relevant details about the author's life to satisfy the curiosity of the general public, who may be wondering about the technical qualifications of the mysterious person whose name appears on the front of the book.

So to satisfy the curiosity of those who have actually managed to read this far: The author has written and co-written several computer books, including *Visual Basic For Dummies, Beginning Programming For Dummies,* and the previous editions of *Microsoft Office For Dummies.* He has has also written numerous magazine articles in his lifetime, including a monthly column for *Boardwatch Magazine.*

In addition to his previous history of technical writing, the author has also been an avid computer user since the early days of MS-DOS 1.25, 2.0, 3.3, 4.01, 5.0, 6.0, Windows 3.1, 95, 98, Millennium Edition, and 2000. When not writing computer books or performing stand-up comedy, the author tries (often unsuccessfully) to keep his Windows operating system from crashing on a daily basis.

Dedication

This book is dedicated to a variety of people, including the following:

All the long-suffering victims forced to learn the arcane features of Microsoft Office, which seem to change with every version, not always for the best. Take heart. You're not stupid — it's the people who write, sell, and encourage the clumsy and complicated computer programs on the market who are the really stupid ones.

All the friendly folks at the Riviera Comedy Club, located at the Riviera Hotel & Casino (www.theriviera.com) in Las Vegas: Steve Schirripa (who appears in HBO's hit show, "The Sopranos"), Don Learned, Bob Zany (www.bobzany.com), Gerry Bednob, Bruce Clark, Tony Vicich, and Kip Addotta. Another big round of thanks go to the people who make the Riviera Comedy Club one of the best places to work: Lynn Snyder, the comedy club manager, and Patricia Weber, the Entertainment Supervisor.

Patrick DeGuire also deserves thanks, not because he helped with this book (he didn't) but because he helped me form Top Bananas Entertainment (www.topbananas.com) — our company devoted to providing clean, quality stand-up comedy for the wonderful people in San Diego. Additional thanks must also go to Chris (the Zooman) Clobber, Michael Elizondo, and Leo (the man, the myth, the legend) Fontaine just because they like seeing their names in print for no apparent reason.

Continuing the theme of thanking people who had nothing to do with this book, the author would also like to dedicate this book to LeStat's, the best little coffeehouse in San Diego, for providing a warm, friendly environment to practice stand-up comedy in the safety and comfort of intelligent people who haven't drowned their inhibitions away in alcohol.

Final thanks go to Cassandra (my wife), Jordan (my son) and Bo, Scraps, Tasha, and Nuit (our cats) for making my life more interesting by the minute.

Author's Acknowledgments

Matt Wagner and Bill Gladstone at Waterside Productions deserve special acknowledgement because if it wasn't for their work, I might never have been hired to write this book and you would be reading some other author's acknowledgements and dedication. These two guys are the best agents an author could hope for, so they deserve all the 15 percent of the book royalties that they get.

Some other people who deserve thanks include Paul Levesque, Rev Mengle (for being an avid sports fan), and the rest of the happy gang of editors, managers, and workers who make Hungry Minds, Inc. the best publisher to work for because they're the complete opposite of their competition across town.

Additional thanks go to Sharon Moxon for making sure that everything in this book is accurate.

A final note of thanks go to anyone who has actually read the About the Author, Dedication, and Author's Acknowledgements page because those pages usually contain useless information that nobody except the author and his closest friends even care about. Thanks for reading this — and say a prayer for all the trees that sacrificed their pulp to allow authors (such as myself) the indulgence to print paragraphs such as this.

Publisher's Acknowledgments

We're proud of this book; please send us your comments through our online registration form located at www.dummies.com/register/.

Some of the people who helped bring this book to market include the following:

Acquisitions, Editorial, and Media Development

Project Editor: Paul Levesque

Acquisitions Editor: Carol Sheehan

Sr. Copy Editor: Barry Childs-Helton

Technical Editor: Sharon Moxon

Editorial Manager: Leah Cameron

Media Development Manager: Laura Carpenter

Media Development Supervisor: Richard Graves

Editorial Assistant: Amanda Foxworth

Production

Project Coordinator: Jennifer Bingham

Layout and Graphics: Gabriele McCann, Kristin Pickett, Brent Savage, Jacque Schneider, Ron Terry, Jeremey Unger, Erin Zeltener

Proofreaders: John Greenough, TECHBOOKS Production Services

Indexer: TECHBOOKS Production Services

Special Help
Teresa Artman, Rebecca Huehls, Amy Pettinella

Publishing and Editorial for Technology Dummies
Richard Swadley, Vice President and Executive Group Publisher
Mary C. Corder, Editorial Director
Andy Cummings, Vice President and Publisher

Publishing for Consumer Dummies
Diane Graves Steele, Vice President and Publisher
Joyce Pepple, Acquisitions Director

Composition Services
Gerry Fahey, Vice President of Production Services
Debbie Stailey, Director of Composition Services

Contents at a Glance

Cartoons at a Glance

By Rich Tennant

page 9

"Did you click the 'HELP' menu bar recently? Mr. Gates is here and he wants to know if everything's alright."

page 265

page 343

page 125

page 223

"See? I created a little felon figure that runs around our Web site hiding behind banner ads. On the last page, our logo puts him in a non-lethal choke hold and brings him back to the home page."

page 313

page 177

page 45

Cartoon Information:
Fax: 978-546-7747
E-Mail: richtennant@the5thwave.com
World Wide Web: www.the5thwave.com

Table of Contents

· ·

Introduction

• •

Microsoft Office XP consists of several programs: a word processor (Word), a spreadsheet program (Excel), a presentation graphics program (PowerPoint), a personal information organizer (Outlook), and a database program (Access). Depending on the version of Microsoft Office XP you have, you may also have bonus programs that include a Web page design and management program (FrontPage).

Although every program shares similar commands and menus to make them all easier to use, you may still find the task of figuring out how to use each program a bit daunting. That's why *Microsoft Office XP For Dummies* gently explains the basics for using each program so you can get started using them right away.

After reading *Microsoft Office XP For Dummies,* you can get more specific information about the programs by reading *Word 2002 For Dummies,* by Dan Gookin; *Excel 2002 For Dummies,* by Greg Harvey; *Access 2002 For Dummies,* by John Kaufeld; *PowerPoint 2002 For Dummies,* by Doug Lowe; *Outlook 2002 For Dummies,* by Bill Dyszel; and *FrontPage 2002 For Dummies,* by Asha Dornfest; all are published by Hungry Minds, Inc.

Who Should Buy This Book

Everyone should buy this book because this sentence says that you should, and you should believe everything you read. But you should especially buy this book if you have any of the following versions of Microsoft Office XP:

- *Standard Edition:* Contains Microsoft Word, Excel, Outlook, and PowerPoint.

- *Small Business Edition:* Contains Microsoft Word, Excel, Outlook, Publisher, and Small Business Edition Tools.

- *Professional Edition:* Contains Microsoft Word, Excel, Outlook, FrontPage, Access, and PowerPoint.

If you have any of these editions of Microsoft Office XP lurking on your hard drive like a computer virus that you can't get rid of, then you can use this book to help you figure out how to get started using Microsoft Office XP today.

This book provides a foundation that you can put to work immediately and then build on later by browsing through the other books in the popular *For Dummies* series.

How This Book Is Organized

This book uses the time-tested method of binding pages and gluing them on one side to form a book. To help you find what you need quickly, this book is divided into eight parts. Each part covers a certain topic about using Microsoft Office XP. Whenever you need help, just flip through this book, find the part that covers the topic you're looking for, and then toss this book aside and get back to work.

Part I: Getting to Know Microsoft Office XP

Even though Microsoft Office XP looks like a bunch of unrelated programs thrown together by Microsoft, it is actually a bunch of unrelated programs that have been tortured over the years into working together.

All the Microsoft Office XP programs provide similar menus, icons, and keystroke commands, so when you know how to use one program, you'll be able to quickly figure out how to use another Office XP program.

Part II: Working with Word

Microsoft Word is the most popular word processor on the face of the earth. Although you can use Word just to write letters, proposals, or apologies, you can also use Word to create fancier documents, such as newsletters that can include graphics and divide text into multiple columns.

If you can't type, don't like to write, or flunked spelling in second grade, you may be glad to know that you can use Word to turn your $2,000 computer into your personal secretary. With the Word spell checker, grammar checker, outliner, and foreign language translator, you can turn your random thoughts into coherent words and sentences that even your boss can understand.

Part III: Playing the Numbers Game with Excel

This part shows you how to design your very own spreadsheets by using Microsoft Excel. You discover what the heck a spreadsheet is, how you can plop numbers and labels into it, how to create your own formulas so that Excel calculates new results automatically, and how to format the whole thing to make it look pleasing to the eye.

After you get the basics of spreadsheet creation, the next step is to convert your raw data into eye-popping graphs, charts, and other colorful images that can amuse everyone from high-powered CEOs of Fortune 500 companies to children roaming around in a day-care center.

Part IV: Making Presentations with PowerPoint

If Word helps you look good in print and Excel helps you convert numbers into attractive charts, PowerPoint can help you create slide shows, overhead transparencies, and on-screen computer presentations that either enhance your information or hide the fact that you don't have the slightest idea what you're talking about in the first place.

Any time you need to make a presentation, let PowerPoint help you develop a dynamic presentation that includes visuals (which can be 35mm slides, overhead transparencies, or screen images), notes (to help you rehearse your presentation), and handouts (to give your audience something to look at instead of staring at you).

Part V: Getting Organized with Outlook

Everyone seems busy all the time (even when doing absolutely nothing but waiting until it's time to go home). In today's fast-moving world where seconds count, you may want to keep track of your tasks, appointments, and schedule so you can effectively manage your time while your peers wander aimlessly through the corporate landscape.

To help you accomplish this task, Microsoft Office XP includes Outlook, a program that combines the features of an appointment book, calendar, and to-do list in one screen. By managing your time with Outlook, you can plan your projects, ration out your time, and effectively squeeze every last productive second out of each day. Unless, of course, you don't turn on your computer that day.

Besides organizing your appointments and tasks, Outlook can also organize all the e-mail that may flood you every day. From within Outlook, you can write, reply to, send, and receive e-mail to and from your friends, whether they're down the hall from you or on another continent.

Part VI: Storing Stuff in Access

If you have the Professional edition of Microsoft Office XP, you have a bonus program called Access. For those of you who like official definitions, Access is a relational database that lets you store and retrieve data, design reports, and actually create your own programs. If you don't have Access in your edition of Microsoft Office XP, you can always buy Access separately and install it on your computer so that this part of the book can be useful to you.

You may find Access handy for saving mailing lists as well as for storing more esoteric information, such as part numbers, Internet addresses, or credit card numbers. If you need to save and retrieve information at a later date, use Access to help you do it quickly and easily.

Part VII: Making Web Pages with FrontPage

Owners of the Professional edition of Microsoft Office XP have an additional bonus programs in the form of FrontPage. With FrontPage, you can create or edit Web pages in much finer detail and with greater control than you can by using Word.

If you ever wanted to create a Web site for personal or business use, FrontPage can simplify the technical details so you can concentrate on making your Web pages look as colorful and exciting as your imagination can create.

Part VIII: The Part of Tens

For those people who just want to find keyboard shortcuts for accessing commonly used commands and tips for working more efficiently with Microsoft Office XP (so they can take the rest of the day off), this part of the book provides common keystrokes for using all the Microsoft programs.

In addition, you can find tips for making Microsoft Office XP seem a lot easier than the incomprehensible manuals may lead you to believe. Just remember: If something in Microsoft Office XP doesn't make sense or confuses you, it's not your fault; it's Microsoft's fault, so feel free to blame the millionaire programmers in Redmond for failing to anticipate your needs and not selling you a more intuitive program.

How to Use This Book

You can use this book as a reference, a tutorial, or a weapon (depending on how hard you throw it at somebody). Unlike novels, this book isn't designed for someone to read from cover to cover (although you could if you wanted). Instead, just browse through the parts that interest you and ignore the rest.

If you plan to take full advantage of Microsoft Office XP, read Part I first so you can acquaint yourself with the more common Office XP features. The other parts of this book are here for your reference and amusement. Although you may not care about making presentations with PowerPoint at first, one day you may want to play around with it just to see what it can do. To your surprise, certain programs you thought you would never use may turn out to be more useful than you ever imagined. Then again, the programs may really turn out to be useless after all, but you'll never find out until you try them.

Foolish assumptions

First of all, you should already have Microsoft Office XP installed on your computer. You should also be running Microsoft Windows 95/98/Me/ NT/2000. If you don't feel comfortable with Windows 95/98/Me, you may want to buy *Windows 95 For Dummies; Windows 98 For Dummies;* or *Windows Millennium Edition For Dummies;* all by Andy Rathbone, published by IDG Books Worldwide, Inc. For more information regarding Windows NT/2000, pick up a copy of *Windows NT 4 For Dummies* or *Windows 2000 Professional For Dummies,* by Andy Rathbone and Sharon Crawford, also published by IDG Books Worldwide, Inc.

Conventions

To get the most out of the information presented in this book, you need to understand the following:

- ✔ The *mouse cursor* or *pointer* appears either as an arrow or as an I-beam pointer (depending on the program you happen to be using at the time). Any time you lose track of the mouse cursor, start moving the mouse around until you see something flashing across your screen. Chances are that what you're seeing is the mouse cursor.

- ✔ *Clicking* refers to pressing the left mouse button once and then letting go. Clicking is how you activate buttons on the toolbar and choose commands from pull-down menus.

✔ *Double-clicking* refers to pressing the left mouse button twice in rapid succession. Double-clicking typically activates a command.

✔ *Dragging* refers to moving the mouse pointer while holding down the left mouse button. To drag an object, select the item by clicking it and then hold the left mouse button and move the item in the desired direction. When you release the mouse button, Windows places the item where you want.

✔ *Right-clicking* means clicking the button on the right side of the mouse. (Some mice have three buttons, so ignore the middle button for now.) Right-clicking usually displays a pop-up menu on the screen.

Note: If you're left-handed and you have changed your mouse settings so that you use your left hand to operate the mouse, *clicking* means pressing the right mouse button, and *right-clicking* means pressing the left mouse button.

Icons used in this book

Icons highlight useful tips, important information to remember, or technical explanations that you can skip if you want. Keep an eye open for the following icons throughout the book:

This icon highlights pieces of information that can be helpful (as long as you remember them, of course).

This icon marks certain steps or procedures that can make your life a whole lot easier when using Microsoft Office XP.

Look out! This icon tells you how to avoid trouble before it starts.

This icon highlights information that's absolutely useless to know for operating Microsoft Office XP but could be interesting to impress your trivia buddies.

Keyboard shortcuts

Microsoft Office XP gives you two ways to choose commands:

✔ Clicking the mouse on a button or menu command

✔ Pressing a keystroke combination, such as Ctrl+S (which means that you hold down the Ctrl key, tap the S key, and then release both keys at the same time)

Most keyboard shortcuts involve holding down the Ctrl or Alt key (typically located to the left and right of the spacebar on your keyboard) in combination with one of the function keys (the keys labeled F1, F2, F3, and so on) or a letter key (A, B, C, and so on).

Microsoft Office XP also displays keyboard shortcuts on its pull-down menus. Whenever you see an underlined letter in a menu title such as File or Edit, you can pull down that menu by pressing Alt followed by the underlined letter. So if you want to pull down the File menu, press Alt+F.

After you display a pull-down menu, Office XP underlines a single letter in every command, such as New in the File menu. To choose a command displayed on a pull-down menu, just type the underlined letter. If you want to choose the New command on the File menu, first pull down the File menu by pressing Alt+F and then type N (because the letter N is underlined in the New command).

You can use whichever method you prefer, just as long as you know what you're doing. Some people swear by the mouse, some swear by the keyboard, and still others just swear at the computer.

Getting Started

By now, you're probably anxious to try out Microsoft Office XP. Turn on your computer and get ready to jump miles ahead of the competition by having the foresight to use the world's most powerful and dominant programs, bundled together in Microsoft Office XP.

Part I
Getting to Know Microsoft Office XP

The 5th Wave   By Rich Tennant

Gee, Richard, you'll have to show me where on the toolbar you found an icon labeled "Overkill".

In this part . . .

At first glance, Microsoft Office XP may seem a compli-cated beast that gobbles up megabytes of hard drive space and offers enough features to overwhelm even the most battle-hardened veteran of the personal computer wars. But after you get over your initial impression (or fear) of Office XP, you can understand (and even admire) the elegant madness behind Office XP's massive bulk.

Despite the fact that Microsoft Office XP contains more commands than any sane person could ever possibly use, Office XP can be conquered. To guide you through the multitude of commands you may need to get your work done, Office XP provides the Office Assistant to answer your questions and provide support.

Want to know how to print mailing labels, save an Excel file in a Lotus 1-2-3 file format, or design your own newsletter in Word? Just ask the friendly Office Assistant. Within seconds, the Office Assistant displays a list of topics that (hopefully) answer your question and get you back to doing productive work.

Besides showing you how to get help within Microsoft Office XP, this part of the book also explains how to get the various programs of Office XP started in the first place. After you start using Office XP, you'll quickly under-stand the basic keystroke and menu commands that all Office XP programs share. That way when you learn how to use one Office XP program, you can quickly learn and use any other Office XP program with a minimum of retraining and hassle and join the ranks of the many happy people already using Microsoft Office XP to get their work done.

Chapter 1

Starting Microsoft Office XP

- -

- -

As usual, the new version of Microsoft Office consists of several programs — so this chapter provides basic instructions to help you start any program and back out of it again. After all, if you can't figure out how to start Microsoft Office XP, the rest of the book might as well be a hefty paperweight.

To give you some freedom of choice (well, okay, a reasonable facsimile thereof), Microsoft offers multiple ways to start any Microsoft Office XP program. You can choose the way you like best. After you find your favorite way to run a Microsoft Office XP program, you can ignore all the other methods if you want. Remember, you're the one in control, not your computer, and not the monster software. They have to do what you tell them to do.

Starting Microsoft Office XP with the Start Button

Windows provides a handy Start button that you can click at any time when you want to choose a program to run. So naturally, one way to start any Microsoft Office XP program is to choose the program after you click the Start button. Just to keep you amused, Microsoft Office XP provides two ways to load an Office XP program:

- ✔ Click the Start button on the taskbar, choose Programs, and then choose the specific program (such as Word) that you want to load.

- ✔ Click the Start button on the taskbar and choose New Office Document or Open Office Document. Then you get to choose what *kind* of document, which starts the program automatically.

Using the Programs pop-up menu

If you don't mind wading through the (sometimes) cluttered appearance of the Programs pop-up menu, you can load and run any Microsoft Office XP program by following these steps:

1. **Click the Start button on the taskbar.**

   A pop-up menu appears.

2. **Choose Programs.**

   The Programs menu appears, as shown in Figure 1-1.

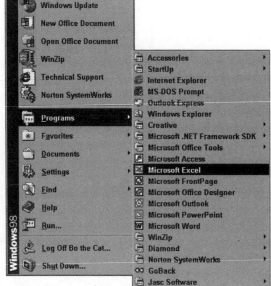

Figure 1-1:
The
Programs
pop-up
menu lists
all the
programs
available
on your
computer.

3. **Click the program that you want to use, such as Microsoft Word or Microsoft PowerPoint.**

   The program you choose appears, ready for you to create a new file or open an existing one.

Clicking New Office Document on the taskbar

If your Programs pop-up menu contains so many programs that you can't easily find the one you want, here's a faster way of loading a Microsoft Office XP program:

1. **Click the Start button on the taskbar.**

   A pop-up menu appears.

2. **Click New Office Document.**

   The New Office Document dialog box appears (as shown in Figure 1-2); you can use it to choose the program you want.

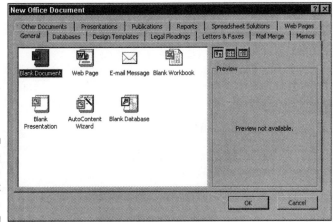

Figure 1-2:
New Office
Document
dialog box.

3. **Click the General tab.**

   If you want to create a specific type of Microsoft Office XP file (such as a fax cover sheet or invoice), click a different tab in this step, such as the Letters & Faxes tab or the Spreadsheet Solutions tab.

4. **Click the type of document that you want to create.**

   If you want to create a new Access database, choose Blank Database. If you want to create a new Word document, choose Blank Document. Besides creating new files, you can also click a Wizard or template icon. A Wizard icon guides you, step by step, into creating a new file. A template provides a preformatted file that you can edit. That way, you don't have to waste time formatting the file yourself.

   You can skip Step 5 if you double-click the file you want to create during Step 4.

5. **Click OK.**

   Your chosen program appears, ready for you to start typing and creating valuable information that you can store on your computer.

Opening an Existing File

Rather than create a brand-new file from scratch, you'll probably spend more time opening and editing existing files. Again, Microsoft Office XP bombards you with different ways to open an existing file. Choose the one that fits your working style.

Clicking Open Office Document on the taskbar

The Windows taskbar provides the quickest way to open an existing Microsoft Office XP file. Just follow these simple steps:

1. **Click the Start button on the taskbar.**

   A pop-up menu appears.

2. **Click Open Office Document.**

   The Open Office Document dialog box appears.

3. **Click the file that you want to open.**

   If the file you want to open is buried in another folder, you may have to open that particular folder by clicking an icon that appears in the Look In box, such as My Documents or Desktop.

   You can skip Step 4 if you double-click the file you want to open during Step 3.

4. **Click Open.**

   Your chosen file appears, ready for you to start viewing and editing the information.

Double-clicking in Windows Explorer

Another way to start a Microsoft Office XP program is to click (or double-click) the Microsoft Office XP file that you want to open and edit. To do that, follow these steps:

1. **Click the Start button on the taskbar.**

   A pop-up menu appears.

2. **Start Windows Explorer.**

   - In Windows 95/98, choose Windows Explorer.

   - In Windows Me/2000, choose Accessories⇨Windows Explorer.

   The Windows Explorer program appears.

3. **Locate the document that you want to open.**

   You may have to double-click a folder (such as My Documents) to find the document you're looking for.

4. **Double-click the icon that represents the document that you want to open.**

   Microsoft Office XP opens your chosen document.

Taking a Shortcut

Rather than wade through pop-up menus or the less-than-intuitive Windows Explorer, just place a shortcut to your favorite Microsoft Office XP program directly on your Windows desktop. That way, you can just double-click your shortcut and run the program right away.

A *desktop shortcut* is nothing more than an icon that represents a specific file. This file can be an actual program (such as Microsoft Word) or a file created by another program (such as your résumé written in Word). Shortcuts appear on your Windows desktop for easy access.

To place a shortcut to your favorite Microsoft Office XP program on the Windows desktop, follow these steps:

1. **Close or minimize any programs you have running so you can see the Windows desktop.**

2. **Right-click the mouse.**

   A pop-up menu appears.

3. **Choose New⇨Shortcut.**

   A Create Shortcut dialog box appears, as shown in Figure 1-3.

4. **Click the Browse button.**

   A Browse dialog box appears.

5. **Locate the Microsoft Office XP program that you want to place on your Windows desktop.**

   For example, if you want to put a shortcut to Excel on the Windows desktop, right-click the Excel icon. By default, Microsoft Office XP stores its program files in the C:\Program Files\Microsoft Office\Office folder.

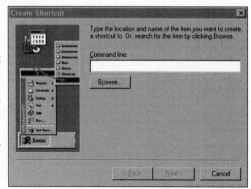

Figure 1-3:
You can use
the Create
Shortcut
dialog box
to place an
icon of your
favorite
program
right on your
Windows
desktop.

To help you decipher the cryptic names Microsoft gives its programs, here's a list you can refer to:

Program	Icon name in the Browse dialog box
Access	Msaccess
Excel	Excel
FrontPage	Frontpg
Outlook	Outlook
PowerPoint	Powerpnt
Word	Winword

6. **Click the program icon you want, such as Frontpg or Powerpnt, and click Open.**

   The Create Shortcut dialog box appears again.

7. **Click Next.**

   The Create Shortcut dialog box asks you for a descriptive name for your desktop icon. If you don't type a name, Windows will use the program icon name by default, such as Msaccess or Winword.

8. **Type a descriptive name for your program, such as Microsoft Word or FrontPage, and click Finish.**

   The Windows desktop appears with your chosen shortcut on the desktop. Shortcuts are easy to spot because they have a little black-and-white arrow in the lower-left corner of the icon.

9. **Double-click your shortcut to run the program.**

If you want to delete a shortcut icon from your desktop, right-click it and choose Delete from the pop-up menu.

Exiting Microsoft Office XP

No matter how much you may like Microsoft Office XP, eventually you have to stop using it so you can go to sleep. Microsoft Office XP provides different ways to exit.

- ✔ If you want to close the current document but still keep the program running, choose File➪Close.

- ✔ If you want to exit the program completely, choose File➪Exit or click the Close box of the program window. (The *Close box* is a little gray box with an X in it, which appears in the upper right-hand corner of a program window.)

If you made any changes since the last time you saved your file, and you try to exit, Microsoft Office XP asks whether you want to save the changes and offers you the following options: Yes, No, or Cancel.

- ✔ Click Yes to save your file.

- ✔ Click No if you don't want to save any recent changes.

- ✔ Click Cancel (or press the Esc key on your keyboard) if you suddenly don't want to exit after all.

The most drastic way to exit from Microsoft Office XP is to turn your computer off. But don't do this! If you turn off your computer without exiting from a Microsoft Office XP program first, you may lose your data. Even worse, if you turn off your computer before letting Windows 95/98/Me/NT/2000 shut itself down, your computer may erase or wreck other files on your hard disk as well.

In case you forget how to shut down Windows 95/98/Me/NT/2000 properly, click the Start button on the Windows taskbar and choose Shut Down. When the Shut Down Windows dialog box appears, click the Shut down option button or choose Shut Down from the list box and then click OK.

For more information about using Windows, pick up a copy *Windows 95 For Dummies, Windows 98 For Dummies, or Windows Me For Dummies* all by Andy Rathbone (published by Hungry Minds, Inc.). For more information regarding Windows NT/2000, pick up a copy of *Windows NT 4 For Dummies* or *Windows 2000 Professional For Dummies,* by Andy Rathbone and Sharon Crawford (also published by Hungry Minds, Inc.).

Chapter 2

Common Office XP Menu and Keystroke Commands

In This Chapter

▶ Using your menus

▶ Displaying toolbars

▶ Working with multiple windows

▶ Using the Office Clipboard

*T*o help you figure out and use the various programs in Microsoft Office XP, all the programs share common menu and keystroke commands. So after you figure out how to use one program of Microsoft Office XP, you should (theoretically) have little trouble figuring out how to use any of the other Microsoft Office XP programs.

Customizing Your Menus

Microsoft Office XP provides three ways to display menu commands on the screen, as shown in Figures 2-1, 2-2, and 2-3. You can

✔ Display every command possible.

✔ Hide the less-frequently-used commands from view (but you can still display the more advanced commands, such as using an auditing feature in Excel, by clicking the downward-pointing arrows at the bottom of the menu).

✔ Hide the less-frequently-used commands from view (but automatically display them as shaded after a few seconds).

Hiding the more-advanced commands from view can be disconcerting to some people; others prefer a cleaner screen, or feel that displaying every possible command on a menu is intimidating. Try experimenting with the way Office XP displays your menus; you can customize the programs to work the way you like best.

To change the way menus work in Microsoft Office XP, follow these steps:

1. **Choose View➪Toolbars➪Customize.**

   A Customize dialog box appears, as shown in Figure 2-4.

2. **Click the Options tab.**

3. **Click or clear one of the following check boxes:**

   • **Always show full menus:** If checked, this option makes the drop-down menus display every possible command (refer to Figure 2-1).

   • **Show full menus after a short delay:** If checked, this option waits a few seconds before showing the less-frequently used commands on a menu (refer to Figure 2-3).

4. **Click Close.**

Figure 2-1:
Menus can display all commands at all times.

Figure 2-2:
Menus can hide infrequently used commands until you tell Office XP to make them visible again.

When you define the way you want your menus to work, it affects the way menus work in *all* Microsoft Office XP programs.

Figure 2-3:
Menus can hide infrequently used commands for a short period of time and then display them again automatically.

Figure 2-4:
The Customize dialog box allows you to modify the way drop-down menus behave in a Microsoft Office XP program.

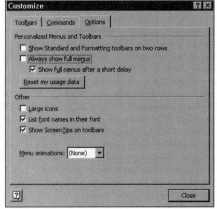

Viewing Your Toolbars

Toolbars contain icons that represent the most commonly used commands. The theory is that it's easier to click a toolbar icon to choose a command than it is to dig through a drop-down menu or press an obscure keystroke combination, such as Ctrl+Shift+D, just to get something done.

Although every Microsoft Office XP displays different toolbar icons, they all work in similar ways and share icons that represent universal commands, such as Save or Print. Naturally, Microsoft Office XP lets you choose how to view your toolbars, where to place them on the screen, and even which icons you want to view.

Smashing (or stacking) the Standard and Formatting toolbars

The two most common toolbars in Microsoft Office XP are the Standard and Formatting toolbars. The Standard toolbar contains icons representing universal commands, such as Save, Cut, or Paste. The Formatting toolbar contains icons representing text-modifying commands, such as changing the font, font size, or underlining.

To save space, Microsoft Office XP can smash both the Standard and Formatting toolbars together as one toolbar. Although this may tuck the toolbars out of the way, smashing two toolbars into one limits the number of icons each toolbar can display. Figure 2-5 shows the Standard and Formatting toolbars smashed together as a single toolbar. Figure 2-6 shows the Standard and Formatting toolbars stacked one on top of the other.

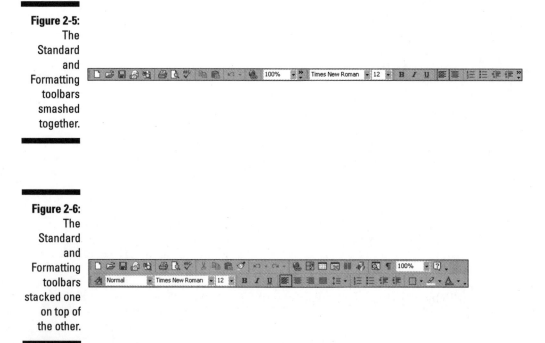

Figure 2-5:
The Standard and Formatting toolbars smashed together.

Figure 2-6:
The Standard and Formatting toolbars stacked one on top of the other.

To combine or stack the Standard and Formatting toolbars, do the following:

1. **Choose View⇨Toolbars⇨Customize.**

   A Customize dialog box appears (refer to Figure 2-4).

2. **Click the Options tab.**

3. **Click or clear the Show Standard and Formatting Toolbars on two rows check box.**

4. **Click Close.**

If you combine the Standard and Formatting toolbars to share one row, you have to click the Toolbar Options button. This displays a drop-down menu that contains any toolbar icons that are not displayed on the toolbar, as shown in Figure 2-7.

Figure 2-7:
When the Standard and Formatting toolbars are smashed together, you have to click the Toolbar Options button to see the rest of the icons.

Toolbar Options button

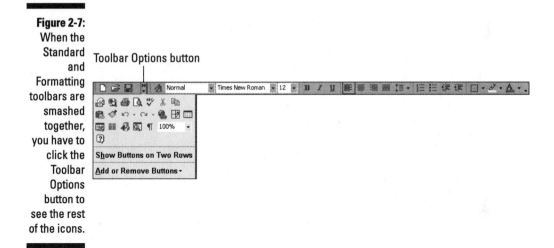

Hiding and displaying toolbars

Another way to use toolbars is to hide them from view or make them display additional toolbars that make available the commands you use most often. For example, if you find yourself creating or editing Web pages frequently using Microsoft Office XP, you may want to display the Web toolbar within Word. That way, all your commands for editing (or creating) Web pages are only one click away.

To hide or display a toolbar, do the following:

1. **Choose View➪Toolbars.**

   The Toolbars drop-down menu appears, as shown in Figure 2-8. Check marks appear next to those toolbars currently displayed.

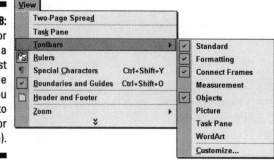

2. **Click the toolbar that you want to display.**

   Or if you want a toolbar to disappear, click the toolbar that you want to hide.

Moving a toolbar

Although most people may be perfectly happy to keep their toolbars at the top of the screen, Microsoft Office XP gives you the option of moving them to the side, bottom, or in the middle of the screen. Figure 2-9 shows a toolbar hovering in the middle of the screen.

To move a toolbar around the screen, do the following:

1. **Move the mouse pointer over the Toolbar handle of the toolbar you want to move. (If the toolbar appears in the middle of the screen, move the mouse pointer over the title bar of the toolbar.)**

   As you hover over the move handle, the mouse pointer turns into a four-way pointing arrow, as shown in Figure 2-9. If you move a toolbar that appears in the middle of the screen, you won't see the four-way pointing arrow mouse pointer until you hold down the left mouse button.

2. **Hold down the left mouse button and drag the mouse.**

   The toolbar appears as a separate window (refer to Figure 2-9).

3. **Release the left mouse button when the toolbar window appears where you want it.**

   If things floating in the middle of the screen make you nervous, you can smash the toolbar to one side or to the bottom of the screen and stick it there.

If you leave the toolbar in the middle of the screen as a floating window, you can resize the toolbar window. Just move the mouse pointer over one edge of the toolbar window, wait until the mouse pointer turns into a double-pointing arrow, and then hold down the left mouse button and drag the mouse to resize the toolbar window.

Toolbar handles

Four-way pointing arrow   Toolbar titlebar

Figure 2-9:
You can drag the Toolbar handle with the mouse to move a toolbar to the middle or side of the screen.

Opening Multiple Windows

To help make you more productive than ever, Microsoft Office XP programs can open several files so you can be working on different data within the same program. If, for example, you've found a new job in Tahiti, one window could display a résumé you're writing in Word while a second window displays your letter of resignation in Word. By opening multiple files in separate windows, you can view several files at the same time.

Although multiple windows let you edit and view the contents of two or more files at the same time, they also gobble up screen space. The more windows you display, the less text each one can hold.

Switching between multiple windows

Every time you open a file (whether by pressing Ctrl+O, clicking the Open icon on the toolbar, or choosing File⇨Open), Microsoft Office XP opens another window.

To avoid cluttering up the screen, Microsoft Office XP normally only displays one window at a time. To switch between multiple windows:

1. **Click the Window menu.**

   A drop-down menu appears, listing all the available windows you can view.

2. **Click the window containing the name of the file that you want to view.**

Office XP displays a button on the Windows taskbar for each window you open. To switch to another window, just click the appropriate button on the taskbar.

Arranging multiple windows

If you open two or more windows, you may want to see the contents of all windows simultaneously. That way, you can view the contents of one window while you edit another.

To display multiple windows on the screen, follow these steps:

1. **Choose Window⇨Arrange All.**

   All your currently open files arrange themselves on the screen as separate windows.

   If you have multiple windows open, you can choose Windows⇨Cascade to neatly stack your windows in layers, like index cards with their edges showing.

2. **Click in the window that you want to edit.**

   The active window (the one you're currently editing) highlights its title bar while the other windows dim their title bar.

After a while, you may not want multiple windows cluttering up your screen. To close a window, do one of the following:

   ✔ Click the Close box of all the windows you want to close. (The Close box is that little X in the upper right-hand corner.)

   ✔ Click the Minimize box of all the windows you want to keep open but hide out of view for the moment. (The Minimize box has a little horizontal line.)

If you click in the Close box at the top of the upper right-hand corner, you may exit out of the program altogether.

You can resize windows or move them by dragging the title bar of a window anywhere on the screen. By doing this, you can arrange your windows in any way you choose.

Saving and closing multiple windows

If you have two or more windows open, you may edit data in any of them, one window at a time. You can close windows individually (by clicking the Close box of each window or choosing File⇨Close). But if you have several windows open, you can close and save windows more conveniently using the Close All commands.

The Close All commands are not available in Access or FrontPage.

To close every open window, do the following:

1. **Hold down the Shift key.**

2. **Choose File⇨Close All.**

   When you hold down the Shift key, the File menu changes the Close command to Close All. If you haven't saved a file, Office XP displays a dialog box that asks whether you want to save your data before closing the file.

Copying and Pasting with the Office Clipboard

When you copy objects (such as text or graphics) in Windows, your computer stores the copied object on the *Windows Clipboard,* which is like an invisible place that temporarily stores items that you can use again in the future. Unfortunately, the Windows Clipboard can hold only one item at a time. The moment you copy a second item, the Windows Clipboard erases anything currently stored on the Clipboard.

To avoid this problem, Microsoft Office XP comes with a special Office Clipboard, which works exactly like the Windows Clipboard except that the Office Clipboard can hold up to 24 (count them, 24) items at a time.

The major limitation of the Office Clipboard is that you can only use this feature while working within one or more Office XP programs. The (ahem) *polite* term for features that work like this is *proprietary technology* — it means the features work only with programs created by a particular maker (in this case, Microsoft) in a bid to make rival programs look obsolete. (Subtle, isn't it?)

Each time you cut or copy an item from within an Office XP program, that cut or copied item appears on both the Office Clipboard and the ordinary Windows Clipboard. That way if you switch to a non-Office XP program, you can paste that item into another program. If you cut or copy another item from an Office XP program, this second item gets stored in the Office Clipboard but erases anything in the Windows Clipboard.

Copying stuff to the Office Clipboard

To copy or cut an object (such as text or a graphic image) to the Office Clipboard, do the following:

1. **Highlight the text or graphic object that you want to copy or cut.**

2. **Click the Copy button (or the Cut button) on the Standard toolbar.**

   Whenever you cut or copy an object, Office XP magically pastes that object onto the Office Clipboard. After you cut or copied 24 items, Office XP starts erasing the oldest item on the Clipboard to make room for each new item you cut or copy.

If you turn off your computer, the Office Clipboard "forgets" (erases) any items stored on it.

Pasting stuff from the Office Clipboard

To paste an object from the Office Clipboard, do the following:

1. **Click where you want to paste an object from the Office Clipboard.**

2. **Choose View➪Task Pane. (You can also double-click the Office Clipboard icon on the Windows taskbar and then skip to Step 5.)**

   The Task Pane appears.

3. **Click the Other Task Panes button.**

   A drop-down menu appears.

4. **Click Clipboard.**

   The Office Clipboard appears, displaying all the items currently available, as shown in Figure 2-10.

5. **Move the mouse pointer over the object you want to paste from the Office Clipboard.**

   Your chosen object appears highlighted and displays a downward-pointing arrow to the right.

6. **Click the downward-pointing arrow.**

   A drop-down menu appears.

7. **Choose Paste. (To paste all the objects from the Office Clipboard, just click the Paste All button in Office Clipboard.)**

Other Tasks button

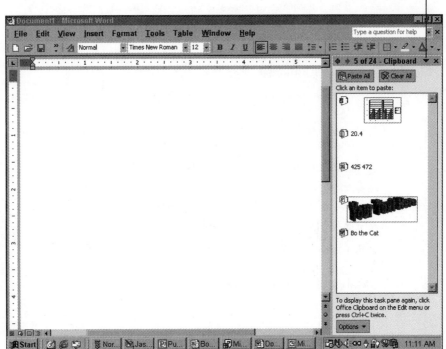

Figure 2-10:
The Office
Clipboard
displays all
items cut or
copied from
an Office XP
program.

Office Clipboard icon

If you press Ctrl+V, choose Edit➪Paste, or click the Paste button on the Standard toolbar, you paste the last object that you cut or copied from another program.

Cleaning out your Office Clipboard

Because Office XP blindly stores everything you cut or copy to the Office Clipboard, you may want to delete some items to make room for items you really want to use again. (If you don't delete an item from the Office Clipboard, Office XP starts deleting the oldest stored items to make room for any new items you copy or cut to the Office Clipboard.) To delete an object from the Office Clipboard, do the following:

1. **Choose View⇨Task Pane. (You can also double-click the Office Clipboard icon on the Windows taskbar and then skip to Step 4. Refer to Figure 2-10.)**

   The Task Pane appears.

2. **Click the Other Task Panes button.**

   A drop-down menu appears.

3. **Click Clipboard.**

   The Office Clipboard appears, displaying all the items currently avilable (refer to Figure 2-10).

4. **Move the mouse pointer over the object you want to delete from the Office Clipboard.**

   Your chosen object appears highlighted and displays a downward-pointing arrow to the right.

5. **Click the downward-pointing arrow.**

   A drop-down menu appears.

6. **Choose Delete.**

   To delete all the objects from the Office Clipboard, just click the Clear All button in Office Clipboard.

Chapter 3

Getting Help from Microsoft Office XP

Microsoft Office XP can be confusing to use. But don't worry. You don't have to master every feature provided in the program; you just need to know the commands that you require to get your job done.

So what happens if you need help using Microsoft Office XP? Before you panic, take some time to get help. Office XP provides two ways to get help: through a cartoon Office Assistant or through a normal Help window.

The Office Assistant is a customizable little cartoon that provides a friendly interface for answering any question you may have about using Microsoft Office XP In case you don't like the Office Assistant, you can always switch back to ordinary Help windows instead. Either way, both the Office Assistant and the ordinary Help windows provide you the same information to any questions you may have using Office XP.

Getting Acquainted with the Office Assistant

Computers frighten nearly everyone, even (believe it or not) the people who design and program them. For that reason, Microsoft created the Office Assistant, an animated figure that puts a friendly face on an otherwise-intimidating program.

Whenever you run any of the programs in Microsoft Office XP (such as Word, Excel, PowerPoint, and so on), you can make the Office Assistant pop up (as shown in Figure 3-1), by pressing F1.

If the Office Assistant does not appear when you press F1, choose Help⇨Show the Office Assistant.

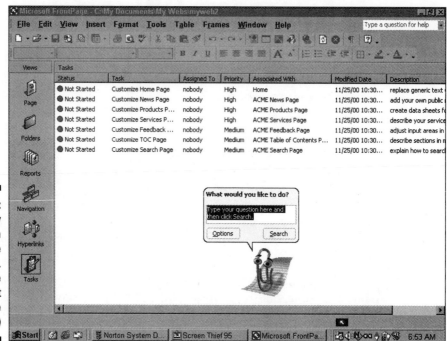

Figure 3-1:
The friendly face of an Office Assistant. (Hey, some of my best *friends* are cartoons.)

Hiding and displaying the Office Assistant

For many people, leaving the Office Assistant on the screen may be amusing, but to others, the cartoon Office Assistants can be more annoying than helpful. If you want, you can hide the Office Assistant from view.

To hide the Office Assistant from view, do either of the following:

- ✔ Choose Help⇨Hide the Office Assistant.
- ✔ Right-click the Office Assistant and choose Hide.

If you hide the Office Assistant, it doesn't appear again unless you choose Help⇨Show the Office Assistant.

Choosing a new Office Assistant

In case you don't like the cartoon character that Microsoft Office XP chooses for you, feel free to choose a different Office Assistant at any time.

To choose a new Office Assistant, do the following:

1. **Click the Office Assistant, press F1, or right-click the Office Assistant.**

    The Office Assistant appears. (Refer to Figure 3-1.)

2. **Click Options.**

3. **Click the Gallery tab.**

    A new window appears, letting you choose a different cartoon Office Assistant, as shown in Figure 3-2.

Figure 3-2:
You can choose a different Office Assistant character at any time.

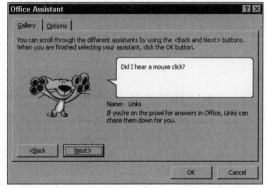

4. **Click Back or Next to see the different animated Office Assistants available.**

    Picking an Office Assistant that you like is purely your choice. They all work the same; they just look different.

5. **Click OK when you find an Office Assistant you like.**

    You may need to insert the Office XP CD each time you choose to install a different Office Assistant.

Getting rid of your Office Assistant for good

Some people love the cute cartoon Office Assistants while others feel like shooting the Office Assistants every time they see one. In case you don't like the Office Assistants and would rather work with ordinary Help windows, here's how you can keep the Office Assistant from appearing:

1. **Click the Office Assistant, press F1, or right-click the Office Assistant.**

2. **Click Options.**

   The Office Assistant dialog box appears as shown in Figure 3-3.

Figure 3-3:
The Office
Assistant
dialog box is
where you
can make
the Office
Assistant go
away for
good.

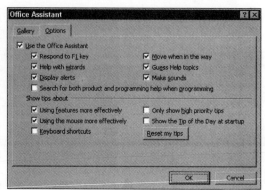

3. **Click the Options tab and click the Use the Office Assistant check box to clear the check box.**

4. **Click OK.**

   The Office Assistant disappears and any time you press F1 to get help, an ordinary Help window appears, as shown in Figure 3-4.

If you want to display the Office Assistant again, choose Help➪Show the Office Assistant.

Animating your Office Assistant

If you get bored while using Office XP (which means it's probably time for you to get another job), you can animate your Office Assistant so it moves on the screen and provides a few seconds of amusement while you stare at the screen and pretend to be doing useful work. To animate your Office Assistant, do the following:

1. **Right-click the Office Assistant.**

2. **Click Animate!.**

   The Office Assistant moves around the screen doing something cute and interesting.

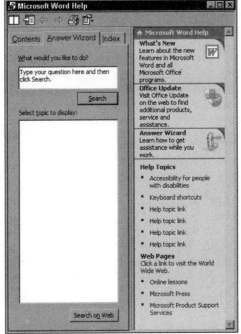

Figure 3-4:
The Help
window that
appears if
you choose
not to
display an
Office
Assistant.

Getting Help from the Office Assistant

The Office Assistant exists for your convenience. (How many things can make that claim?) Whenever you need help, just click the Office Assistant and type a question. The Office Assistant responds by displaying a list of relevant topics.(If you turned off the Office Assistant, you can still type a question into the ordinary Help window by using the Answer Wizard as explained below.)

When you type a question to the Office Assistant, make sure you spell everything correctly; otherwise, the Office Assistant doesn't know what type of help you need.

Asking the Office Assistant for help

To get help from the Office Assistant by typing a question, do the following:

1. **Click the Office Assistant, press F1, or click the Help icon in the toolbar.**

   A yellow balloon, similar to a cartoon dialog balloon, pops up. (Refer to Figure 3-1.)

2. **Type your question (such as Indent paragraph or Graphics) and click Search.**

   The yellow dialog balloon displays a list of topics related to your question, as shown in Figure 3-5.

   When you ask for help by typing a question, the Office Assistant scans your sentence to look for relevant words that it can recognize, such as *format*, *save*, or *stylesheet*. So, rather than type complete sentences such as "I want to know how to format a paragraph," just type "Format paragraph."

3. **Click the topic you want more help with.**

   A Help window appears, displaying more detailed information about your chosen topic, as shown in Figure 3-6.

4. **Click the Close box (the X in the window's upper-right corner) to get rid of the Help window.**

If you click the Print icon in the Help window, you can print a hard copy of the step-by-step instructions the Office Assistant provides. That way, you can save the instructions for future reference.

Asking for help through the Answer Wizard

In case you turned off the Office Assistant, you can still type in a question and get help by using the Answer Wizard. To get help from the Answer Wizard by typing a question, do the following:

1. **Press F1.**

   The Help window appears (refer to Figure 3-4).

2. **Click the Answer Wizard tab.**

3. **Type your question (such as Indent paragraph or Graphics) in the What Would You Like To Do? text box and click Search.**

   A list of topics, related to your question, appears in the Select topic to display box.

4. **Click the topic you want more help with.**

   The Help window displays help for your chosen topic in the right pane of the Help window.

5. **Click the Close box (the X in the window's upper-right corner) to get rid of the Help window.**

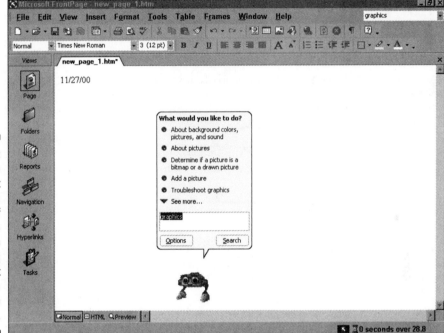

Figure 3-5:
The Office
Assistant
displays a
list of
related help
topics
according
to what
question
you type in
the text box.

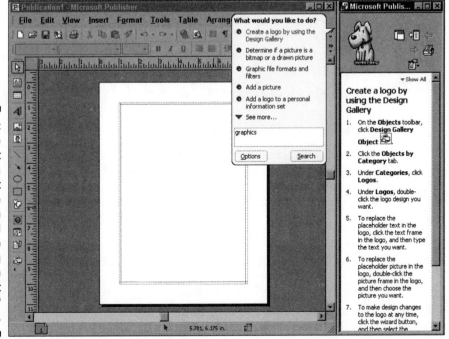

Figure 3-6:
The Office
Assistant
displays a
window that
displays the
information
you need
to keep
working
with
Microsoft
Office XXP
(hopefully).

Identifying Icons with the What's This? Command

Although all the programs in Microsoft Office XP use similar menus, toolbars, and commands, you may still find the user interface cryptic, confusing, and completely mystifying. But don't worry because Microsoft provides a handy What's This? command.

The What's This? command lets you point at any strange icon on the screen to have Office XP politely display a short description explaining the purpose of that particular icon.

To use the What's This? command, do the following:

1. **Choose Help⇨What's This? or press Shift+F1.**

   A question mark appears next to the mouse pointer. (In case you suddenly decide you don't want to use the What's This? command, press the Esc key.)

2. **Move the mouse pointer over a toolbar icon or menu command and click the mouse button.**

   Office XP displays a tiny window that provides a brief explanation about the toolbar icon or menu command you choose.

3. **Press any key (such as the Esc key) or click the mouse to remove the tiny explanation window.**

Getting Help on the World Wide Web

To provide you with the latest software updates, patches, bug fixes, program news, tips, and software add-ons, Microsoft runs its own Web site (www. microsoft.com). To help you reach Microsoft's Web site quickly and easily, every Office XP program has a special *Office on the Web* command.

Before you can use this Office on the Web command, you must have an existing Internet account or be willing to create (and pay for) an Internet account.

To access the Microsoft Web site, which is full of useful Microsoft Office XP information, software, news, or bug updates, do the following:

1. **Choose Help⇨Office on the Web.**

   Office XP starts up your Internet browser and loads the Microsoft Office XP Web page.

2. **Browse the pages until you find the information you need.**

3. **Choose File⇨Exit or click the close box of your browser to make the browser go away.**

Exiting from your Web browser may not always disconnect you from the Internet. To make sure you disconnect from the Internet, click on the Dial-Up Connection icon, which appears in the lower right-hand corner of the Windows Taskbar. When a dialog box appears, click Disconnect.

Recovering From Crashes with Office XP

One of the most common problems with using a computer is having the computer freeze, crash, or act erratically for no apparent reason. When this happens, don't blame yourself; blame all the people who make computers so unreliable in the first place. Because computers aren't likely to become more reliable in the future, Microsoft Office XP offers two ways to protect yourself:

- Repairing Microsoft Office XP programs
- Protecting documents corrupted during a computer crash

Repairing Microsoft Office XP

Each program (Word, Excel, PowerPoint, and so on) consists of several files with cryptic file extensions, such as .EXE, .DLL, and .OLB. If you accidentally delete or modify one of these files, your Microsoft Office XP program may no longer work.

To protect you from this problem, Microsoft Office XP contains a special Detect and Repair command that — what else? — checks to make sure that all those important files still exist on your hard disk and are in working order.

(Of course, the big problem is that if a file is missing or corrupted, you may not be able to run any Microsoft Office XP programs in the first place in order to use the Detect and Repair command. In that case, you may have to go back to reinstalling the entire program all over again. Be sure to make backups of your important data just in case the installation procedure goes awry and messes up your hard disk completely.)

So, the next time any Office XP program starts acting flaky, try to fix it by using the Detect and Repair command:

1. **Run a Microsoft Office XP program, such as Word or PowerPoint.**

2. **Choose Help⇨Detect and Repair. (You may have to click the double rightward-pointing arrow in the Help menu before you can see the Detect and Repair command.)**

   The Detect and Repair dialog box appears, as shown in Figure 3-7.

Figure 3-7:
The Detect and Repair dialog box can help fix most problems you may have with Office XP.

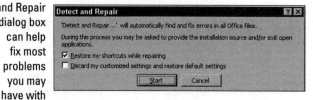

3. **Click the check boxes to choose any options you want.**

   The two options for repairing Microsoft Office include the following:

   - **Restore my shortcuts while repairing:** Makes sure any desktop shortcuts you may create continue pointing to the right programs and documents.

   - **Discard my customized settings and restore default settings:** Returns your copy of Office XP back to its original settings, wiping out any custom changes you may make to menus or toolbars.

4. **Click Start.**

   Follow the on-screen instructions as Microsoft Office XP valiantly tries to fix itself if it detects any problems. You may have to insert the Microsoft Office XP CD into your CD-ROM drive.

Protecting files from a computer crash

One common source of frustration (besides the computer itself) is when the computer crashes while you're working on a document. That's why everyone recommends that you save your document at frequent intervals. Because you can't predict computer crashes (except knowing that it *will* crash on you one day), Microsoft Office XP provides several options for minimizing the chance of losing data during a computer crash:

✔ **Timed saving of files:** Automatically saves information about your document at specific time intervals. By saving document information, you can increase the chances that Office XP can recover your data in the event of a crash. Available only in Word, Excel, PowerPoint, and Outlook.

✔ **Hang manager:** Allows you to attempt to restart Word, Excel, or PowerPoint if they crash.

✔ **Corrupt document recovery:** Attempts to recover a file that may have been corrupted when the program crashed. Available only in Word and Excel.

The best way to protect your data is to save your files often and store backup copies of your data in separate locations, such as on a rewritable CD or ZIP disk.

Saving files automatically

For your first line of defense in protecting your data, you can make Word, Excel, PowerPoint, and Outlook save your files automatically at specific intervals, such as every ten minutes, by following these steps:

1. **Choose Tools⇨Options.**

   The Options dialog box appears.

2. **Click the Save tab.**

   The Save tab displays the Save AutoRecover Info check box, as shown in Figure 3-8.

3. **Make sure a check mark appears in the Save AutoRecover Info check box.**

Figure 3-8: The Save Auto-Recover Info check box gives you the option of saving your files at specific intervals.

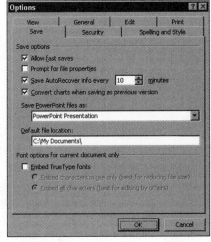

4. **Click the <u>m</u>inutes text box and type the number of minutes you want to wait before saving your document information automatically, such as every ten minutes.**

5. **Click OK.**

Restarting a frozen application

Instead of crashing, Word, Excel, or PowerPoint may *hang* or *freeze*, which means the program still appears on the screen although nothing seems to work (such as the keyboard or the mouse). When this happens (notice the emphasis on *when* and not *if*), you can attempt to restart Word, Excel, or PowerPoint by running the Microsoft Office Application Recovery Tool, as follows:

1. **Click the Start button on the Windows taskbar.**

   A pop-up menu appears.

2. **Choose <u>P</u>rograms⇨Microsoft Office Tools⇨Microsoft Office Application Recovery.**

   The Microsoft Office Application Recovery dialog box appears, as shown in Figure 3-9.

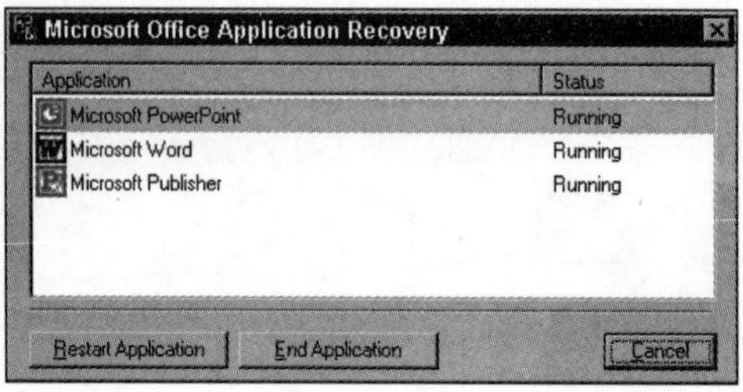

Figure 3-9:
The
Microsoft
Office
Application
Recovery
dialog box
shows you
which Office
programs
are running
and which
ones have
crashed.

3. **Click the crashed program you want to restart and click Restart Application.**

   If you're lucky, Microsoft Office XP restarts your chosen application. If nothing happens, click End Application and try to restart the application again.

After a program crashes, there's a greater chance that it'll crash again. So, after you restart a crashed application such as Word, you should immediately save any opened documents and exit the previously crashed application before you start the application up again. For extra safety, consider also restarting your entire computer.

Recovering corrupted files

No matter how careful you may be, if Microsoft Office XP crashes, it could mangle any documents that you were working on at the time of the crash. If this happens, Word, Excel, and PowerPoint can attempt to recover your files the next time you start the program. To attempt to recover your files, do the following:

1. **Load Word, Excel, or PowerPoint immediately after your Office XP program crashed.**

   A Document Recovery pane appears, as shown in Figure 3-10.

2. **Click the document you want to recover.**

   A downward-pointing arrow appears to the right.

3. **Click the downward-pointing arrow.**

   A pop-up menu appears.

4. **Click Open or Save As.**

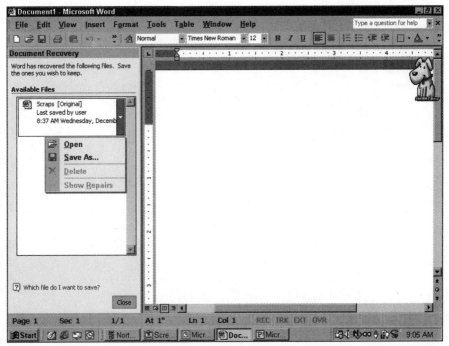

Figure 3-10:
The Document Recovery pane displays a list of all files that may have been corrupted during the last crash.

Both Word and Excel offer another way to recover files corrupted during a computer crash. To use this option, follow these steps:

1. **Load either Word or Excel.**

2. **Choose File➪Open (or press Ctrl+O).**

   The Open dialog box appears.

3. **Click the file you want to recover.**

4. **Click the downward-pointing arrow that appears to the right of the Open button in the lower right-hand corner.**

   A pop-up menu appears, as shown in Figure 3-11.

5. **Click Open and Repair.**

   Word or Excel attempts to load your chosen file and repair any problems that may have occurred during a crash.

Figure 3-11:
The Open dialog box in Word and Excel offers an alternate way to recover files corrupted during a crash.

Part II
Working with Word

The 5th Wave — By Rich Tennant

"THE FUNNY THING IS, I NEVER KNEW THEY HAD DESKTOP PUBLISHING SOFTWARE FOR PAPER SHREDDERS."

In this part . . .

Word processing remains the most popular use for a personal computer (right after playing games and wasting hours exploring the Internet), so this part of the book gently guides you into using the powerhouse word processor known as Microsoft Word. By using the 2002 version of Word, you can create anything from a simple letter to a resume or business report.

Along the way to discovering how to use Word's powerful features, you also encounter the more basic features, such as how to write, edit, spell-check, and grammar-check your writing, and how to format text to make it look really pretty.

Word may seem like an ordinary word processor at first glance, but this part of the book unlocks the techniques that summon Word to help you write, create, and print your ideas as fast as you care to type them. (Just as long as your computer doesn't crash on you, that is.)

Chapter 4

Working with Word Documents

As its name implies, Word lets you write words so that you can create letters, reports, proposals, brochures, newsletters, pink slips, ransom notes, and practically anything else that requires a rudimentary command of the written language. Because Word may look intimidating at first glance, this chapter guides you through opening, saving, and printing your work along with helping you understand the general appearance of Word.

Creating a New Word Document

Word gives you four ways to create a new document:

✔ When you first run Word, it automatically creates a new document, ready for you to start typing. (So stop reading this and start typing.)

✔ You can click the New Blank Document button on the Standard toolbar.

✔ You can choose File➪New.

✔ You can press Ctrl+N.

If you choose File➪New, a New Document pane opens and gives you the option of opening an existing document, creating a blank document, or creating a document based on a template, as shown in Figure 4-1.

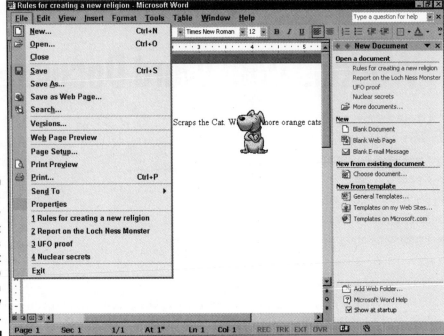

Figure 4-1:
The New
Document
pane gives
you different
ways to
create a
new
document.

Using a template

Staring at a blank page intimidates many people, so Word offers you the choice of creating a new document based on a template, which provides you with preformatted headings and paragraphs. That way, instead of typing text and formatting everything yourself, you can just type text into a template to create a fax cover sheet, business report, or résumé. To use a template, do the following:

1. **Choose File⇨New.**

   The New Document pane appears (refer to Figure 4-1).

2. **Click the General Templates icon.**

   The Templates dialog box appears, as shown in Figure 4-2.

3. **Click the template that you want to use and click OK.**

   Word displays the template, and you're ready to start typing.

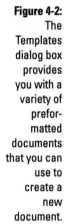

Figure 4-2:
The
Templates
dialog box
provides
you with a
variety of
prefor-
matted
documents
that you can
use to
create a
new
document.

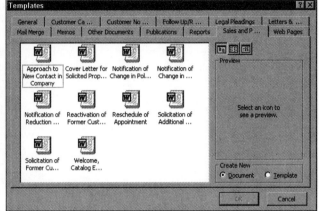

Creating a document from an existing document

Templates can help you create new documents quickly, but sometimes you may not want to use one of the predefined templates that Office XP provides. In that case, you can create a new document based on the formatting of one of your previously created documents. To do this, follow these steps:

1. **Choose File⇨New.**

   The New Document pane appears (refer to Figure 4-1).

2. **Click the Choose Document icon (it's under the New from Existing Document heading).**

   A New from Existing Document dialog box appears.

3. **Click the document that you want to base your new document on and click Create New.**

   Word displays a copy of your chosen document. At this point, you can start modifying any text or formatting.

Opening a Previously Saved File

Instead of creating new documents, you may want to spend more of your time editing documents that you already created. To open a previously saved file, Word gives you four choices:

- ✔ Press Ctrl+O.

- ✔ Click the Open button on the Standard toolbar.

- ✔ Choose File➪Open.

- ✔ Choose one of the last four files you saved; their names appear at the bottom of the File menu or inside the New Document pane (refer to Figure 4-1).

If you choose one of the first three opening methods, the Open dialog box appears. Just double-click the file that you want to open, and it should unfold before you in all its glory and greatness.

Putting Text into a Document

After you open an existing document (or create a new one), you still need to add text into your document. Two common ways to add text to a Word document include:

- ✔ Typing text
- ✔ Importing text from another program

Typing text

Typing is the most obvious way to add text to a document, but because not everyone feels comfortable typing accurately, Word provides the helpful AutoCorrect tool, which recognizes common misspellings and automatically corrects them as you type. (Just to see the AutoCorrect feature in action, type "teh" and watch Word automatically retype it as "the.")

Word recognizes misspellings of most common words, such as *the, about,* and *again,* but just in case you constantly misspell a word that Word doesn't recognize, you can teach Word to recognize your misspelling and the correct spelling by doing the following:

1. **Choose Tools➪AutoCorrect**

   The AutoCorrect dialog box appears as shown in Figure 4-3.

2. **Click in the Replace text box and type the way you commonly misspell a word.**

   Make sure you type the misspelled word exactly as you normally misspell it.

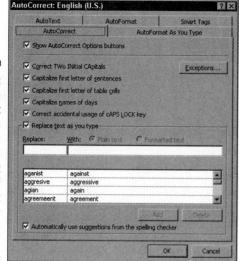

Figure 4-3:
The
AutoCorrect
dialog box is
where you
teach Word
the correct
spelling of
your most
commonly
misspelled
words.

3. **Click in the With text box and type the correct spelling of the word you typed in Step 2.**

   Make sure you type the correct spelling of your word in Step 3 or else Word will mindlessly correct your misspelling with the misspelled word you type in Step 3.

4. **Click OK.**

   Word is now trained to recognize and automatically correct your chosen word.

Importing text from another program

Sometimes you may want to convert or transfer text stored in another program into a Word document. One simple way to import text is to copy the text from the other program to the Windows Clipboard (or to the new Office Clipboard, if you're transferring several items from another Office XP program), and then paste the text into your Word document.

However, if the text is stored on another computer, such as a Macintosh, you must follow these steps to import the text into a Word document:

1. **Save the text trapped in the other computer into one of the file formats listed in Table 4-1.**

   Most programs allow you to save files in a different file format by choosing File⇨Save As and then specifying the file format you want to use.

51

If you want to keep the original formatting — such as font, size, and spacing — then use the file format listed at the top of Table 4-1; it retains most formatting. If the text itself is all you want to import, then use the file format listed at the bottom of the table — it retains virtually no formatting.

Table 4-1 Some Popular File Formats That Word Can Understand

File Format Type	Common File Extension
Word 2000	.DOC
Word 6.0/95	.DOC
Word 4.0-5.1 for Macintosh	.DOC
Works 5.0 for Windows	.WPS
Works 4.0 for Windows	.WPS
WordPerfect 5.x/6.x	.WP
Excel	.XLS
Rich text format	.RTF
HTML Web page	.HTML or .HTM
Lotus 1-2-3	.WKx (such as .WK4)
ASCII or text file	.TXT or .ASC

2. Copy the file in Step 1 to your computer.

You can save it to a floppy disk and then copy it to your hard disk from the floppy, or use the direct approach — your friendly neighborhood local-area network.

3. Load Word and choose File⇨Open, or press Ctrl+O.

The Open dialog box appears.

4. Click in the Files of Type: list box and choose the file type that you saved your text in during Step 1, such as WordPerfect 5.x.

5. Click the file that contains the text you want to import and click Open.

Word loads your text. You may have to do some minor (or major) reformatting to tidy up the text, but at least you won't have to retype it letter by letter (at least we can hope so).

Viewing Microsoft Word Documents

Because word processing involves staring at text for long periods of time, Word provides several different ways to view your documents. Word can make your text easier to read by displaying it in different views — enlarging the text or revealing spaces and paragraph marks — so you can see exactly how your writing will look when printed.

Choosing a different view of a document

Word lets you see your document from four perspectives, each showing a different amount of text and graphics on-screen. To change the view of your document, choose View from the menu bar and then choose one of the following:

- **Normal:** Great when you want to write in a clean screen without worrying about headers, footers, or vertical rulers getting in your way.
- **Web Layout:** Shows you what your document looks like when displayed as a Web page.
- **Print Layout:** Shows you exactly how your document will look when printed, including headers and footers.
- **Outline:** Comes in handy when you don't have the slightest idea what to write and you want to create an outline to help organize your thoughts. While in Outline view (see Figure 4-4), you can organize your thoughts into topics and subtopics.

In case you really don't like the clutter of toolbars or drop-down menus, Word gives you the option of switching to the Full Screen view, which shows nothing but a blank screen and any text you type. To switch to the Full Screen view, choose View➪Full Screen. To switch out of the Full Screen view, press Esc or click the Close Full Screen button.

As a quick way to switch document views, just click the Normal, Web Layout, Print Layout, and Outline View buttons that Word 2000 displays along the far left of the horizontal scroll bar (see Figure 4-4).

Hiding (or showing) the scroll bars

To give you a little bit more room on the screen to see your text, you can get rid of both the horizontal and vertical scroll bars. To hide the scroll bars, do the following:

1. **Choose Tools➪Options.**

   The Options dialog box appears, as shown in Figure 4-5.

2. **Click the View tab.**

3. **Click the check boxes next to Horizontal Scroll Bar and Vertical Scroll Bar.**

4. **Click OK.**

   Voilà! Word hides your scroll bars, giving you another few millimeters of space. If you later want to display your scroll bars, just repeat Steps 1 through 4 and replace the check marks in the check boxes.

Changing screen magnification

For many people, the way Word displays text may be too small to see. To enlarge (or shrink) text, you can change the screen's magnification until the text fills the entire screen.

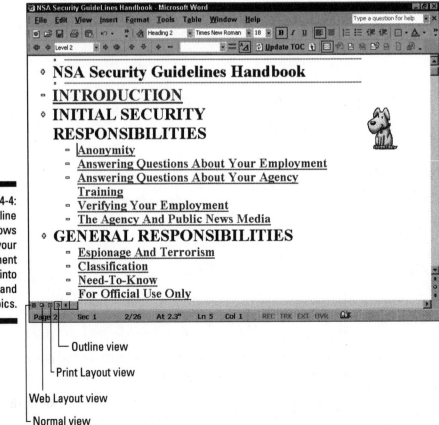

Figure 4-4:
The Outline
view shows
your
document
divided into
topics and
subtopics.

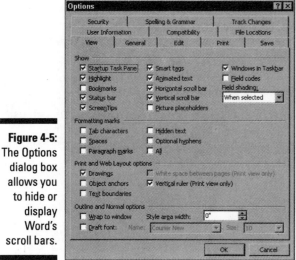

Figure 4-5:
The Options dialog box allows you to hide or display Word's scroll bars.

To change your screen's magnification, follow these steps:

1. **Choose View⇨Zoom.**

   The Zoom dialog box appears, as shown in Figure 4-6.

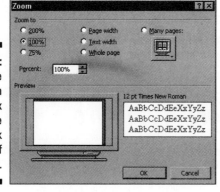

Figure 4-6:
You can use the Zoom dialog box to enlarge or shrink your view of your text.

2. **Click one of the following option buttons in the Zoom To list:**

   • **200%:** Makes your text appear at twice its normal size.

   • **100%:** Makes your text appear at the normal, default size.

   • **75%:** Makes your text appear smaller.

   • **Page Width:** Makes your text line appear just as wide as the currently open window displayed in Word.

• **Text width:** Blows up or squeezes the page so all the text fits on the screen (available only in Print Layout view).

• **Whole page:** Squeezes the whole page on the screen (available only in Print Layout view).

• **Many pages:** Shows miniature versions of all the pages of your entire document (available only in Print Layout view).

You free spirits who absolutely must express your individuality can use the Percent list box to specify an exact-percentage magnification at which to display your document. The Percent list box can even handle oddball percentages, such as 57%, 93%, or 138%.

3. Click OK.

Showing spaces and paragraph marks

If your document ever exhibits strange spacing between words or paragraphs, you may need to know whether you inadvertently entered two spaces between words (or none at all) or pressed the Enter key twice after paragraphs. To make Word show spaces and paragraph marks in your document, do the following:

1. Click the Show/Hide Paragraph Marks button (which looks like a backwards P with two vertical parallel lines) on the Standard toolbar.

Word displays the spaces (as dots), paragraph marks (those double-stemmed backwards *P*s), and any hidden text in your document.

2. Click the Show/Hide Paragraph Marks button again to hide spaces, paragraph marks, and any hidden text.

Deciphering the Word Toolbars

Rather than force you to memorize obscure keystroke combinations or wade through multiple layers of drop-down menus, Word lets you choose common commands by clicking buttons stored on toolbars.

The two most common toolbars are the Standard and Formatting toolbars. (Word actually offers over a dozen different toolbars, but the Standard and Formatting toolbars are the main ones you use.) These two toolbars automatically appear when you first install and start Word. You can hide them later to make your screen less cluttered, if you want. (But then you could *find* everything on the screen — where's the challenge in that? Just kidding.)

Exploring the Standard toolbar

The Standard toolbar offers access to the program's most frequently used commands, arranged from left to right in roughly the order of their frequency of use, as shown in Figure 4-7.

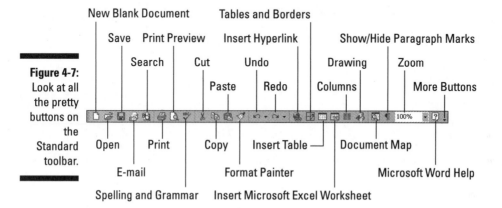

Figure 4-7: Look at all the pretty buttons on the Standard toolbar.

New Blank Document — Tables and Borders
Save — Print Preview — Insert Hyperlink — Show/Hide Paragraph Marks
Search — Cut — Undo — Drawing — Zoom
Paste — Redo — Columns — More Buttons
Open — Print — Copy — Insert Table — Document Map
E-mail — Format Painter — Microsoft Word Help
Spelling and Grammar — Insert Microsoft Excel Worksheet

To quickly find out what each button on the Standard toolbar does, put the mouse pointer over a button and wait a second or two until the ScreenTip — a brief explanation of the button — appears. (These handy labels also go by the name *tooltips* when they identify particular tools in a software program.)

Looking good with the Formatting toolbar

The Formatting toolbar contains commands to make your text look pretty with different fonts, type sizes, and typefaces (such as bold, italics, and underline). Figure 4-8 shows the Formatting toolbar.

To use any command on the Formatting toolbar, just select the text that you want to format and then click the appropriate button (or the downward-pointing arrow next to any list box on the Formatting toolbar). Chapter 5 explains how to select text so you can format it with the Formatting toolbar at a later time.

Exploring the Word Ruler

The *ruler* defines the margins and tabs of your document. If you create a multicolumn document, the ruler also shows the column placement and the distance between the columns. By using the ruler, you can make margins wider (or smaller) and change the indentation of paragraphs.

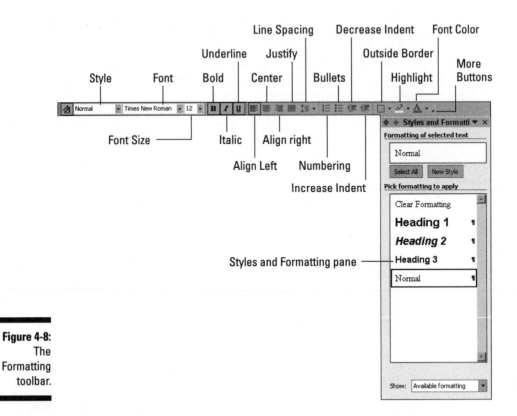

Hiding and displaying the ruler

If you don't want to see the ruler on your screen (or if you want to display the ruler after you hide it), you can hide it (or display it) by choosing View➪Ruler.

If you switch to Print Layout view, Word displays a vertical ruler along the left-hand side of the screen. To hide this vertical ruler, switch to a different view, such as Normal or Web Layout view.

Setting tabs on the ruler

Word provides five different types of tabs (shown in Figure 4-9) that you can set on the ruler.

The five tab types (no, they're not a '60s vocal group) have five different functions:

- ✔ **Left tab (looks like an *L*):** Moves text toward the right edge of the page as you type

- ✔ **Center tab (looks like an upside-down *T*):** Centers text around the tab

- ✔ **Right tab (looks like a backward *L*):** Moves text toward the left edge of the page as you type

- ✔ **Decimal tab (looks like an upside-down *T* with a dot next to it):** Aligns decimal numbers in a column on the decimal point, as in this example:

  24.90

  1.9084

  58093.89

- ✔ **Bar tab (looks like a straight line, like |):** Draws a vertical line on the document

To place a tab on the ruler, follow these steps:

1. **Click the Tab Selection button (which appears to the left of the ruler) until it displays the tab that you want to use.**

2. **Click the ruler where you want to place the tab.**

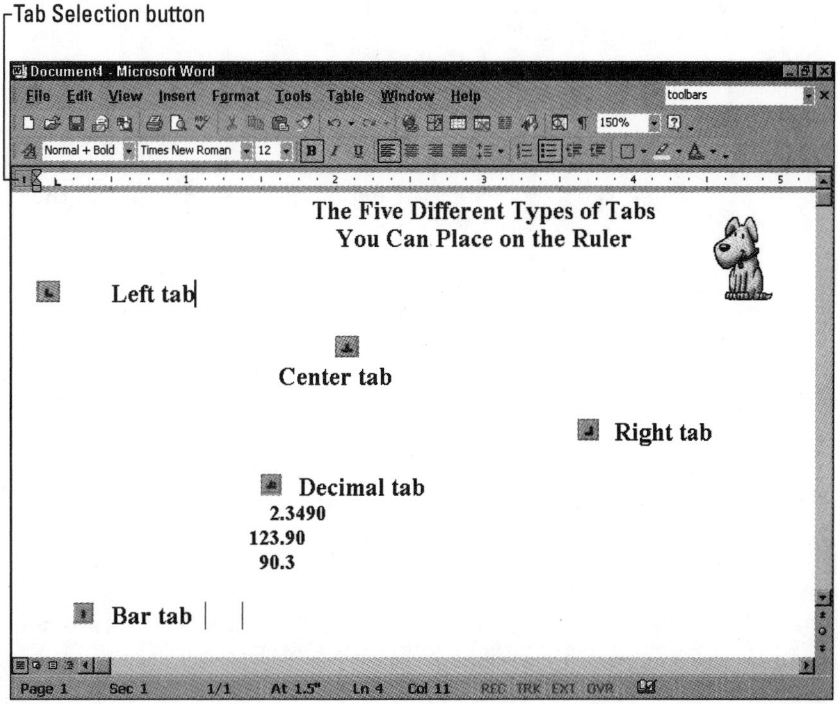

Tab Selection button

Figure 4-9:
The five different types of tabs you can place on a ruler.

To move an existing tab on the ruler, do the following:

1. **Put the mouse pointer on the tab you want to move.**

2. **Hold down the left mouse button until you see a dotted line appear directly below the tab.**

3. **Move the mouse to where you want to move the tab.**

4. **Release the left mouse button.**

To remove a tab from the ruler, do the following:

1. **Put the mouse pointer on the tab you want to remove.**

2. **Hold down the left mouse button until you see a dotted line appear directly beneath the tab.**

3. **Move the mouse off the ruler.**

4. **Release the left mouse button.**

Indents on your ruler

To help you indent paragraphs, the Tab Selection button also displays two types of indentation icons, as shown in Figure 4-10:

- ✔ **First Line Indent icon:** This icon looks like an upside-down house and defines the left margin of the first line in a paragraph.

- ✔ **Hanging Indent icon:** This icon looks like a big U on the Tab Selection button and as a right-side-up house above the Left Indent icon on the ruler. The icon defines the left margin of every line but the first line in a paragraph.

To provide more indentation options, the ruler displays two indent icons that can indent your text left and right, as shown in Figure 4-10.

- ✔ **Left Indent icon:** This icon does not appear in the Tab Selection button, and it defines the left margin of every line of a paragraph.

- ✔ **Right Indent icon:** This icon does not appear in the Tab Selection button, and it defines the right margin of every line of a paragraph.

The ruler can display only one indent (whether First Line, Hanging, Left, or Right) per paragraph.

To indent paragraphs with the First Line Indent, Hanging Indent, Left Indent, and Right Indent markers, follow these steps:

1. **Select the paragraphs that you want to indent.**

   Skip this step if you haven't written any paragraphs to indent yet. Any indentation that you apply to a blank document affects the entire future document.

2. **Put the mouse pointer on a marker (First Line Indent, Hanging Indent, Left Indent, or Right Indent) and hold down the left mouse button.**

   Word displays a dotted vertical line directly under the marker.

3. **Move the mouse where you want to indent the paragraph and then release the mouse button.**

Instead of moving the indent markers on the ruler, you can click the Tab Selection button until the First Line or Hanging Indent icon appears, and then click the ruler where you want to put the First Line or Hanging Indent marker.

Figure 4-10:
Using the ruler, you can indent text.

Moving through a Word Document

You can navigate through a Word document by using the mouse or the keyboard. Although the mouse is easier to master, the keyboard can be more convenient to use, because you don't have to keep reaching for the mouse when your fingers are already on the keyboard.

Using the mouse to jump around in a document

The mouse is often the quickest way to move around a document. When you use the mouse, you can use the vertical scroll bar, as shown in Figure 4-11.

Figure 4-11:
The vertical
scroll bar.

Down Arrow

Scroll Box

Up Arrow

Next Page

Selectg Browser Object

Previous Page

You can use the scroll bar to do the following:

✔ Click the up or down arrow to scroll up or down, one line at a time.

✔ Drag the scroll box in the desired direction to jump to an approximate location in your document.

✔ Click the scroll bar above or below the scroll box to page up or down one window at a time.

✔ Click the Previous Page or Next Page arrows at the bottom of the scroll bar to jump to the top of the previous or next page.

If your mouse doesn't have a wheel in the middle, you can also roll the middle wheel on your mouse to scroll a line at a time up or down.

Using the keyboard to jump around in a document

For those who hate the mouse (or just like using the keyboard), here are the different ways to jump around in your document by pressing keys:

✔ Press the ↓ key to move down one line in your document.

✔ Press the ↑ key to move up one line in your document.

✔ Hold down the Ctrl key and press ↑ or ↓ to jump up or down a paragraph at a time.

✔ Press the PgDn key (or Page Down, on some keyboards) to jump down the document one window at a time.

✔ Press the PgUp key (or Page Up, on some keyboards) to jump up the document one window at a time.

✔ Press Ctrl+Home to jump to the beginning of your document.

✔ Press Ctrl+End to jump to the end of your document.

Using the Go To command

When you want to jump to a specific part of your document, the Go To command is much easier and faster than either the mouse or the keyboard. Besides jumping to a specific page number, the Go To command can also jump to the following:

✔ A specific line number

✔ A comment written by a specific person

✔ A bookmark that you or someone else placed in the document

To use the Go To command, do the following:

1. **Choose Edit⇨Go To or press Ctrl+G.**

   The Go To tab of the Find and Replace dialog box appears, as shown in Figure 4-12.

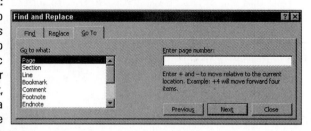

2. **Type a page number (or click the item you want to find, such as a specific line number, and then type what you want to find) and press Enter.**

   Word jumps to your chosen item, such as a page number or line number.

3. **Click Close or press Esc to make the Go To dialog box go away.**

Saving Your Stuff

Normally, if you're going to take the time and trouble to write something in Word, you probably want to save your work so you can use it again in the future. Word provides three ways to save your stuff.

Always save your work periodically in case your computer crashes, the power goes out, Windows 95/98/Me/NT/2000 inexplicably freezes on you, or some jerk comes along and starts messing around on your computer. Chapter 3 provides information on how to recover a document in case your computer crashes.

Saving your document

To save your document, choose one of the following methods:

  ✔ Press Ctrl+S.

  ✔ Click the Save button on the Standard toolbar (the button that looks like a floppy disk).

  ✔ Choose File➪Save.

If you're saving a document for the first time, Word asks you to choose a name for your file. Ideally, you should make your file name as descriptive as possible, such as Letter To Dad or Subpoena To Ex-Spouse, so it jars your memory about the document's contents when you haven't looked at the file for a while.

If you have multiple documents open and want to save them all in one keystroke, hold down the Shift key and choose File➪Save All.

The longest file name that Word can handle is 255 characters. File names must not include the forward slash (/), backslash (\), greater-than sign (>), less-than sign (<), asterisk (*), question mark (?), quotation mark ("), pipe symbol (|), colon (:), or semicolon (;).

Saving your document under a new name or as a different file type

Suppose you wrote a report that took five days to write and now you have to write a similar report, due on Monday. Rather than starting from scratch, you can open your old report, save it as a new document, and then edit this new document while leaving the original document intact.

To save your document under a different name, follow these steps:

1. **Choose File➪Save As.**

   The Save As dialog box appears.

2. **Type a new name for your file in the File Name box.**

3. **(Optional) Click in the Save as Type list box and choose a file format to use, such as WordPerfect 5.0 or Works 4.0 for Windows.**

4. **Click Save.**

Word documents are compatible with Word 2000 documents, but not always completely compatible with older versions of Word, such as those created by Word 97 or Word 6.0. If you want to save a Word document so someone else can edit it using an older version of Word, choose the Save As command and choose a file format (such as Word 6.0/95), in the Save as Type list box of the Save As dialog box.

To ensure maximum compatibility between Word documents and older versions of Word such as Word 97, you can turn off specific Word features that aren't supported by older versions of Word. To turn off these features, follow these steps:

1. **Choose Tools➪Options.**

2. **Click the Save tab.**

   The Save tab in the Options dialog box appears, as shown in Figure 4-13.

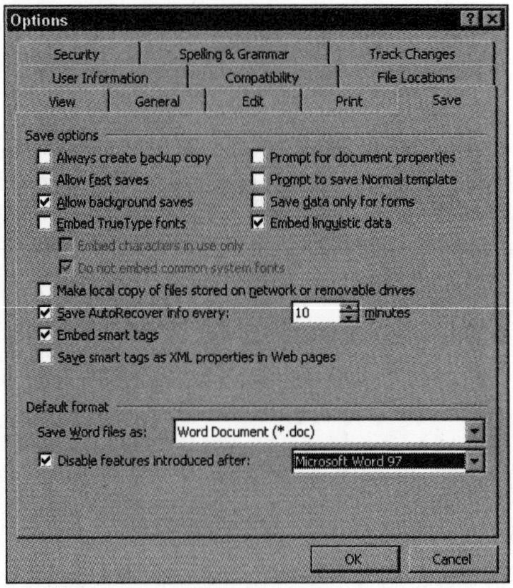

Figure 4-13: You can disable certain features in Word so your documents remain compatible with older versions of Word.

3. **Click the Disable Features Introduced After check box.**

4. **Click in the list box and choose a version of Word, such as Microsoft Word 97.**

5. **Click OK.**

Making backups of your file automatically

In case you're terrified of losing data (a completely justified fear, given the penchant of Windows 95/98/Me/NT/2000 for crashing), you may want to use Word's backup feature.

The *backup feature* creates a second copy (a backup) of your document every time you save your document. This backup file is called "Backup of (name of original document)." So if you save a document called "Plan for world domination," the backup file is called "Backup of Plan for world domination" and is stored in the same folder as your original document. (This also means if you accidentally wipe out the folder containing the original document, you also wipe out the backup copy as well.)

To turn on Word's backup feature, follow these steps:

1. **Choose Tools⇨Options.**

   The Options dialog box appears (refer to Figure 4-13).

2. **Click the Save tab.**

3. **Make sure a check mark appears in the Always Create Backup Copy check box.**

4. **Click OK.**

Word also provides an Allow Fast Saves check box that you can click after Step 3. The Fast Saves option saves your files quickly (hence the name Fast Save) because it only stores any changes you make in a smaller, separate, temporary file on the disk. If you choose the Fast Saves option, you should clear the Allow Fast Saves check box periodically so Word consolidates all changes into a single file.

Previewing and Printing Your Masterpiece

If you don't mind contributing to global deforestation, you're free to print every chance you get, just to see whether your documents are properly aligned. But if you're one of the growing crowd of grownups who cringe at the thought of wasting precious resources on unnecessary printing, use the Word Print Preview feature before you actually print out your work.

Putting Print Preview to work

Print Preview enables you to see how your document looks before you print it. That way, you can check to see whether your margins are aligned properly and your page numbers appear in the right place — and detect any print that's trying to escape from the page.

To use the Print Preview feature, do the following:

1. **Choose File⇨Print Preview.**

   Word displays your document in minuscule print, as shown in Figure 4-14, and displays the cursor as a magnifying glass.

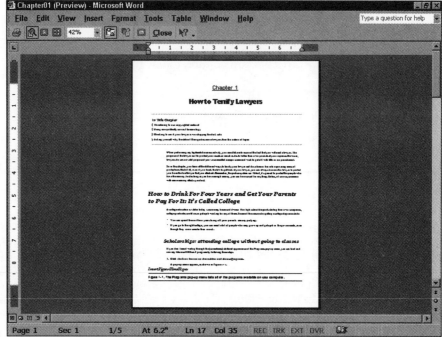

Figure 4-14:
Print
Preview
shows you
what your
document
will look like
when you
eventually
print it.

2. **Move the mouse cursor (the magnifying glass) over the document and click to view your document in its full size.**

3. **Click Close to close Print Preview.**

Defining your pages

Before you print your Word documents, you may want to define your page margins and paper size. To define your pages, do the following:

1. **Choose File⇨Page Setup.**

   The Page Setup dialog box appears.

2. **Click the Margins tab and click the Top, Bottom, Left, or Right boxes to define the margins you want to set.**

   The Margins tab appears in Page Setup dialog box as shown in Figure 4-15.

3. **Click the Paper tab and then click in the Paper Size list box to define the paper size (such as Legal or A4).**

   You may also want to define the specific width and height of your pages.

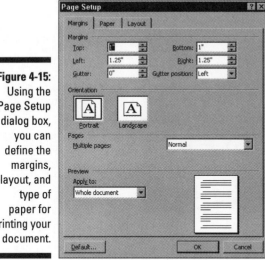

Figure 4-15:
Using the
Page Setup
dialog box,
you can
define the
margins,
layout, and
type of
paper for
printing your
document.

4. **Click in the First Page and Other Pages list boxes under the Paper Source group to define the location of the paper you want to use for your printer.**

5. **Click the Layout tab.**

   The Layout tab lets you define if you want your headers and footers to appear differently on odd or even pages, or whether they should appear on the first page or not.

6. **Click OK.**

   After this exhaustive and tedious process of defining the paper you're going to use, you're ready to actually print your Word documents.

Printing your work

Sooner or later, you must succumb to the need to print something that you created in Word (call it a hunch). To print a Word document, follow these steps:

1. **Choose File⇨Print or press Ctrl+P.**

   The Printer dialog box appears, as shown in Figure 4-16.

2. **Click the Name list box and choose the printer to use.**

3. **In the Page range group, click an option button to choose the pages you want to print, such as All or Current page.**

   If you click the Pages option button, you can selectively choose the pages you want to print, such as page 1, 3, and 5 through 12.

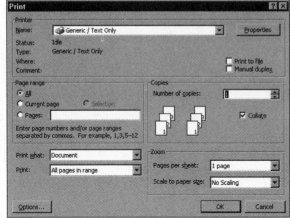

Figure 4-16:
You can use
the Print
dialog box
to define the
number of
copies and
the page
range you
want to
print.

4. **Click the Number of Copies box and type the number of copies you want.**

5. **Click the Print What list box and choose what you want to print, such as your Document or any comments you've added to the document.**

6. **Click the Print list box and choose what you want to print, such as Odd or Even pages.**

7. **Click OK.**

When you click the Print button (the button that looks like a printer) on the Standard toolbar, Word immediately starts printing your entire document, bypassing the Print dialog box. If you want to print specific pages or a certain number of copies, go through the menu instead (or press Ctrl+P).

Chapter 5

Manipulating Your Words

*E*ven the best writers in the world need to edit their writing once in a while to delete text, rearrange paragraphs, or check their spelling and grammar. Fortunately, Word can simplify (or even automate) most of these tasks for you. That way, you can concentrate on writing rather than worrying about the trivial tasks of spelling and using grammar correctly.

Selecting Text

Before you can delete, move, copy, or format text, you must *select* it first. Selecting text tells Word, "See this text that I just highlighted? That's what I want you to change."

You can select text in two ways:

✔ Drag or click the mouse.

✔ Use the keyboard.

Dragging or clicking the mouse to select text

Dragging the mouse is the easiest and most intuitive way to select text (provided you're already comfortable using the mouse).

To select text with the mouse:

1. **Move the mouse pointer to the beginning (or end) of the text that you want to select.**

2. **Hold down the left mouse button and move the mouse to the other end of the text, highlighting all the text you want to select.**

3. **Release the left mouse button.**

If you trust your mouse-clicking abilities, try these other ways to select text with the mouse:

✔ Double-click a word (selects the word as well as the space that follows it).

✔ Hold down the Ctrl key and click inside a sentence to select the entire sentence.

✔ Triple-click inside a paragraph to select the entire paragraph.

✔ Click to the far left (where the cursor changes to an arrow) of the first word in a line to select the entire line.

✔ Double-click to the far left of a paragraph to select the entire paragraph.

✔ With your mouse to the far left of the text, vertically drag (that is, hold down the mouse button and move the mouse) to select multiple lines, whether those lines are part of a single paragraph or multiple paragraphs.

Using the keyboard to select text

Instead of reaching for the mouse, you may find one of the keyboard shortcuts shown in Table 5-1 easier for selecting text. If you repeat the key combination, you select more text in the direction indicated.

Table 5-1	Keyboard Shortcuts for Selecting Text
Pressing This	*Selects This*
Shift+→	Character to right of insertion point
Shift+←	Character to left of insertion point
Shift+Home	All the current line to the left of the insertion point
Shift+End	All the current line to the right of the insertion point
Shift+PgUp	A screenful of text from the insertion point up

Pressing This	Selects This
Shift+PgDn	A screenful of text from the insertion point down
Ctrl+Shift+→	One word to the right of the insertion point
Ctrl+Shift+←	One word to the left of the insertion point
Ctrl+Shift+Home	All text from the insertion point to the beginning of the document
Ctrl+Shift+End	All text from the insertion point to the end of the document
Alt+Ctrl+Shift+Page Down	All text from the insertion point to the end of the displayed window
F8 and an arrow key	From the insertion point in the direction of whichever arrow you choose. F8 puts you in selection mode, which you get out of by pressing Esc.
Ctrl+Shift+F8 and an arrow key	Highlights a block of text (the size of the highlighted text varies depending on how many times you press the up/down or right/left arrow keys)
Ctrl+A	Entire document — all text, including footnotes (but excluding headers and footers); good for making a font change throughout the whole document

Editing Text

Not even the greatest authors can write their masterpieces in one draft. Most people need to edit their writing until it means exactly what they want to say. To make this (usually disagreeable) task easier, Word lets you edit text in several ways: deleting text, copying or moving text (even between different documents), or using drag-and-drop editing.

Deleting text

Two keys can delete individual characters and selected text:

✔ The Backspace key (typically gray, with an arrow pointing to the left), at the top of the keyboard, eliminates characters to the *left* of the insertion point.

✔ The Delete key, which you find in more than one place — below the Insert key (above the arrow keys) and below the 3 key on the numeric keypad — eliminates characters to the *right* of the insertion point.

Avoid pressing the Insert key (or Ins on some keyboards). The Word default mode is Insert mode, which means that when you type, your newly typed words push any existing words to the right. If you accidentally press the Insert key, you enter Overtype mode. When you're in Overtype mode, typing new text simply wipes out any existing text that gets in the way.

Here are a few things you may want to note:

✔ Choosing Edit⇨Clear does the same thing as pressing the Delete key.

✔ You can delete entire blocks of text (or graphics) by selecting the text (or graphics) first and then pressing either the Backspace or Delete key.

✔ Rather than delete text and then type something new, you can delete and replace text at the same time by selecting the text and then typing your new text.

People have a tendency to change their minds (especially politicians). In case you delete text (or do almost anything else, for that matter) and suddenly realize that you didn't want to perform that particular action after all, you have three options:

✔ Press Ctrl+Z.

✔ Choose Edit⇨Undo.

✔ Click the Undo button on the Standard toolbar.

By choosing one of the three Undo options, Word takes back the last command that you did. For example, if you delete a paragraph and suddenly realize you made a mistake, press Ctrl+Z, and Word restores your text.

Copying and moving text

If you want to copy text and place the copy in a different part of the document, or simply move text from one place to another:

1. **Select the text that you want to copy.**

   Use the mouse or keyboard as explained in the "Selecting Text" section earlier in this chapter.

2. **Copy or cut the selected text.**

   Copying text lets you keep the original text in its current location but paste a copy of that text in another part of your document. To copy the text, you can do any of the following:

   - Choose Edit⇨Copy.
   - Press Ctrl+C.
   - Click the Copy button on the Standard toolbar.
   - Click the right mouse button and choose Copy from the pop-up menu.

   Cutting text removes the text so you can move it to another part of your document. To cut the text, you can do any of the following:

   - Choose Edit⇨Cut.
   - Press Ctrl+X.
   - Click the Cut button on the Standard toolbar.
   - Click the right mouse button and choose Cut from the pop-up menu.

3. **Move the cursor to where you want to place the copied or cut text.**

4. **Choose the Paste command in one of the following ways:**

   - Choose Edit⇨Paste.
   - Press Ctrl+V.
   - Click the Paste button on the Standard toolbar.
   - Click the right mouse button and choose Paste from the pop-up menu.

Each time you copy or cut text, Windows stores this text on the Office Clipboard, which is a temporary storage place that holds up to 24 copied or cut objects. For more information about the Office Clipboard, see Chapter 2.

Discovering drag-and-drop editing

Although *drag-and-drop* sounds like something you may do when shopping at the last minute during the holidays, it's actually a shortcut for cutting and pasting. Instead of copying or cutting text and pasting it somewhere else, drag-and-drop editing lets you drag text to a new location. Then you can drop the text by releasing the mouse button.

Drag-and-drop editing works within a document as well as between documents. If you have two documents open, you can simply drag and drop text between the two documents.

Drag-and-drop editing can be a bit tricky to master at first. You may want to experiment on a document that you can afford to mess up, such as your boss's résumé. If you do make a mistake using drag-and-drop editing, you can always use the Undo command (press Ctrl+Z) to fix it.

To drag and drop selected text to a new location, do the following:

1. **Select the text to move by using the mouse or one of the keyboard commands.**

2. **Place the mouse pointer inside the selected text and hold down the left mouse button.**

   The mouse pointer displays a box underneath, and a gray, vertical dotted line shows you where Word will put your selected text when you let go of the left mouse button.

3. **Drag the text to the new location.**

   Word displays a vertical gray line to show you where your selected text will appear the moment you release the left mouse button.

4. **Release the left mouse button.**

If you'd rather copy text than move it, follow these steps:

1. **Select the text that you want to copy by using the mouse or one of the keyboard commands.**

2. **Hold down the Ctrl key.**

3. **Place the mouse pointer on the selected text and hold down the left mouse button.**

4. **Drag the text to the new location.**

5. **Release the mouse button and the Ctrl key.**

Checking Your Grammar and Spelling

Some of the best writers in the world can't spell correctly — just look at all the weird spellings in Shakespeare's original plays. To make sure that your high-powered business presentation doesn't look like the scribblings of a five-year-old, let Word check your grammar and spelling before you show your document to anyone else.

Checking grammar and spelling as you write

As you type, Word acts like a grammar-school teacher and immediately underlines possible problems to call them to your attention. A green, wavy line appears under possible grammar errors, and a red, wavy line highlights possible spelling mistakes.

To address grammatical problems that Word underlines:

1. **Place the mouse pointer over the word underlined by a green wavy line.**

2. **Click the right mouse button.**

   A pop-up menu appears, as shown in Figure 5-1.

3. **Choose one of the boldface suggestions Word provides, or click Grammar for more information.**

   If you click Grammar, the Grammar dialog box appears (as shown in Figure 5-2), offering suggestions and giving you the option of choosing whether to ignore a particular grammar rule.

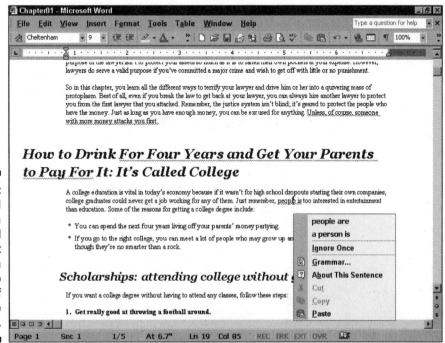

Figure 5-1:
When Word finds a grammatical error, it displays a pop-up menu of possible suggestions.

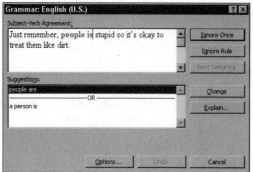

Figure 5-2:
The
Grammar
dialog box.

4. Choose one of the following options, depending on your opinion of the matter in question:

- Click Resume.

- Click Ignore Rule.

- Click a suggestion displayed in the Suggestions list box and click change.

5. Click Cancel, click the close box in the upper-right corner of the window, or press Esc to dismiss the Grammar dialog box.

To address spelling problems that Word underlines:

1. Place the mouse pointer over the word underlined by a red wavy line.

2. Click the right mouse button.

A pop-up menu appears, listing words that Word thinks you meant instead of the misspelled word, as shown in Figure 5-3.

3. Choose one of the following:

- Click one of the boldface words that Word suggests.

- Click Add to Dictionary to add the underlined word to the dictionary so it won't be flagged as an error ever again.

- Click Ignore All. *Note:* Ignore All makes Word bypass all future instances of this spelling in this document.

If having Word automatically check your spelling or grammar as you type gets on your nerves, you can turn it off by following these steps:

1. Choose Tools⇨Options.

The Options dialog box appears.

2. Click the Spelling & Grammar tab.

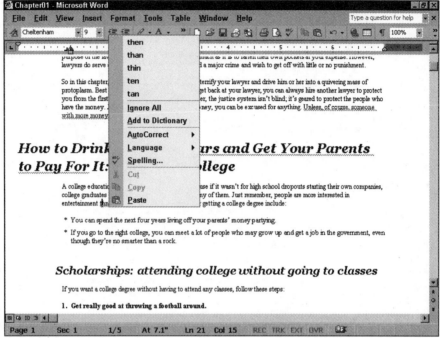

Figure 5-3:
Word
displays a
list of words
that come
close to
matching
your
misspelled
word.

3. **Click the Check Spelling as You Type or Check Grammar as You Type check box so that the check mark disappears.**

    When the check box is empty, the feature is turned off.

4. **Click OK.**

Checking your entire document for spelling and grammar

Rather than correcting spelling and grammatical mistakes while you type, you may want to finish writing and then check your spelling and grammar. To check the spelling and grammar of your entire document, do the following:

1. **Choose one of the following:**

    • Choose Tools⇨Spelling and Grammar.

    • Press F7.

    • Click the Spelling and Grammar button on the Standard toolbar (the one with the check mark and the letters *ABC* on it).

    Each time Word finds a possible problem, it stops and displays the Spelling and Grammar dialog box, as shown in Figure 5-4.

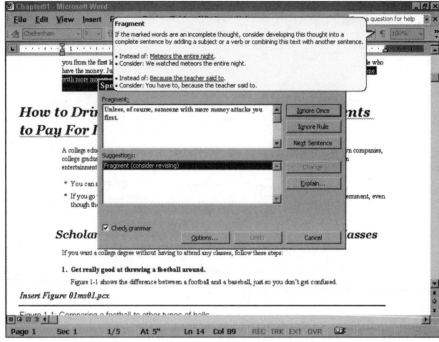

Figure 5-4:
The Spelling
and
Grammar
dialog box
can help
correct
mistakes in
your
document.

2. Choose one of the following, depending on your opinion of the matter at hand:

- Click Ignore Once.

- Click Ignore All (if spell-checking) or Ignore Rule (if grammar checking).

- Click Add to Dictionary to add the underlined word to the dictionary so it won't be flagged as an error ever again. (The Add to Dictionary button only appears when spell-checking.)

- Click a suggestion displayed in the Suggestions list box and click Change or Change All.

After Word finishes checking your document, it displays the message, "The spelling and grammar check is complete."

3. Click OK to return to your document.

Instead of highlighting a suggested word from the Suggestions list box and clicking Change, you can accept a suggested word by double-clicking that word. As another alternative, just type your own correction directly in the top window of the Spelling and Grammar dialog box.

If you don't want Word to check your grammar while checking spelling, you can turn off just the grammar checker by following these steps:

1. **Choose Tools⇨Options.**

   The Options dialog box appears.

2. **Click the Spelling & Grammar tab.**

3. **Click the Check Grammar with Spelling check box so the check box is empty.**

4. **Click OK.**

Saving time with AutoCorrect

AutoCorrect contains a list of common typographical errors along with their corrections. The moment you type a word matching AutoCorrect's list of typographical errors (such as *teh* instead of *the*, or *adn* instead of *and*), AutoCorrect springs into action and corrects the misspelling right away (giving you the illusion that you actually spell everything correctly).

✔ You can add your own common spelling mistakes to the AutoCorrect dictionary so it corrects them automatically.

✔ If you use a lot of bizarre technical terms or proper names, you can store shorthand references in AutoCorrect. For example, instead of typing *Massachusetts Institute of Technology* each time, just store the letters *MIT* in AutoCorrect. Each time you type *MIT,* AutoCorrect automatically replaces it with *Massachusetts Institute of Technology.* (If you really want to type *MIT,* you'll have to retype it again and then Word leaves your typing alone.)

To modify AutoCorrect, do the following:

1. **Choose Tools⇨AutoCorrect.**

   The AutoCorrect dialog box appears, as shown in Figure 5-5.

2. **In the Replace box, type a word that you frequently misspell.**

   Or type a shorthand word to represent a longer word or phrase, such as **MIT**.

3. **Type the correct spelling of the word in the With box.**

   Or type the longer word or phrase that you want AutoCorrect to use, such as **Massachusetts Institute of Technology**.

4. **Click Add.**

5. **Click OK.**

If you enter a misspelled word in the With box, AutoCorrect misspells the word consistently — which goes to show you that (a) computers aren't that smart after all, and (b) you can actually call your new janitorial invention "X-punge" or "KleenitOOPS" and teach AutoCorrect to accept the name as correct.

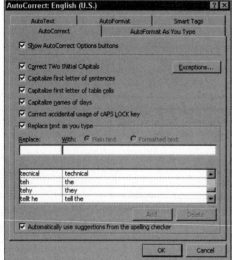

Figure 5-5:
The
AutoCorrect
dialog box
displays a
list of
common
misspellings
— and their
correct
spellings
(which
Word offers
to use
instead).

To remove a word from AutoCorrect, follow these steps:

1. **Choose Tools⇨AutoCorrect.**

   The AutoCorrect dialog box appears (refer to Figure 5-5).

2. **In the two-column list box at the bottom of the dialog box, click the word that you want to remove from AutoCorrect.**

   Word highlights the entire row.

3. **Click Delete.**

4. **Click OK.**

If you want to turn off AutoCorrect so it doesn't annoy you as you write, follow these steps:

1. **Choose Tools⇨AutoCorrect.**

   The AutoCorrect dialog box appears.

2. **Click the AutoCorrect tab.**

3. **Click all the check boxes that currently have check marks.**

   The check boxes should appear empty when you finish.

4. **Click OK.**

Counting Your Words

Because many writers get paid by the word and need to create documents with a certain number of words (say, 1,500 to 2,500 words), you may want to know how many words are in your document. Fortunately, Word is smart enough to know how to count all the words in your document. To count your words, follow these steps:

1. **Choose Tools⇨Word Count.**

   The Word Count dialog box appears, as shown in Figure 5-6.

2. **Click Close.**

You can also display the word count of a document by choosing View⇨Toolbars⇨Word Count. This displays a Word Count toolbar that shows the word count each time you click the Recount button.

Word Count toolbar

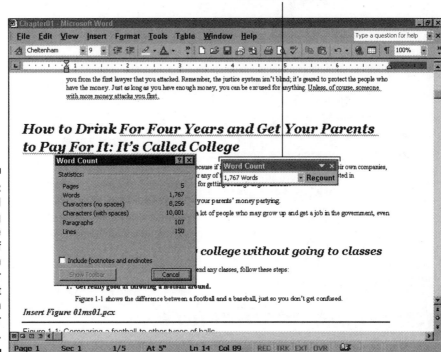

Figure 5-6:
The Word Count dialog box lists the number of words in your document (along with other information).

Translating Your Words

Because not everyone speaks (or writes) in the same language, Word is smart enough to know how to translate words and phrases from English into French or Spanish (or from French or Spanish to English). So, the next time you need to translate some words, do the following:

You may need to install Word's foreign language dictionaries from the installation CDs.

1. **Choose Tools⇨Language⇨Translate.**

   The Translate pane appears (as shown in Figure 5-7), giving you options for translating individual words, phrases, or entire documents into another language.

2. **Click a radio button to define what you want to translate: Text, Current selection, or Entire document.**

   If you click the Text radio button, you have to type a word that you want to translate.

3. **Click in the Dictionary list box and choose a translation option, such as English (U.S.) to French.**

4. **Click Go.**

   The Translate pane displays several translations.

5. **Click Replace.**

   If you chose the Text radio button in Step 2, you need to follow Steps 6 through 8. Otherwise, you can click the close box in the Translation pane to make it go away.

6. **Move the cursor to the part of your document where you want the translated word to appear.**

7. **Highlight the translated word(s) that you want to use and click Replace.**

   Word displays your chosen translated word in your document.

8. **Click the close box of the Translation pane to make it go away.**

Using Find and Replace

To find a certain word or phrase in your document, you can scroll through and examine the document line by line yourself, or you can do it the easy way and let Word find the word or phrase for you.

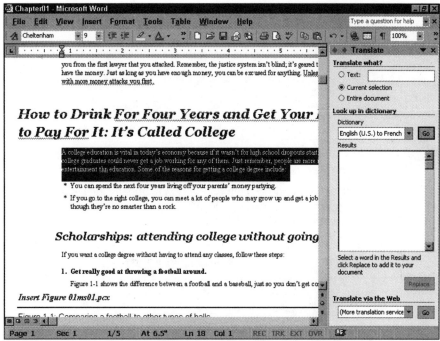

Figure 5-7:
The
Translate
pane.

The Find and Replace feature can also come in handy when you want to replace certain words or phrases, but don't feel like doing it yourself. For example, you may have a prenuptial agreement with the name *Frank* written everywhere. If you want to find all references to *Frank* and replace them with *Bob,* the Find and Replace feature can do it for you faster and more accurately than a high-priced lawyer (who probably uses the Find and Replace feature anyway).

Using the Find feature

To find a word or phrase, follow these steps:

1. **Choose Edit⇨Find or press Ctrl+F.**

   The Find and Replace dialog box appears (as shown in Figure 5-8), ready to search through your document for specific words or phrases.

2. **Type the word or phrase that you want to find within your document in the Find What box.**

   If you're repeating a previous search, click the downward-pointing arrow next to the Find what box to display a list of your last four searches.

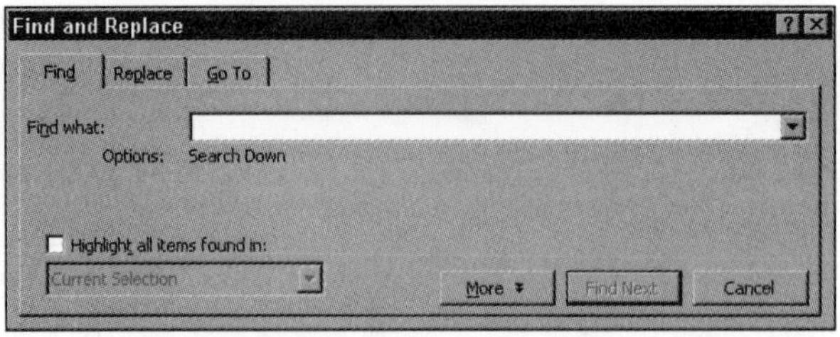

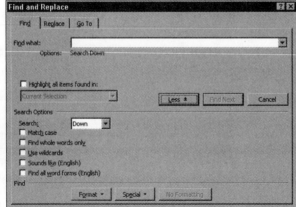

Figure 5-8:
The Find
and Replace
dialog box.

3. **Click More to customize your search, or skip to Step 8 if you want to start your search right away.**

   The Find and Replace dialog box magically grows larger (as shown in Figure 5-9), providing more options that you can use to search your document for specific text.

Figure 5-9:
The larger
version of
the Find and
Replace
dialog box.

4. **Click the Search list box if you want to limit what part of the document Word checks. Choose from the following:**

   - **All:** Searches the entire document.

   - **Down:** Searches from the current location of the cursor to the end of the document.

   - **Up:** Searches from the current location of the cursor to the beginning of the document.

5. **If you want to limit your search to specific criteria, check the appropriate check boxes:**

   - **Match case:** Searches for the exact upper- and lowercase word or phrase that you type in the Find What box.

- **Find whole words only:** Searches for complete words and doesn't flag words that contain the text you're searching for (for example, searching for *Ann* won't bring up *Anniversary*).

- **Use wildcards:** Lets you use wildcards in your search (for example, type ***te** to find all words that end with *te*).

- **Sounds like:** Searches for words phonetically.

- **Find all word forms:** Searches for different forms of a word (a search for *sing* would bring up *sang,* for example).

6. **Click Format if you want to search for words in a specified Font, Paragraph, Language, or Style.**

7. **Click Special if you want to search for particular punctuation marks or section breaks.**

8. **Start the search by clicking Find Next.**

9. **After you reach the first selection, use one of the following options:**

- To search for the next occurrence of the object of your search, click Find Next again.

- To close the Find and Replace dialog box and work on your document, click the Cancel button.

Using the Find and Replace feature

To find a word or phrase and replace it with another word or phrase, follow these steps:

1. **Choose Edit⇨Replace or press Ctrl+H.**

   The Find and Replace dialog box appears.

2. **In the Find What box, type the word or phrase that you want to find within your document.**

3. **In the Replace With box, type the word or phrase that you want to use in place of the Find What text.**

4. **Click More to customize your find-and-replace operation, or skip to Step 5 if you want to start finding and replacing text right away.**

   If you click More, a larger version of the Find and Replace dialog box appears (as shown in Figure 5-10), offering more options that you can use to search for (and yes, replace) specific text.

   For a description of all the options you have for narrowing your find and replace, refer to Steps 4 through 7 in the preceding section, "Using the Find feature."

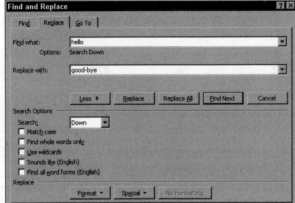

Figure 5-10:
The larger
version of
the Find and
Replace
dialog box.

5. **Start the search and replace by clicking Find Next.**

6. **When Word locates the desired word or phrase, choose one of the following options:**

   • To do nothing and continue searching, click Find Next.

   • If you want Word to replace the found text with what you have in the Replace With box, click Replace.

   • To replace every occurrence of the selected text with the replacement text, click Replace All. (Such trust between human and computer is a beautiful thing. I hope.)

   • If you want to quit the search, click Cancel.

Be careful when choosing the Replace All command. To prevent Word from replacing words buried inside other words (such as replacing the letters *can* inside the word *cannon*), click the Find Whole Words Only check box to put a check mark in it.

Chapter 6

Making Your Words Look Pretty

● ●

In This Chapter

▶ Formatting your document by hand

▶ Formatting your document with themes and style templates

▶ Creating tables and lists

▶ Adding borders

● ●

*W*ords alone don't always sway an audience. Besides writing clearly (something you rarely see in most computer manuals), you should also format your writing so that people want to look at it. The better looking your document is, the more likely that someone will take the time to read it.

Microsoft Word gives you two ways to format text: by hand or by using something called a *style template* (explained later in this chapter, so don't worry about the exact meaning for now). Formatting text by hand takes longer but gives you more control. Formatting text using a style template is faster but may not format the text exactly the way you want, which means you may have to go back and format the text slightly on your own.

So which method should you use? Both. If you're in a hurry, use a style template. If you just need to do a little formatting, do it yourself.

Formatting Text Manually

To modify the appearance of your text, you can change one of the following options: the font and font sizes, the type *styles* (bold, italics, underline, and so on), and the color of the text.

Picking a font and font size

Your computer probably comes with a variety of fonts that you don't even know exist. A *font* defines the appearance of individual letters. Depending on which fonts your computer has, you can make your text look like it was printed in a newspaper or written with a feather quill. Some examples of different fonts are

> ✔ Times New Roman
>
> ✔ Courier
>
> ✔ Arial

When you click the Font list box on the Formatting toolbar, Word conveniently displays a list of all available fonts and shows you what they look like, as shown in Figure 6-1.

Figure 6-1:
The Font list box allows you to view and pick the font you want for your text.

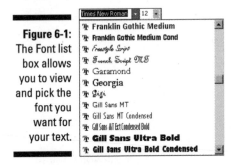

The font size makes your text bigger or smaller, regardless of the type of font you choose. Some fonts look better large, some fonts look good small, and some fonts look horrible no matter what font size you choose.

If you're not sure whether or how to change the font or font size of your text, experiment with a few font and font size combinations to see whether they improve the readability of your text.

If you plan to share documents with others, stick to common fonts, such as Times New Roman or MS Sans Serif. Not all computers have some of the more bizarre fonts installed so if you use those fonts, your text may look really weird on someone else's computer.

To change the font and font size of text, do this:

1. **Highlight the text that you want to modify.**

   If you need help highlighting text, review the section on selecting text in Chapter 5.

2. **Click the Font list box on the Formatting toolbar and choose a font.**

   Depending on how your toolbars look, you may have to click the double rightward-pointing arrows on the Formatting toolbar to display the Font list box.

3. **Click the Font Size list box on the Formatting toolbar and choose a font size.**

Word displays the selected text in your chosen font and font size.

If you choose a font and font size without selecting any text first, Word automatically uses your chosen font and font size on whatever text you type next.

Choosing a type style

Just to give you a little extra control over your text, Word also lets you display text as bold, italicized, or underlined, regardless of the font or font size you choose.

✔ **This sentence appears in bold.**

✔ *This sentence appears in italics.*

✔ This sentence is underlined.

✔ **This sentence shows that you can combine styles — bold and underlined *with italics*, for example.**

To change the type style of text, follow these steps:

1. **Highlight the text that you want to modify.**

2. **Choose one or more of the following, depending on how you want your text to look:**

   • Click the Bold button (which looks like a B) on the Formatting toolbar or press Ctrl+B.

   • Click the Italic button (which looks like an I) on the Formatting toolbar or press Ctrl+I.

   • Click the Underline button (which looks like a U) on the Formatting toolbar or press Ctrl+U.

   Word displays the selected text in your chosen style.

If you choose a type style without selecting any text, Word automatically uses your chosen style, such as italic or underline, on whatever text you type next.

Making a splash with color

Because the cost of color printers is falling as rapidly as the net worth of the United States government, you may want to experiment with using different colors to display text. (By the way, adding color doesn't have to be just an aesthetic choice. Color is very useful when you want to highlight portions of text or strain the eyes of the people forced to read your document.)

Depending on how your toolbars look, you may have to click the double rightward-pointing arrows on the Formatting toolbar to display the Highlight and Font Color buttons.

To change the background color of your text (which makes your text look like someone colored it with a highlighting marker), do the following:

1. **Select the text that you want to modify.**

2. **Click the downward-pointing arrow to the right of the Highlight button on the Formatting toolbar.**

   A palette of different colors appears.

3. **Click the color that you want to use on the background.**

   Word magically changes the background color of your text.

To change the color of the actual letters that make up your text, do the following:

1. **Select the text that you want to modify.**

2. **Click the downward-pointing arrow to the right of the Font Color button on the Formatting toolbar.**

   A palette of different colors appears.

3. **Click the color that you want to use on the text.**

   Word changes the color of your text.

Painting text with the Format Painter

Suppose you have a chunk of text formatted perfectly — font, font size, type style, and so on. Do you have to go through the whole laborious process again to make another chunk of text look exactly the same? Of course not! Use the Format Painter.

The Format Painter tells Word, "See the way you formatted that block of text I just highlighted? I want you to use that same formatting on this other chunk of text."

By using the Format Painter, you don't have to format the individual characteristics of text yourself, which saves time so you can do something that's more important (like make plans for lunch or print your résumé).

To use the Format Painter, follow these steps:

1. **Select the text containing the formatting that you want to use on another chunk of text.**

2. **Click the Format Painter button (it looks like a paintbrush and appears to the right of the Paste icon) on the Formatting toolbar.**

   The mouse cursor turns into an I-beam cursor with a paintbrush to the left. The paintbrush lets you know that Word automatically formats the next chunk of text that you select.

3. **Select the text that you want to format.**

   As soon as you release the left mouse button, Word formats the text with all the formatting characteristics of the text you selected in Step 1.

If the text that you select in Step 1 contains a variety of formatting characteristics, Word copies only the formatting characteristics that the entire chunk of selected text has in common. For example, if you select text that's in Times New Roman font with one sentence underlined, a second sentence in bold, and a third sentence with a yellow background, Word formats your new text with the only shared formatting characteristic — the Times New Roman font.

Aligning text to the right and the left

Word lets you choose an alignment for your text, which can be left, center, right, or justified, as shown in Figure 6-2. Most of the time you probably want to left-align text, but occasionally, you may want to center a heading in the middle of the page or justify an entire paragraph. Don't worry too much about right-aligning text unless you like displaying your text in strange ways.

In a nutshell, here's what the four alignment possibilities do to your text:

- ✔ **Left-align text:** The left margin is a straight line, and the right margin is uneven.

- ✔ **Center text:** Each line is centered in the middle of the page. Consequently, both the left and right margins look ragged when you have several lines of unequal length centered.

- ✔ **Right-align text:** The right margin is a straight line, and the left margin is uneven.

- ✔ **Justify text:** Both the left and right margins are straight, and the letters in between look somewhat spaced apart.

To align text, do the following:

1. **Click anywhere inside the paragraph that you want to align.**

2. **Click the Align Left, Center, Align Right, or Justify button on the Formatting toolbar, depending on how you want the text to look.**

   As soon as you click a button, Word aligns your text.

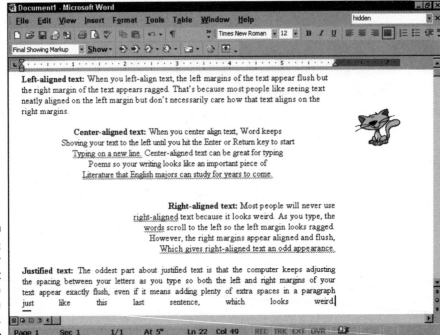

If you choose an alignment without selecting any text first, Word applies your chosen alignment to whatever text you type next.

Indenting text

Similar to aligning text is indenting text. Indenting text can make a block of text stand out so it's easy to find and read.

To indent text, do the following:

1. **Highlight the paragraph that you want to indent.**

   You can just highlight part of a paragraph, and when you choose the Indent command, Word is smart enough to indent the entire paragraph.

2. **Click the Increase Indent or Decrease Indent buttons on the Formatting toolbar.**

   Clicking the Increase Indent button moves the text to the right. Clicking the Decrease Indent button moves the text to the left.

Formatting Your Document the Easy Way

If you really love using Word, you can format your text manually. However, Word provides three shortcuts for changing the appearance of your documents:

- ✔ **Themes:** Define the color and graphical appearance of bullets, text, horizontal lines, and the background of a document

- ✔ **Style templates:** Provide one or more styles for creating common types of documents, such as résumés, business letters, or fax cover pages

- ✔ **Styles:** Define the format for a paragraph using specific margins, font sizes, or underlining

Choosing a theme

A *theme* lets you choose the decorative appearance of your document. If you don't choose a theme, your text appears in boring black and white. Themes mostly make your document look pretty. If you don't care about appearances, you probably don't need to use themes.

To choose a theme, follow these steps:

1. Choose Format⇨Theme.

The Theme dialog box appears, as shown in Figure 6-3.

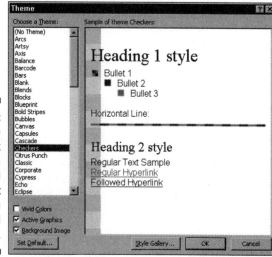

Figure 6-3:
The Theme dialog box can create a formatted document for you quickly and easily.

2. **Click the theme you want to use in the Choose a Theme list.**

   Each time you click a theme, Word politely shows you a sample of how that theme can change the appearance of your document. You may need to insert your Office XP CD in your computer to install your chosen theme.

3. **Select or clear one or more of the following check boxes:**

   - **Vivid Colors:** Adds (or removes) additional colors to text
   - **Active Graphics:** Adds (or removes) additional graphics to make bullets and horizontal lines look more interesting
   - **Background Image:** Adds (or removes) the background graphic

4. **Click OK after you find and define a theme to use.**

   Word displays your chosen theme on the currently displayed document.

Choosing a style template

A *style template* provides formatting for common types of documents (faxes, reports, proposals, memos, and so on). So, if you need to write a fax cover sheet or a business letter, you could write the whole thing from scratch and waste a lot of time in the process. Or, you could use a special fax or business letter template that provides the formatting (styles) for creating a fax or business letter. Then all you have to do is type the text and let Word worry about the formatting.

To choose a style template, follow these steps:

1. **Choose Format⇨Theme.**

   The Theme dialog box appears (refer to Figure 6-3), showing you the theme used in your current document.

2. **Click the Style Gallery button.**

   The Style Gallery dialog box appears, as shown in Figure 6-4.

3. **Click one of the style templates listed in the Template box, such as Elegant Fax or Contemporary Report.**

   You can scroll up or down the list under the Template box to see more style templates.

4. **Click one of the following option buttons in the Preview group:**

   - **Document:** Shows what your current document looks like with the selected style template
   - **Example:** Shows how a typical document can look with the selected style template
   - **Style Samples:** Shows the different styles that make up the style template

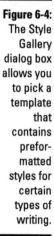

Figure 6-4:
The Style
Gallery
dialog box
allows you
to pick a
template
that
contains
prefor-
matted
styles for
certain
types of
writing.

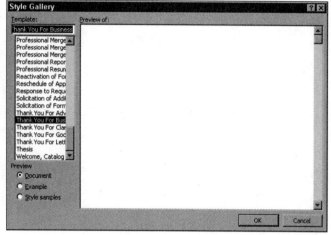

5. **Click OK after you find a style template that you want to use.**

Formatting paragraphs with different styles

Styles define the overall appearance of the text, such as the fonts used to display text or the size of text. By using different styles in a document, you can keep your document from looking like a boring typewritten page (provided, of course, that you still remember what a typewriter is).

To choose a style, use the Style list box on the Formatting toolbar as described in the following steps:

1. **Click in the paragraph that you want to format with a particular style.**

   If you haven't typed any text yet, Word applies the style to whatever text you type in Step 4.

2. **Click the Style list box on the Formatting toolbar to choose a style.**

   A list of different styles appears, as shown in Figure 6-5. (Depending on how your toolbars look, you may have to click the double rightward-pointing arrows on the Formatting toolbar to display the Style list box.)

   If you can't see the Style box on the Formatting toolbar, click the Toolbar Options button on the Formatting toolbar.

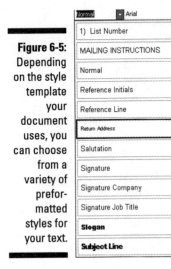

Figure 6-5:
Depending
on the style
template
your
document
uses, you
can choose
from a
variety of
prefor-
matted
styles for
your text.

3. **Click the style that you want to use.**

4. **Type your text and watch Word format it before your eyes. (Or Word formats your text right away, if you moved the cursor to an existing block of text in Step 1.)**

Aligning Text with Tables

Tables organize information in rows and columns, which can be useful for displaying information in an easy-to-read format. With a table, you can organize essential text so people can find and read it easily, rather than trying to find important information buried inside a paragraph.

Before you start working with tables, you need to know some things about rows and columns, including the following:

- ✔ A *row* displays information horizontally.

- ✔ A *column* displays information vertically.

- ✔ A *cell* is a single box formed by the intersection of a row and a column.

Making a table

You may be happy to know that Word provides two different ways to make a table in your documents:

✔ Draw the table in your document with the mouse

✔ Define the size of a table by typing in the exact number of rows and columns

Drawing a table with the mouse

If you want to create tables right away, you can draw the table's approximate size by using the mouse. You can modify its height and width later. To create a table using the mouse, do the following:

1. **Choose Table⇨Draw Table.**

   The Tables and Borders toolbar appears, and the mouse pointer turns into a pencil icon.

2. **Move the mouse where you want the table to appear.**

3. **Hold down the left mouse button and drag the mouse to draw the table, as shown in Figure 6-6.**

4. **Release the left mouse button.**

   Word displays your table as a solid line.

Tables and Borders toolbar

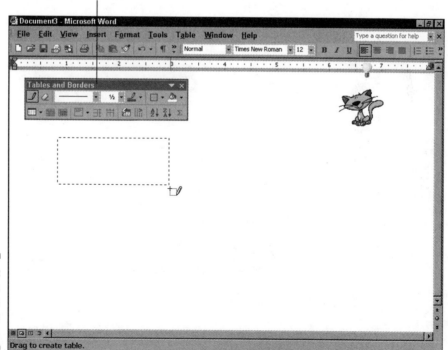

Figure 6-6:
You can draw a table with the mouse.

5. **Drag the mouse inside the table where you want to draw a row or column. You can draw a dotted line vertically, horizontally, or diagonally to define your cells.**

   Word draws a dotted line, as shown in Figure 6-7. Repeat this step as many times as necessary.

   In case you make a mistake, just click the Eraser icon on the Tables and Borders toolbar and click the line that you want to erase. Then click the Draw Table icon again to start drawing your table once more.

6. **Press Esc when you finish drawing your rows and columns.**

   The mouse cursor changes from a pencil icon back to an I-shaped icon. At this point, you can click inside a cell and type text in your newly created table.

7. **Click the Close box of the Tables and Borders toolbar to make it go away.**

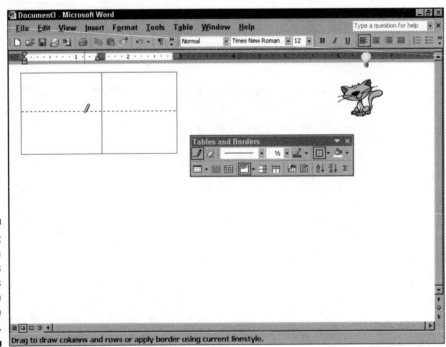

Figure 6-7:
You can draw rows and columns in a table with the mouse.

Defining a table from the Table menu

If you want to create a table the slower way, which gives you more control over your table's appearance, use the Word main menu:

1. **Choose Table⇨Insert⇨Table.**

   The Insert Table dialog box appears, as shown in Figure 6-8.

2. **In the Number of Columns box, type the number of columns you want.**

3. **In the Number of Rows box, type the number of rows you want.**

Figure 6-8:
The Insert Table dialog box allows you to precisely define the size of a table.

4. **In the AutoFit Behavior area, select one of the following option buttons:**

   • **Fixed Column Width:** You can choose Auto to force Word to make column widths the size of the longest item stored in the entire table, or you can define a specific value, such as 0.5 inches.

   • **AutoFit to Contents:** Adjusts column widths depending on the longest item in each column.

   • **AutoFit to Window:** Adjusts the table based on the size of the window used to display the table.

5. **Click the AutoFormat button.**

   The Table AutoFormat dialog box appears, as shown in Figure 6-9.

6. **Click one of the table formats (such as Classic 3 or Simple 1) in the Table Styles list and try out the various formatting options available in the dialog box.**

   The Preview window shows a sample of the selected table format. When you select any check boxes in the Apply Special Formats To group in the Table AutoFormat dialog box, the Preview window shows how these options affect the selected table format's appearance.

7. After you select your table format preference and any optional formatting options, click OK.

The Insert Table dialog box appears again (refer to Figure 6-8).

8. Click OK.

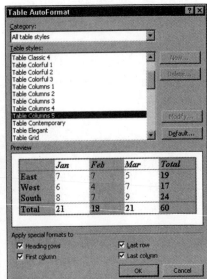

Figure 6-9:
The Table
AutoFormat
dialog box
allows you
to make
your tables
look pretty.

Entering and editing table data

A blank table is pretty useless, so you may want to add data inside the tables you create. To enter and edit data, just click the desired cell and use the keyboard to type or edit. You can also use the following methods to move around within the table:

- ✔ Press the Tab key to move the cursor to the next cell to the right in the same row.
- ✔ Press Shift+Tab to move backward (to the left) in the row.
- ✔ Use the ↑ and ↓ keys to move from row to row.

Deleting tables

Word gives you two ways to delete a table:

✔ Delete just the contents of the table (leave the blank cells and formatting intact).

✔ Delete the entire table, including the contents of the table.

To delete only the contents of the table but not the table itself, do the following:

1. **Click the mouse anywhere inside the table containing the data you want to delete.**

2. **Choose Table⇨Select⇨Table.**

   Word highlights your chosen table.

3. **Press Delete.**

   Word deletes the data inside your chosen table.

To delete the contents of the table and the table itself, do the following:

1. **Click the mouse anywhere inside the table.**

2. **Choose Table⇨Delete⇨Table.**

   Word deletes your chosen table and any data inside of it.

Adding or deleting rows, columns, and cells, oh my!

After you create a table, you may want to make it bigger or smaller by adding or deleting rows and columns. To delete a row or column, do the following:

1. **Put the cursor in the row or column that you want to delete.**

   You can either use the keyboard arrow keys or click the table using the mouse.

2. **Choose Table⇨Select⇨Column (or Row).**

   Word highlights your chosen row or column.

3. **Choose Table⇨Delete⇨Columns (or Rows).**

To delete a single cell, which may make your table look funny, do the following:

1. **Put the cursor in the cell that you want to delete.**

   You can either use the keyboard cursor keys or click in the cell.

2. **Choose Table⇨Delete⇨Cells.**

   The Delete Cells dialog box appears.

3. **Select an option button (such as Shift Cells Left) and click OK.**

To add a row or column to your table, do this:

1. **Put the cursor in any row or column.**
2. **Choose Table⇨Insert⇨Columns to the Left (or Columns to the Right or Rows Above or Rows Below).**

To add a single cell, do the following:

1. **Put the cursor in the table where you want to add a cell.**
2. **Choose Table⇨Insert⇨Cells.**

   The Insert Cells dialog box appears.

3. **Select an option button (such as Shift Cells Right) and click OK.**

Changing the dimensions of a table's columns and rows

Normally, Word displays all columns with the same width and all rows with the same height. However, if you want some rows or columns to be a different size, Word gives you two options for changing them:

- Use the mouse to change the height or width of rows and columns visually.
- Define exact dimensions for the height or width of rows and columns.

Changing the height of a row or the width of a column visually

To change the row height or column width of a table visually, do the following:

1. **Choose View⇨Print Layout or click the Print Layout View button in the bottom left-hand corner of the screen.**

   Word displays a vertical ruler on the left side of the screen and a horizontal ruler at the top of the screen.

2. **Click inside the table that you want to modify.**

   The Adjust Table Row and Adjust Column markers appear, as shown in Figure 6-10.

3. **Place the mouse cursor over one of the Adjust Table Row or Adjust Column markers on the vertical or horizontal ruler.**

4. **Hold down the left mouse button and drag the mouse up or down (or right and left).**

   Word displays a dotted line to show you how your chosen row or column will look when you release the mouse button.

5. **Release the left mouse button when you're happy with the height of your row or width of your column.**

Adjust Table Column markers

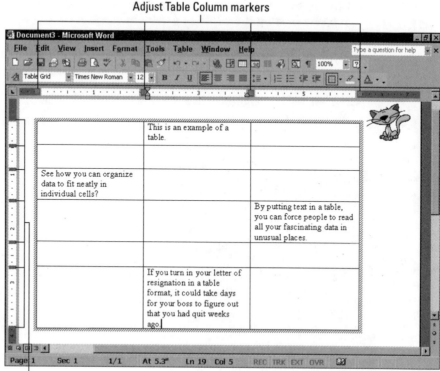

Figure 6-10:
You can use
the markers
to adjust the
rows and
columns.

Adjust Table Row markers

Defining exact dimensions for the height of a row or the width of a column

To tell Word to use exact dimensions for the height of a row or width of a column, do this:

1. **Click in the row or column that you want to adjust.**

2. **Choose Table⇨Table Properties.**

   The Table Properties dialog box appears, as shown in Figure 6-11.

3. **Click the Row or Column tab.**

   The Row or Column tab appears in the Table Properties dialog box.

4. **Click in the Specify Height (or Preferred Width) box and click the up or down arrows to choose a height or width, such as 0.74 inches.**

5. **Click in the Row Height Is box and choose At Least or Exactly. (If you're adjusting the width of a column, click in the Measure In box and choose Inches or Percent.)**

If you choose the At Least option for the row height, your rows will never be smaller than the dimensions you specify, but may be larger, depending on the amount of text you type in it. If you want rows to remain a fixed height, choose the Exactly option instead.

6. **Click OK.**

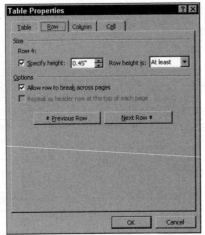

Figure 6-11:
The Table Properties dialog box can help you precisely define the widths and heights of your table's columns and rows.

Making Lists

Some people like making lists so they know what they're supposed to do, what they're supposed to buy, and what they really don't feel like doing but feel guilty enough about that they try to do it anyway. To help accommodate list makers all over the world, Word creates lists quickly and easily.

Word lets you make two types of lists: numbered and bulleted. As their names suggest, a numbered list displays each item with a number in front, while a bulleted list displays a bullet in front of each item, as shown in Figure 6-12.

You can left-align, right-align, center, or justify any of your bulleted or numbered lists. Aren't computers an exciting example of how technology can empower the average user?

To create a numbered or bulleted list, do this:

1. **Select the text that you want to turn into a list.**

2. **Choose Format⇨Bullets and Numbering.**

   The Bullets and Numbering dialog box appears, as shown in Figure 6-13.

3. **Click the Bulleted tab to create a bulleted list or the Numbered tab to create a numbered list.**

   The dialog box displays two rows of boxes that show the various numbering or bullet styles.

4. **Click inside the box that shows the type of bullets or numbering that you want to use; then click OK.**

   Word automatically converts your selected text into a list.

If you choose a numbering or bullet option without first selecting text, Word automatically formats whatever you type next into the type of list you chose.

If you don't care about the style of bullets or numbering that Word uses, just click the Numbering or Bullets button on the Formatting toolbar and then start typing your text. Word applies its default numbering (using numbers such as 1 and 2) or bullet style (displaying a simple black dot) to your text as you type.

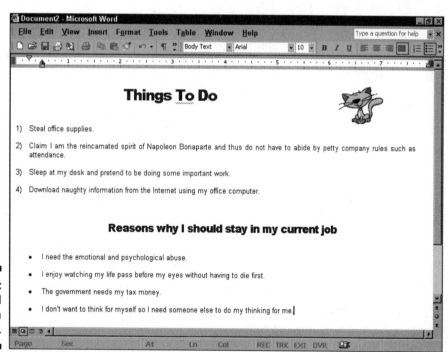

Figure 6-12: A numbered list and a bulleted list.

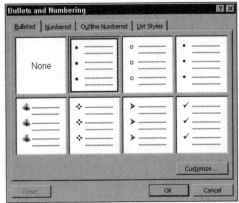

Figure 6-13:
The Bullets
and
Numbering
dialog box
shows you
different
bullet and
numbering
styles you
can choose.

In case Word's automatic list-making feature is more annoying than useful, you can turn it off by choosing Tools⇨AutoCorrect. Then click the AutoFormat As You Type tab and click the Automatic Bulleted List or Automatic Numbered Lists check boxes to clear them. Finally, click OK.

Putting a Border on Your Pages

Another way to make your document look visually appealing is to put borders around the edges, top, or bottom of your page. Borders can consist of solid or dotted lines that thickness and appear in color.

Adding borders to your text

To add a border to your document, do the following:

1. **Choose Format⇨Borders and Shading.**

   The Borders and Shading dialog box appears, as shown in Figure 6-14.

2. **Click the Borders or Page Border tab.**

   Use the Borders tab to put a border around a paragraph. Use the Page Border tab to place a border around one or more pages of your document.

3. **In the Setting area, click an option, such as Box or Shadow.**

   The Preview box shows you what the border will look like.

4. **Click a line style in the Style list box, such as a solid or dotted line.**

5. **Click the Color list box and choose a color, such as red or black.**

Top Border button

Bottom Border button

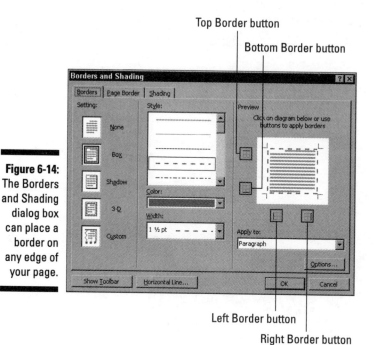

Figure 6-14:
The Borders
and Shading
dialog box
can place a
border on
any edge of
your page.

Left Border button

Right Border button

6. **Click in the Width list box and choose a width such as 1 pt or 3 pt.**

7. **Click the top-, bottom-, right-, and/or left-edge button in the Preview section to define where you want the border to appear.**

8. **Click in the Apply To list box and choose an option such as Whole Document or This Section.**

9. **Click OK.**

Word displays your border around your page. If you cannot see your borders, you may have to switch to Print Layout view by choosing View⇨Print Layout.

Shading your text

To give your pages a little extra bit of visual appeal, consider adding a color background to your text:

1. **Highlight the text that you want to shade.**

If you want to shade an entire paragraph, you can just move the cursor into that paragraph by clicking the mouse or moving the cursor with the arrow keys.

2. **Choose Format⇨Borders and Shading.**

   The Borders and Shading dialog box appears (see Figure 6-15).

3. **Click the Shading tab.**

   The Shading tab appears within the Borders and Shading dialog box, as shown in Figure 6-15.

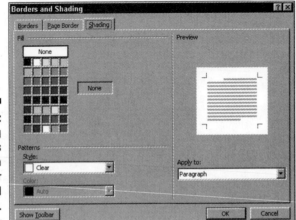

Figure 6-15:
The Shading tab allows you to put a color background behind text.

4. **(Optional) Click a color in the Fill section, such as yellow or green.**

   If you choose a color in this step, your chosen color completely fills up the background of your chosen text.

5. **(Optional) Click in the Style list box under the Patterns section and choose an option such as 10% or Lt Grid.**

   A pattern displays a series of dots or lines behind your highlighted text. A light percentage (10%) displays spots sporadically, while a higher percentage (50%) displays more spots in the background of your text.

6. **Click OK.**

   Word displays shading behind the paragraph you chose in Step 1.

Chapter 7

Creating Fancy Pages

● ●

In This Chapter

▶ Adding headers and footers

▶ Dividing text into columns

▶ Putting pictures into your documents

▶ Polishing your document

● ●

*Y*ou can use Word to write letters, reports, or threatening notes to people you don't like. With a little bit of creativity and a lot of patience, you can also use Word to format and publish those letters, reports, and notes. You can use Word's limited desktop publishing features to make simple newsletters, brochures, and flyers without having to wrestle with a separate desktop publishing program (such as Microsoft Publisher).

Playing with Footers and Headers

Headers and footers are chunks of text that appear at the top and bottom of your pages. *Headers* appear at the top of the page (think of where your head appears in relation to your body), while *footers* appear at the bottom (think of where your feet appear).

Both headers and footers can appear on each page of a document and contain information, such as the publication title, the section or chapter title, the page number, and/or the author's name. If you look at the odd-numbered pages in this book, you can see that the chapter number, chapter title, and page number appear at the top of the page as a header. Headers and footers are useful for displaying identical (or nearly identical) text on two or more pages — for example, document titles or page references (such as *Page 4 of 89*). Although you can type this same text over and over again on each page (but why?), letting Word do the work for you is much easier.

You have two ways to view a document's headers and footers:

- ✔ Choose <u>V</u>iew⇨<u>H</u>eader and Footer.
- ✔ Choose <u>V</u>iew⇨<u>P</u>rint Layout (or click the Print Layout View button in the bottom-left corner of the screen).

If you switch to Print Layout view, you can see how your headers and footers will look on each page, but you won't be able to edit them in that view.

Adding headers and footers

To add a header or footer, follow these steps:

1. **Choose <u>V</u>iew⇨<u>H</u>eader and Footer.**

   Word displays the Header and Footer toolbar along with a Header (or Footer) text box where you can type a header (or footer), as shown in Figure 7-1.

2. **Type your header (or footer) text in the Header (or Footer) text box and/or click a toolbar button to have Word insert the page number, number of pages, date, or time.**

   - If you press Tab once, Word moves the cursor to the center of the header text box. If you press Tab again, Word moves the cursor to the right of the head text box.

   - If you click the Insert Page Number, Insert Number of Pages, Insert Date, or Insert Time buttons to insert the page number, date, or time in your header, Word automatically updates this information from page to page (for the page number information) or each time you open the document (for the date and time information).

   - You can also click Insert AutoText on the toolbar to have Word insert commonly used text for headers and footers (for example, Page X of Y).

3. **Click the Switch between Header and Footer button.**

   Word displays the Footer text box (or the Header text box if you created a header in Step 2).

4. **Type your text in the Footer (or Header) text box and/or click a toolbar button.**

   Refer to Step 2 for directions.

5. **Click <u>C</u>lose on the Header and Footer toolbar to dismiss the toolbar.**

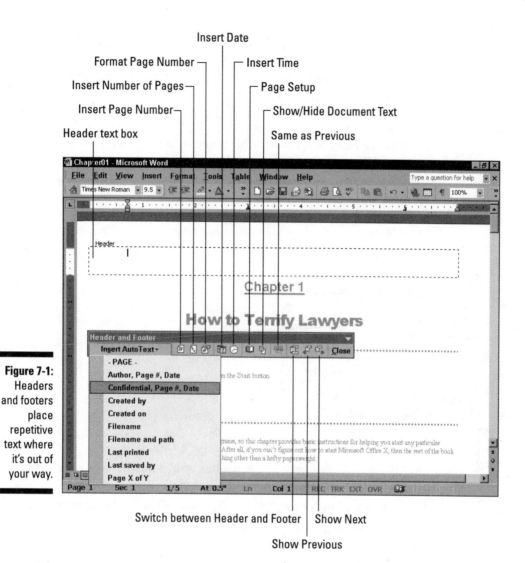

Figure 7-1:
Headers
and footers
place
repetitive
text where
it's out of
your way.

Switch between Header and Footer | Show Next

Show Previous

Modifying page numbering

When you tell Word to include page numbers in your headers or footers,
Word starts numbering from page one and displays Arabic numerals such as
1, 3, and 49. If you want to number your pages differently (for example, numbering them as i, ii, iii, or a, b, c), or you want Word to make 97 the first page
number in your document, you have to use the Page Number Format button
on the Header and Footer toolbar. To use the Page Number Format button,
follow these steps:

1. **Choose View⇨Header and Footer.**

   The Header and Footer toolbar appears (refer to Figure 7-1).

2. **Highlight the page numbers that appear in your Header (or Footer) text box.**

   The page number appears shaded gray. If page numbers do not appear in your Header (or Footer) text box, click the Insert Page Number button on the Header and Footer toolbar and then highlight the number that appears.

3. **Click the Format Page Number button on the Header and Footer toolbar.**

   The Page Number Format dialog box appears (as shown in Figure 7-2) offering ways to change the way Word displays numbers or starts numbering in your header or footer.

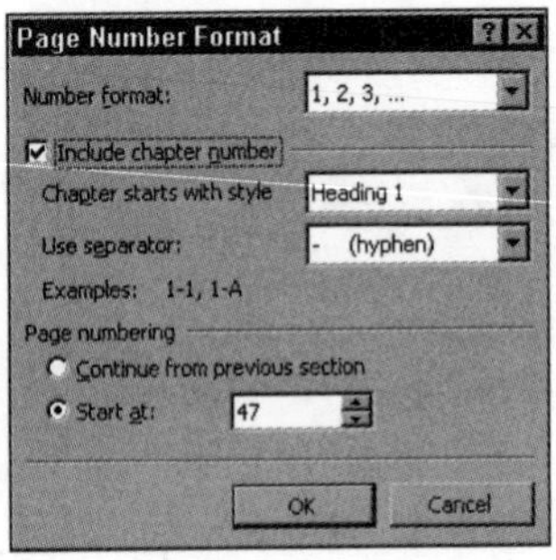

Figure 7-2:
The Page
Number
Format
dialog box.

4. **Click in the Number Format list box and choose a page numbering style (such as 1, 2, 3 or i, ii, iii).**

5. **In the Page Numbering group, select one of the following option buttons:**

   - **Continue from Previous Section:** Numbers pages sequentially

   - **Start At:** Lets you define the starting page number as a number other than 1

6. **Click OK.**

Setting Up Multicolumn Documents

To create a newsletter or brochure, you may want to display text in two or more columns to give it a professional look. Word can divide your documents into multiple columns — but remember that if you use more than four columns on a single page, none of the columns can display much text.

Making columns the fast way

To create multiple columns quickly, follow these steps:

1. **Choose Edit⇨Select All or press Ctrl+A.**

2. **Click the Columns button on the Standard toolbar.**

   The Column menu appears, giving you the choice of dividing a page into two, three, or four columns.

3. **Highlight the number of columns you want by dragging the mouse to the right.**

   Word immediately converts your document into a multicolumn document.

Making custom columns

To create customized columns, follow these steps:

1. **Choose Edit⇨Select All or press Ctrl+A.**

2. **Choose Format⇨Columns.**

   The Columns dialog box appears (as shown in Figure 7-3), offering ways to define column widths and space between columns.

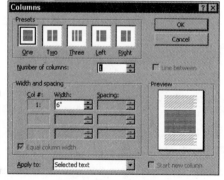

Figure 7-3:
The
Columns
dialog box.

3. **Click one of the column types shown in the Presets group or type the number of columns you want in the Number of Columns box.**

4. **Click (or clear) the Equal column width check box.**

   If the Equal Column Width check box is clear, you can define the width of each column individually.

5. **Click the Width box in the Width and Spacing group and click the up or down arrow to specify the exact dimension of each column width.**

   You can also type a specific column width if you want.

6. **Click the Spacing box in the Width and Spacing group and click the up or down arrow to specify the exact dimension of the spacing between each column.**

   You can also type a specific spacing width if you want.

7. **Click OK.**

   Word displays your document in multiple columns, customized to your specifications.

Adding Pictures to a Document

Not only can you add text boxes to your documents, you can add graphics as well. Word gives you several choices for inserting graphics into a document:

- **Clip Art:** Gives you the option of inserting any picture from the Microsoft Office Clip Art gallery
- **From File:** Adds a picture stored in a graphic file created by another program (for example, PaintShop Pro or Adobe Photoshop)
- **AutoShapes:** Draws one of many shapes (such as an oval, rectangle, or star) on your screen
- **WordArt:** Creates text that appears in different colors and shapes

Talk about versatility. Word gives you three additional ways to put graphics in your document:

- **New Drawing:** Use this option to create your own drawings from geometric shapes, lines, or WordArt.
- **From Scanner or Camera:** Use this option to add digital images or photographs created by a scanner or digital camera.
- **Chart:** Lets you add a business graph, such as a pie, line, or bar chart.

Creating a clip-art library

Clip art consists of ready-made pictures that someone else (or maybe even you) has already created in digital form for use with Word documents. To help you organize your clip art, Office XP offers a special Media Gallery, which can keep track of any images scattered around various folders on your hard drive.

The first time you try to insert clip art into a document, the Media Gallery asks you to define the folders that contain all the clip-art images you want to use, as follows:

1. **Choose Insert➪Picture➪Clip Art.**

   The Add Clips to Gallery dialog box appears, as shown in Figure 7-4, offering to organize your clip-art images.

Figure 7-4: The Add Clips to Gallery dialog box offers to organize your clip-art images.

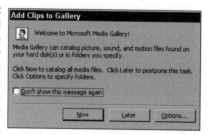

2. **Click Options.**

   An Auto Import Settings dialog box appears, as shown in Figure 7-5, displaying all the folders that Word's Media Gallery feature ransacks for clip art.

Figure 7-5: The Auto Import Settings dialog box displays all the folders where the Media Gallery looks for clip art.

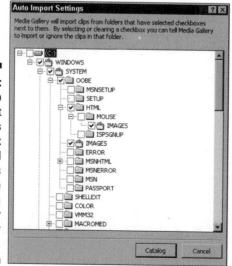

3. **Select the check box next to each folder that contains images you want to include in the Media Gallery.**

If you don't want images from a particular folder, clear the folder's check box.

4. **Click Catalog.**

A Microsoft Media Gallery dialog box appears, informing you that it's organizing your clip art. When the Media Gallery is finished organizing your clip art, the Microsoft Media Gallery dialog box disappears.

Putting clip art into your document

To add clip art to a document, follow these steps:

1. **Choose Insert⇨Picture⇨Clip Art.**

The Insert Clip Art pane appears, as shown in Figure 7-6, offering to help you find the right clip-art image for your document. (If you haven't followed the instructions in the "Creating a clip-art library for the first time" section, the Microsoft Media Gallery dialog box pops up. You can click Later if you want to ignore this dialog box.)

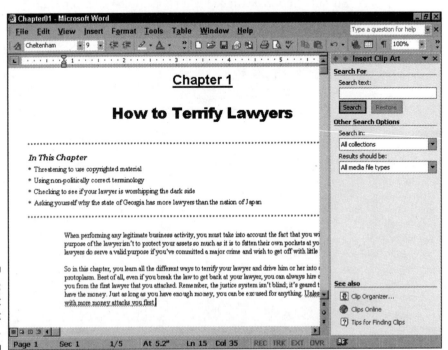

Figure 7-6:
The Insert
Clip Art
pane.

2. **Click in the Search text box and type a word or two describing the type of clip art you want to use.**

   You may want to keep the description simple at first — *sailboat,* for example, instead of *catamaran,* or *hot dog* instead of *bratwurst.*

3. **Click Search.**

   The Insert Clip Art pane displays all the clip-art images that match your search.

4. **Click the mouse cursor in your Word document where you want to insert the clip-art image.**

5. **Move the mouse over the image you want to use.**

   A downward-pointing arrow appears to the right of your chosen image.

6. **Click the downward-pointing arrow to display a menu, as shown in Figure 7-7, and choose Insert.**

   Word inserts your chosen clip art in your document.

7. **Click the Close box in the Insert Clip Art pane to make it go away.**

   Word inserts your chosen clip art in your document.

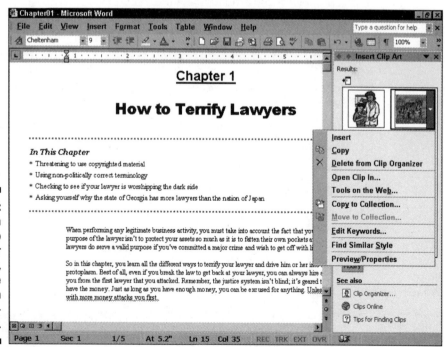

Figure 7-7: To insert an image into your document, choose Insert from the drop-down menu.

Putting existing graphic files into a document

If you've already drawn, copied, bought, or created a graphic file (for example, with a digital camera), you can shove it into a Word document.

To add an existing graphic file to a document, follow these steps:

1. **Move the cursor where you want to insert the image.**

2. **Choose Insert➪Picture➪From File.**

   An Insert Picture dialog box appears.

3. **Click the folder containing the graphic file you want to add.**

4. **Click the file you want to use.**

   Word displays your chosen image.

5. **Click Insert.**

   Word inserts your chosen image into your document. If you need to wrap words around your picture, follow the instructions in the "Wrapping words around a picture" section later in this chapter.

Putting an AutoShape into a document

AutoShapes are geometric objects, such as arrows, hearts, and moons that Word has already drawn for you. To add an AutoShape to a document, follow these steps:

1. **Move the cursor where you want to insert the AutoShape.**

2. **Choose Insert➪Picture➪AutoShapes.**

   An AutoShapes toolbar appears, as shown in Figure 7-8.

3. **Click the type of AutoShape you want to add, such as Block Arrows or Lines.**

   A pull-down menu of different shapes appears.

4. **Click the AutoShape image you want to use.**

   The mouse turns into a crosshair.

5. **Move the mouse to where you want to draw your AutoShape, hold down the left mouse button, and drag the mouse to define the size of your AutoShape.**

   Your chosen image appears in your document.

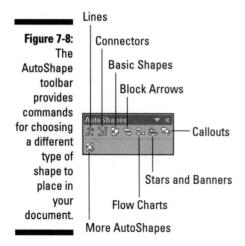

Figure 7-8:
The
AutoShape
toolbar
provides
commands
for choosing
a different
type of
shape to
place in
your
document.

Lines

Connectors

Basic Shapes

Block Arrows

Callouts

Stars and Banners

Flow Charts

More AutoShapes

6. Click the Close box to make the AutoShapes toolbar go away.

If you need to wrap words around your AutoShape, follow the instructions in the section "Wrapping words around a picture" later in this chapter.

Using WordArt in a document

WordArt is a fancy way to make your text look pretty by combining colors, shapes, and fonts in a unique appearance. To add WordArt to a document, follow these steps:

1. Move the cursor where you want to insert the WordArt.

2. Choose Insert⇨Picture⇨WordArt.

A WordArt Gallery dialog box appears.

3. Click the type of WordArt that you want to add and click OK.

An Edit WordArt Text dialog box appears, as shown in Figure 7-9.

4. Type the text you want to display and click OK.

You may want to change the font, adjust the size, or add bold or italics to your text before clicking OK.

Wrapping words around a picture

A picture in your document may cover up any text underneath. Unless hiding your words is the effect you're looking for, you should make sure that nearby text wraps around your pictures.

Figure 7-9:
The Edit
WordArt
Text dialog
box is
where you
can modify
the
appearance
of your text.

To wrap text around a picture, such as clip art or Word Art, follow these steps:

1. **Click the picture that you want words to wrap around.**

2. **Click the right mouse button.**

   A pop-up menu appears.

3. **Choose Format.**

   The Format dialog box appears.

4. **Click the Layout tab.**

5. **Click an icon in the Wrapping Style group, such as Square or Tight.**

   The different icons in the Format dialog box show you how your text will wrap around your chosen object. For example, the Tight option makes text appear very close to the edges of your picture.

6. **Click an option in the Horizontal Layout group, such as Left or Right.**

   The horizontal alignment defines how your picture appears next to any text that wraps around it. For example, choosing the Right option makes your picture align to the right of your text.

7. **Click OK.**

If you click the Advanced button after Step 6, you can define the exact distance that separates text from the border of your picture.

Moving a picture in a document

After you place a picture in a document, you can always move it to a new location later. To move a picture, follow these steps:

1. **Click the picture that you want to move.**

   Handles appear around your chosen picture.

2. **Hold down the left mouse button and drag the mouse.**

   As you move the mouse, a gray vertical line appears in your text to show you where Word will move your picture the moment you release the left mouse button.

3. **Release the left mouse button when the picture appears where you want it.**

Putting the Final Touches on a Document

Before printing your document, you might want to take one last look at your document to make sure your margins are correct or that all text is formatted the way you want. If you spot some text that looks a bit odd for some reason, you can use the Reveal Formatting pane to show you exactly how that particular text is formatted. That way if you see something wrong, you can correct it and make sure your words look exactly the way you want them to.

To use the Reveal Formatting pane, follow these steps:

1. **Highlight the text you want to examine.**

2. **Choose Format➪Reveal Formatting.**

   The Reveal Formatting pane appears, as shown in Figure 7-10.

   If you select the Show All Formatting Marks check box, Word displays spaces and paragraph marks in your document so you can see if you have an extra space that doesn't belong or an extra paragraph that shouldn't be there.

3. **Click a formatting link, such as Alignment or Font, to modify that particular formatting for your text.**

   If you click a formatting link, the appropriate dialog box pops up so you can make any changes.

4. **Click the close box of the Reveal Formatting pane to make the pane go away.**

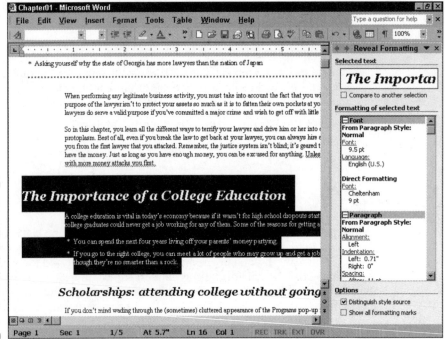

Figure 7-10:
The Reveal
Formatting
pane shows
you how
your
highlighted
text is
formatted.

Part III

Playing the Numbers Game with Excel

The 5th Wave — By Rich Tennant

"MY GIRLFRIEND RAN A SPREADSHEET OF MY LIFE, AND GENERATED THIS CHART. MY BEST HOPE IS THAT SHE'LL CHANGE HER MAJOR FROM 'COMPUTER SCIENCES' TO 'REHABILITATIVE SERVICES.'"

In this part . . .

If adding, subtracting, multiplying, or dividing long lists of numbers sounds scary, relax. Microsoft endowed Office XP with the world's most popular spreadsheet program, dubbed Microsoft Excel. By using Excel, you can create budgets, track inventories, calculate future profits (or losses), and design bar, line, and pie charts so you can see what your numbers are really trying to tell you.

Think of Excel as your personal calculating machine that plows through your numbers for you — whether you need to manage something as simple as a home budget or something as wonderfully complex as an annual profit-and-loss statement for a Fortune 500 corporation.

By tracking numbers, amounts, lengths, measurements, or money with Excel, you can quickly predict future trends and likely results. Type in your annual salary along with any business expenses you have, and you can calculate how much income tax your government plans to steal from you in the future. Or play "What if?" games with your numbers and ask questions, such as "Which sales region sells the most useless products," "How much can I avoid paying in taxes if my income increases by 50 percent," and "If my company increases sales, how much of an annual bonus can I give myself while letting my employees starve on minimum wages?"

So if you want to get started crunching numbers, this is the part of the book that shows you how to use Excel effectively.

Chapter 8

The Basics of Spreadsheets: Numbers, Labels, and Formatting

. . . .

In This Chapter

▶ Finding out what the heck a spreadsheet is

▶ Typing stuff into a worksheet

▶ Moving around a worksheet

▶ Formatting a worksheet

▶ Sending a worksheet to the printer

. . . .

*S*preadsheets, such as Microsoft Excel, help you track budgets, inventories, or embezzlements (kidding!) on your own personal computer. Of course, if you need to store formulas and plug in different numbers on a regular basis, you *could* use a pencil and calculator (whoa, way retro!). But besides the problems of punching in the wrong numbers, you have the added nuisance of recalculating every formula all by yourself.

Because Microsoft Office XP comes with Excel, you may as well get your money's worth and use a spreadsheet to help you calculate numbers, instead. To use a spreadsheet, just type in numbers, create formulas, and then add labels to help you understand what specific numbers represent. After you do that, you may want to format your numbers and labels to make them look pretty.

What Is a Spreadsheet, Anyway?

In the old days, accountants wrote long columns of numbers on sheets of green ledger paper divided by lines to ease the task of entering and organizing information in neat rows. At first, computer spreadsheets were just the electronic equivalent of green ledger paper. You could see rows and columns on your computer screen instead of on paper. Over time, the programs got a lot smarter. (Ah, progress.)

These days the terms *spreadsheet* and *worksheet* get bandied about inter-changeably. When people talk about a spreadsheet, they may mean a soft-ware program (such as Excel or Lotus 1-2-3), or a single document created in that program, or the actual data typed into that document. (For shame, for shame; don't they realize that ambiguity is habit-forming?) In Excel-speak, worksheet normally means a particular set of data typed into a spreadsheet, or a single page in a workbook, which can contain several worksheets. There. Now isn't that clearer?

As it presents itself on-screen, a spreadsheet consists of the following items (shown in Figure 8-1):

- ✔ **A worksheet divided into rows and columns.** A *worksheet* acts like a page on which you can type numbers and labels. Each worksheet contains up to 256 vertical columns and 65,535 horizontal rows. Columns are identified by letters (A, B, C, and so on). Rows are numbered (1, 2, 3, and so on).

- ✔ **Cells.** A *cell* is the intersection of a row and a column. When you type data into a worksheet, you have to type it in a cell. Cells are identified by their column letters followed by their row numbers. For example, the cell at the intersection of column G and row 12 is called cell G12.

- ✔ **Numbers.** *Numbers* can represent amounts, lengths, or quantities, such as $50.54, 309, or 0.094.

- ✔ **Labels.** *Labels* identify what your spreadsheet numbers mean, in case you forget. Typical labels are "May," "Western Sales Region," and "Total Amount We Lost Through Fred's Stupidity."

- ✔ **Formulas.** *Formulas* let you calculate new results based on the numbers you type in. Formulas are as simple as adding two numbers together or as complicated as calculating third-order differential equations that nobody really cares about. (Chapter 10 provides more information about creating formulas.)

Spreadsheets may look like boring paper ledgers, but they also offer addi-tional forecasting and budgeting capabilities. These capabilities let you ask what-if questions such as, "What would happen if the cost of oil went up 10 percent?" "What would happen if our sales plummeted 90 percent?" "What would happen if I gave myself a million-dollar raise despite the fact that sales have plummeted 90 percent?"

Excel also lets you organize multiple worksheets in a collection called a *work-book*. Each workbook can hold several thousand individual worksheets (the limit depends on your computer's memory and your willingness to keep cre-ating more worksheets). For more information about using workbooks, see Chapter 12.

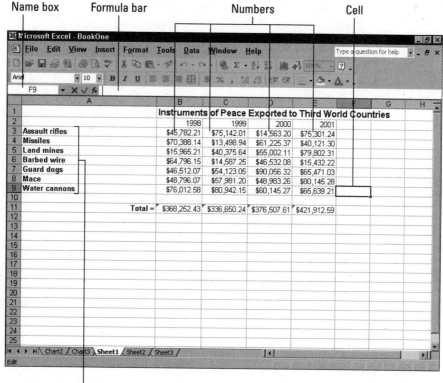

Name box   Formula bar   Numbers   Cell

Figure 8-1:
The parts of
a typical
spreadsheet
as seen
in Excel.

Labels

Putting Stuff in a Worksheet

Before you can type any information into Excel, you have to start the program (details, details). In case you forget how to load Excel, refer to Chapter 1 to refresh your memory.

After you start Excel, an empty worksheet appears on the screen. Because an empty worksheet is useless by itself, you need to type data into the worksheet's cells. The three types of data that you can type into a cell are numbers, labels, and formulas.

Entering information in a cell

To type data into a cell, follow these steps:

1. **Click in the cell where you want to type data.**

   Excel highlights your cell with a dark border around the edges. The high-lighted cell is called the *active cell* and is the Excel way of telling you, "If you start typing something now, this is the cell where I'm going to put it."

2. **Type a number (such as** 8.3**), label (such as** My Loot**), or formula (such as** =A1+F4-G3**).**

   As you type, Excel displays what you're typing in your chosen cell and in the Formula Bar (refer to Figure 8-1).

   Excel is also smart enough to display dates and times in a cell. If you want to type a time based on a 12-hour time clock, type a time in a cell, such as **7:45** followed by a space and **a** or **p** for AM or PM, respectively. To put the current time in a cell, press Ctrl+Shift+: (colon). To type a date, use either slashes or dashes, such as **4/7/2001** or **4-Mar-2000**. To put the current date in a cell, press Ctrl+; (semicolon).

3. **Do any one of the following actions to make your typed data appear in your chosen cell:**

   • Press Enter.

   • Click the Enter (green check mark) button, next to the Formula Bar.

   • Press an arrow key to select a different cell.

   • Click a different cell to select it.

Normally when you type text, Excel displays your text as a single line. If you want to display your text in a cell as multiple lines, press Alt+Enter to start a new line in the cell. So if you type **My income**, press Alt+Enter, and type **for 2001**, then Excel displays two lines in the cell. *My income* appears as the first line and *for 2001* appears as the second line in that same cell.

If you suddenly decide that you don't want your data to appear in the cell before you perform Step 3, press Esc or click the Cancel (red X) button, next to the Formula Bar. If you already typed data in a cell and want to reverse your action, press Ctrl+Z or click the Undo button.

If you need to type the names of successive months or days in adjacent cells (such as January, February, March, and so on), Excel has a handy shortcut that can save you a lot of typing. To use this shortcut, follow these steps:

1. **Click a cell and type a month or day, such as** March **(or** Mar.**) or** Tuesday **(or** Tue.**).**

   The Fill handle — a black box — appears at the bottom-right corner of the cell that you just typed in.

2. **Place the mouse cursor directly over the Fill handle so that the cursor turns into a black crosshair.**

3. **Hold down the left mouse button and drag the mouse to the right or down.**

   As you move the mouse, Excel displays the successive months or days in each cell that you highlight, as shown in Figure 8-2.

4. **Release the left mouse button.**

   Excel automatically types the name of the months or days in the range of cells that you selected.

Deleting and editing the contents of a cell

Sometimes you may need to edit what you typed in a cell, because you made a mistake, you just want to express your creative urges by typing something else in the cell, or you want to get that data out of there altogether.

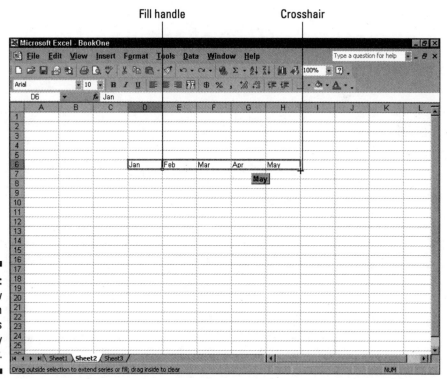

Figure 8-2: Filling a row or column with labels the easy way.

To edit data in a cell, follow these steps:

1. **Click or use the arrow keys to select the cell containing the data that you want to edit.**

2. **Press F2, click in the Formula Bar, or double-click the cell containing the data that you want to edit.**

3. **Press Backspace to delete characters to the left of the insertion point or press Delete to erase characters to the right of the insertion point.**

4. **Type any new data.**

5. **To make your typed data appear in your chosen cell, press Enter, click the Enter button (the green check mark next to the Formula Bar), or select a different cell.**

To delete data in a cell or cells, follow these steps:

1. **Highlight the cell or cells containing the data that you want to delete.**

2. **Press Delete, or choose <u>E</u>dit⇨<u>C</u>lear⇨<u>C</u>ontents.**

Navigating a Worksheet

A single worksheet can contain up to 256 columns and 65,536 rows. Obviously, your tiny computer screen can't display such a large worksheet all at once, so you can see only part of a worksheet at any given time, much like viewing the ocean through a porthole.

Using the mouse to jump around a worksheet

If you create a huge worksheet, you need a way to navigate through the whole thing. Fortunately, Excel provides several different ways to use the mouse or the keyboard to jump around a worksheet without breaking a sweat.

To navigate a worksheet with the mouse, you have two choices:

- Click the vertical and horizontal scroll bars.
- Use the wheel on your mouse (provided, of course, your mouse has a wheel; not all mice have discovered it).

To jump around a document by using the vertical or horizontal scroll bar, you have these choices:

✔ Click the up/down, right/left scroll buttons at the ends of the scroll bars to scroll up and down one row or right and left one column at a time.

✔ Drag the scroll box along the scroll bar in the desired direction to jump to an approximate location in your document.

✔ Click the vertical scroll bar above or below the scroll box to page up or down one screen-length at a time.

✔ Click the horizontal scroll bar to the right or left of the scroll box to page right or left one screen-width at a time.

Using the keyboard to jump around a document

For those who hate the mouse or just prefer using the keyboard, here are the different ways to jump around your document by pressing keys:

✔ Press the ↓ key to move one row down in your worksheet.

✔ Press the ↑ to move one row up in your worksheet.

✔ Press the → to move one column to the right in your worksheet.

✔ Press the ← to move one column to the left in your worksheet.

✔ Hold down the Ctrl key and press ↓, ↑, →, or ← to jump up/down or right/left one adjacent row or column of data at a time.

✔ Press the PgDn key (or Page Down on some keyboards) to jump down the worksheet one screen-length at a time.

✔ Press the PgUp key (or Page Up on some keyboards) to jump up the worksheet one screen-length at a time.

✔ Press Ctrl+Home to jump to the A1 cell in your worksheet, which appears in the upper-left corner of every worksheet.

✔ Press Ctrl+End to jump to the last cell in your worksheet.

✔ Press the End key and then press ↓, ↑, →, or ← to jump to the end/ beginning or top/bottom of data in the current row or column.

You can open any Excel worksheet (even a blank one will do) and practice using all the different methods of navigating around a worksheet. Then you can memorize the commands you find most useful and forget about the rest.

Using the Go To command

When you want to jump to a specific cell in your worksheet, the Go To command is a lot faster than the mouse or the keyboard.

To use the Go To command, follow these steps:

1. **Choose Edit⇨Go To or press Ctrl+G.**

   The Go To dialog box appears.

2. **Type a cell reference (such as A4 or C21) or click a cell reference or cell name displayed in the Go To list box.**

3. **Click OK.**

Each time you use the Go To command, Excel remembers the last cell reference(s) you typed in. If you have any named cells or cell ranges (see the next section, "Naming cells and ranges"), Excel automatically displays these cell names in the Go To dialog box.

Naming cells and ranges

If you don't like referring to cells as E4 or H31, you can assign more meaningful names to a single cell or range of cells. Assigning names can make finding portions of a worksheet much easier. For example, finding your budget's 2001 income cell is a lot easier if it's called "income2001" instead of F22.

To assign a name to a cell or range of cells, follow these steps:

1. **Click the cell that you want to name, or select the range of cells that you want to name by dragging (holding down the left mouse button while moving the mouse) over the cells.**

   The cell is highlighted as the active cell. (Or the range is highlighted, and the first cell in the range becomes the active cell.) The active cell's address appears in the Name Box.

2. **Click in the Name Box.**

   Excel highlights the cell address.

3. **Type the name that you want to assign to the cell or cell range.**

4. **Press Enter.**

   The name that you assigned appears in the Name Box.

Names must start with a letter, must be one word, and cannot contain more than 255 characters. "MyIncome" is a valid cell name, but "My Income for 1999" is not, because of the spaces between the words. Rather than use a space, use underscores — for example, "My_Income_for_1999."

Jumping to a named cell or cell range

After you name a cell or cell range, you can jump to it from any other cell by following these steps:

1. **Click the downward-pointing arrow to the right of the Name Box.**

   Excel displays a list of all named cells or cell ranges in the current workbook.

2. **Click the cell name that you want to jump to.**

   Excel highlights the cell or range of cells represented by the name you chose.

Deleting a named cell or cell range

You may later decide that you don't need a name to represent a particular cell or cell range. To delete a cell name, follow these steps:

1. **Choose Insert⇨Name⇨Define.**

   The Define Name dialog box appears.

2. **Click the cell name that you want to delete and click Delete.**

   Repeat this step for each cell name that you want to delete.

3. **Click OK.**

Deleting a cell name doesn't delete the contents of any cells in the worksheet.

Using the Excel Toolbars

Like all the Microsoft Office XP programs, Excel provides several ways to choose a command. You can press a keystroke combination, use pull-down menus, or click an icon displayed on a toolbar.

The two most common toolbars are the Standard toolbar and the Formatting toolbar. (Excel actually offers over a dozen different toolbars, but the Standard and Formatting toolbars are the main ones you use.) These two toolbars automatically appear when you first install and start Excel. You can hide them later to make your screen look less cluttered, if you want.

Exploring the Standard toolbar

The Standard toolbar offers access to the program's most frequently used commands, arranged from left to right in roughly the order of their frequency of use, as shown in Figure 8-3.

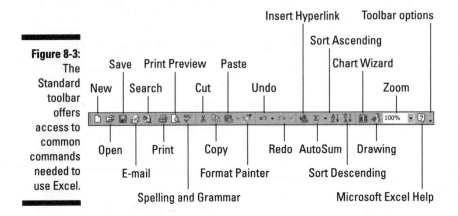

Figure 8-3:
The
Standard
toolbar
offers
access to
common
commands
needed to
use Excel.

To quickly find out what each button on the Standard toolbar does, move the mouse pointer over a button and then wait a second or two until the *ScreenTip* — a brief explanation of the button — appears.

Using the Formatting toolbar to change the way worksheets look

The Formatting toolbar contains commands to make your text look pretty with different fonts, type sizes, and typefaces (such as bold, italics, and underline), as shown in Figure 8-4.

To use any of the commands on the Formatting toolbar, select the text that you want to format, and then click the appropriate button or the downward-pointing arrow of the list box on the Formatting toolbar.

Excel offers more toolbars than just the Standard and Formatting toolbars, but these two toolbars contain the most common commands you need. In case you get curious and want to see all the Excel toolbars, choose View➪ Toolbars to open a menu that lists all the toolbars available with names like Drawing, PivotTable, and Web.

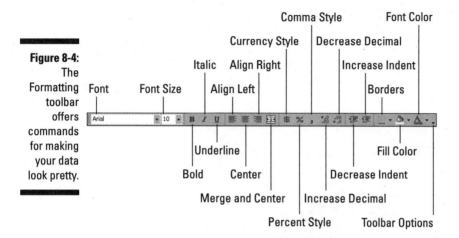

Figure 8-4:
The Formatting toolbar offers commands for making your data look pretty.

Making Your Worksheet Pretty with Formatting

Rows and columns of endless numbers and labels can look pretty dull. Because a plain, boring worksheet can be as hard to understand as a tax form, Excel gives you the option of formatting your cells.

By formatting different parts of your worksheet, you can turn a lifeless document into a powerful persuasion tool that can convince your boss to approve your budget proposals — and give him or her the impression that you gave it more thought than you really did. (Well, we can hope . . .)

Excel offers an almost unlimited variety of formatting options. You can change fonts, borders, number styles, and alignment to make your worksheets look pretty.

Formatting just defines the way data looks but doesn't affect the way Excel manipulates that data in formulas.

Using AutoFormat

If you aren't a designer but want fancy formatting without having to sweat artistic bullets, use the Excel AutoFormat feature. AutoFormat can automatically format a range of cells for you, according to one of many formatting styles.

To use AutoFormat, follow these steps:

1. **Highlight two or more adjacent cells that you want to format.**

2. **Choose Format⇨AutoFormat.**

   The AutoFormat dialog box appears, as shown in Figure 8-5.

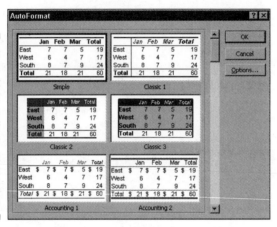

3. **Click a format that you want to use.**

4. **Click OK.**

   Excel automatically formats the range of cells that you selected in Step 1.

If you want to restrict the types of formatting that AutoFormat can apply, click the Options button in the AutoFormat dialog box. Deselect the formats that apply options you don't want AutoFormat to use. For example, if you don't want Excel to change fonts, remove the check from the Font check box by clicking it.

Manually formatting your cells

For more control over the appearance of your cells, you may prefer to format them yourself. To format one or more cells, follow these steps:

1. **Highlight the cell or range of cells that you want to format.**

2. **Choose Format⇨Cells, or press Ctrl+1.**

   The Format Cells dialog box appears, as shown in Figure 8-6.

Figure 8-6:
The Format
Cells dialog
box
provides
different
ways to
modify
numbers,
alignment of
data, fonts,
borders, or
background
patterns of
a cell or
multiple
cells.

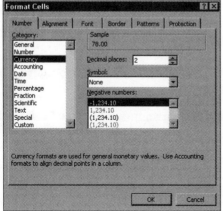

3. **Click one of the following tabs to view different options available:**

   • **Number:** Defines the way numbers appear in cells, such as with a currency sign or in scientific notation.

   For a faster way to format numbers, click in a cell and then click the Currency Style, Percent Style, Comma Style, Increase Decimal, or Decrease Decimal button on the Formatting toolbar.

   • **Alignment:** Defines the way labels appear in a cell, using (for example) word wrapping within a cell or displayed at an angle.

   • **Font:** Defines the font, size, and colors of your text or numbers.

   • **Border:** Defines borders around the cells.

   For a faster way to create borders around a cell, click in a cell and then click the Borders button on the Formatting toolbar. When a menu of different border styles appears, click the border style you want to use.

   • **Patterns:** Defines background colors and patterns of cells.

   • **Protection:** Protects cells from change if the entire worksheet is also protected by choosing the Tools⇨Protection⇨Protect Sheet or Protect Workbook.

4. **Make any changes, such as choosing a different color or font, and then click OK.**

   Excel displays your cells with your chosen formatting.

If you don't like the way your cells look, you can undo any formatting changes you made by pressing Ctrl+Z or clicking the Undo button right away.

Removing formatting

If you decide you want to remove formatting from one or more cells, you can do so at any time:

1. **Highlight one or more cells that you want to clear from any formatting.**

2. **Choose Edit⇨Clear⇨Formats.**

   Excel clears all formatting from your chosen cells.

Adjusting column widths

Unless you specify otherwise, Excel displays all columns in equal widths. However, you may soon find that some of your data appears truncated, scrunched, weird, or otherwise not displayed the way you intended. This problem occurs when your columns are too narrow.

To fix this problem, you can adjust columns to make them wider or narrower. To adjust the column widths quickly, follow these steps:

1. **Place the mouse cursor directly over one of the vertical borders of the column heading that you want to modify.**

   For example, if you want to adjust the width of column B, move the mouse cursor over the border between columns B and C.

2. **Hold down the left mouse button and drag the mouse to the left or right.**

   The mouse cursor appears as a double-headed arrow. Excel also displays a dotted vertical line to show you the approximate width of your column.

3. **Release the left mouse button when the column is the width you want.**

If you double-click the border between column headings, Excel automatically modifies the column on the left to make it just wide enough to display the longest entry in that column.

If you want to get real precise about defining your column widths, follow these steps:

1. **Click somewhere in the column you want to modify.**

   (Well, okay, this step doesn't have to be *all* that precise.)

2. **Choose Format⇨Column⇨Width.**

   A Column Width dialog box appears.

3. **Type a number to specify the column width (such as** 14.5**) and click OK.**

   Excel modifies your columns.

If you want to adjust the width of a column to match the width of data in a single cell, click that cell and choose Format⇨Column⇨AutoFit Selection.

Adjusting row heights

Excel normally displays all rows in equal heights. However, you may want to make some rows taller or shorter.

To change the height of a row quickly, follow these steps:

1. **Place the mouse cursor directly over one of the horizontal borders of the row that you want to modify.**

   The mouse cursor turns into a double-pointing arrow.

2. **Hold down the left mouse button and drag the mouse up or down.**

   Excel displays a dotted vertical line along with a small box that tells you the exact height of the row.

3. **Release the left mouse button when the row is the height you want.**

For people who want to define the row height exactly, these steps are precisely the ones to follow:

1. **Click in the row you want to modify.**

2. **Choose Format⇨Row⇨Height.**

   A Row Height dialog box appears.

3. **Type a number to specify the column width (such as** 12.95**) and click OK.**

   Excel modifies your rows.

If you want to adjust the height of a row based on the height of data in a single cell, click that cell and choose Format⇨Row⇨AutoFit.

Saving Worksheets for Posterity

Saving your work is important so that you can edit and review it later. When you save a file, you can give copies of that file to others so they can see and use your data on their computers as well.

Saving your worksheets in a file

After you type numbers, labels, or formulas into a worksheet, how about saving the worksheet in a file so you won't have to type everything all over again? (What a concept.)

To save a workbook, including all its worksheets, follow these steps:

1. **Choose one of the following:**
   - Click the Save button (the picture of a disk) on the Standard toolbar.
   - Press Ctrl+S.
   - Choose File⇨Save.

   If you haven't saved the file before, the Save As dialog box appears.

2. **Click in the File Name box and type a name for your Excel workbook, such as** Fake Accounting **or** Bribery Records.

3. **Click Save.**

Saving your file under a new name

After you've created some worksheets, you may want to create a new one based on the design of an existing worksheet. Rather than starting from scratch, you can save an existing worksheet under a different name and then modify that new named file.

To save your file under a different name, follow these steps:

1. **Choose File⇨Save As.**

   The Save As dialog box appears.

2. **Click in the File Name box and type a name for your Excel workbook, such as** Fake Accounting, My Favorite Swindles, **or** Bribery Records.

3. **Click in the Save as Type list box and choose a file format to use.**

   At this point you can choose some really weird file formats like WK4 (1-2-3) or DBF 3 (dBASE III).

4. **Click Save.**

Excel worksheets are compatible with Excel 2000 files, but not with those created by older versions of Excel (such as Excel 5.0). If you want to save an Excel worksheet so someone else can edit it using an older version of Excel, choose the Save As command and choose the appropriate version of Excel (say, Excel 5.0/95, 97, or Microsoft Excel 4.0 Worksheet) in the Save as Type list box of the Save As dialog box.

If, for some reason, you need to share your Excel files with a spreadsheet program that isn't listed in the Save As dialog box, use a universal file format such as SYLK (Symbolic Link), DIF (Data Interchange Format), or CSV (Comma delimited). These file formats may lose some formatting, but they keep your numbers and formulas intact so you can export Excel data to another spreadsheet — or to another computer altogether.

Printing a Worksheet

After you type numbers, labels, and formulas into a worksheet, you eventually want to print it out so you don't have to drag everyone else over to look at your worksheet on your tiny computer screen. Before printing out a worksheet (and possibly wasting precious natural resources such as paper and ink), use the Print Preview feature first.

Using Print Preview to see your worksheet

Excel's Print Preview lets you see how your worksheet looks before you actually print it. That way, you can see things like whether your margins are aligned properly and whether columns or rows fit on a single page.

To use Print Preview, follow these steps:

1. **Choose File⇨Print Preview.**

   Excel displays your worksheet in minuscule print and displays the cursor as a magnifying glass, as shown in Figure 8-7.

2. **Move the mouse cursor (the magnifying glass) over the document and click to view your document in its full size.**

3. **Click Close to exit Print Preview or Print to start printing right away.**

Printing worksheets

When you decide to print your worksheet, Excel gives you a variety of ways to do so:

1. **Make sure your printer is turned on, properly connected to your computer, loaded with paper, hasn't been drop-kicked through the third-story window out of frustration, and so on.**

2. Choose one of the following ways to open the Print dialog box:

- Press Ctrl+P.
- Choose File⇨Print.

3. Click in the <u>N</u>ame list box and choose the printer you want to use.

4. In the Print Range group, click an option button to choose the pages you want to print.

You can select All, or type a page number or range to print in the <u>F</u>rom and <u>T</u>o boxes.

5. Click in the Number of <u>C</u>opies box and type the number of copies you want.

6. Select a radio button in the Print What area to choose what you want to print, such as Selectio<u>n</u> (which prints any cells you've already high-lighted), <u>E</u>ntire Workbook, or Acti<u>v</u>e Sheet(s).

7. Click OK.

If you want to print your entire worksheet right away, click the Print button on the Standard toolbar. If you want to specify which pages you want to print and how many copies, choose one of the other methods (Ctrl+P or File⇨Print).

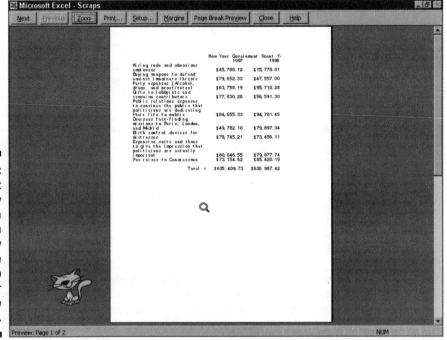

Figure 8-7:
The Print Preview feature can show you how many pages are needed to print your entire worksheet.

Printing part of a worksheet

You may not always want to print your entire worksheet. Instead, you may want to selectively choose which parts of the worksheet to print. To do this, you first need to define something mysterious that Excel calls a *print area*. Here's the drill:

1. **Highlight one or more cells that you want to print.**

2. **Choose File⇨Print Area⇨Set Print Area.**

   Excel displays dotted lines around your chosen print area. You can define only one print area at a time.

With your print area established, you can now print out the selected portion of your worksheet as if it were just a regular worksheet. See the "Printing worksheets" section for the details.

To clear any print areas you have defined, choose File⇨Print Area⇨Clear Print Area.

Chapter 9

Having Fun with Formulas and Functions

● ●

In This Chapter

▶ Making your own formulas

▶ Editing your formulas

▶ Choosing the right function to use

▶ Checking your formulas for mistakes

● ●

*F*ormulas represent the heart of spreadsheets because they allow you to type in different numbers and have Excel automatically calculate the results.

Besides doing your chores of addition, subtraction, division, and multiplication, Excel can also create more complicated calculations — statistical results, scientific calculations, or financial formulas to compare how much money you're losing in the stock market every month to how much cash you're spending on collectible baseball cards.

Creating Formulas

Excel works like a fancy calculator; it can whip up any type of result — as long as you know what you're doing in the first place. (And of course you do, right?) To tell Excel what to do, you create a formula by using the following steps:

1. **Click the cell where you want to display the results of a calculation.**

2. **Type = (the equal sign) followed by your formula.**

   For example, if you want a formula that multiplies the contents of cell B3 by the contents of cell C3, type **=B3*C3**.

   Instead of typing a cell reference, such as C3, you can just click the cell containing the data you want to use.

3. Press Enter.

Excel displays the results of your calculation.

If your formula has an error in it, such as trying to add a number to a label, Excel displays an error message so that you can fix your mistake.

To give you an idea of all the different types of formulas that you can create, Table 9-1 shows the most common calculations performed with a formula. The numbers shown in the Example column represent data stored in other cells. For example, in the Addition row, you may actually type **=B3+G12**, where B3 contains the number 5 and G12 contains the number 3.4.

Table 9-1	Common Formula Calculations		
Operator	*What It Does*	*Example*	*Result*
+	Addition	=5+3.4	8.4
-	Subtraction	=54.2-2.1	52.1
*	Multiplication	=1.2*4	4.8
/	Division	=25/5	5
%	Percentage	=42%	0.42
^	Exponentiation	=4^3	64
=	Equal	=6=7	False
>	Greater than	=7>2	True
<	Less than	=9<8	False
>=	Greater than or equal to	=45>=3	True
<=	Less than or equal to	=40<=2	False
<>	Not equal to	=5<>7	True
&	Text concatenation	="Bo the" & "Cat"	Bo the Cat

When you create a formula, you can either type numbers in the formula (such as 56.43+89/02) or use mysterious things called *cell references* (such as B5+N12). Although you may need to type numbers in a formula occasionally, the real power of Excel comes from using cell references.

Cell references let you take the contents of a specific cell and use those contents as part of your calculation. That way you can create multiple formulas that feed data into several other formulas.

What the heck are references?

In the working world, you give references to employers who want to check up on your background. In the world of Excel, you use references to identify cells containing numbers that you want to use in a formula to calculate a result.

Referencing a single cell

In Excel, you can reference a cell in one of two ways:

- Use the column and row labels, such as A4 or C7.
- Use your own column and row labels, such as Feb or Sales.

For example, suppose you have numbers stored in cells B5 and B6, as shown in Figure 9-1. In this example, cell B7 contains the formula

```
=B5+B6
```

When you reference another cell, that cell can contain either data (such as numbers) or a formula (that calculates a result based on data obtained from other cell references).

The cell references in the above formula are B5 and B6, so the formula tells Excel, "Find the number stored in cell B5 and add it to the number stored in B6."

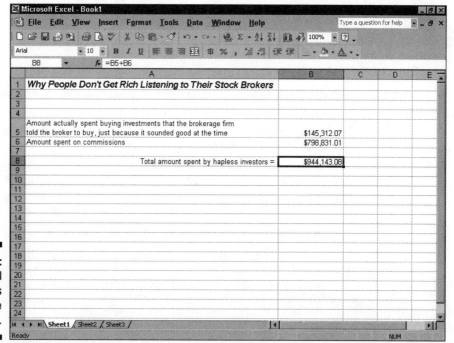

Figure 9-1: Using cell references to calculate a result.

Using cell references in a formula

To create a formula using a cell reference

1. **Click the cell where you want the results of the formula to appear.**

2. **Type = (the equal sign).**

3. **Choose one of the following methods:**

   - Type the cell reference, such as B4.

   - Click the cell containing the number that you want to use in your formula, such as B4.

4. **Type an operator, such as + (the plus sign).**

5. **Repeat Steps 3 and 4 as often as necessary to build your formula.**

6. **Press Enter.**

Now if you change the number in a cell that's referenced in another cell's formula, such as B4 in this example, Excel automatically calculates a new result.

To help you create the most common formulas, Excel has a special feature called *AutoSum.* By using the AutoSum button that appears on the Standard toolbar, you can quickly add or find the average of a row or column full of numbers.

The AutoSum feature only calculates numbers stored in cells that appear in the same row or column. The moment the AutoSum feature finds an empty cell, it assumes there are no more numbers to include in its calculation.

To use AutoSum:

1. **Click in the cell that you want to hold the result of your calculation.**

   This cell must appear underneath a column of numbers or to the right of a row of numbers.

2. **Click the downward-pointing arrow that appears to the right of the AutoSum button on the Standard toolbar.**

   A drop-down menu appears, displaying the common functions you can choose, such as Sum or Count, as shown in Figure 9-2. (Functions contain built-in formulas; to find out what the functions on this menu can do for you, see the "Common Excel functions" sidebar in this chapter.)

3. **Click the function you want to use, such as Sum or Max.**

   Depending on the function you choose, Excel automatically calculates and displays the result at the bottom of the column or to the right of the row that you selected. Figure 9-3 shows AutoSum adding cells B3 through B9.

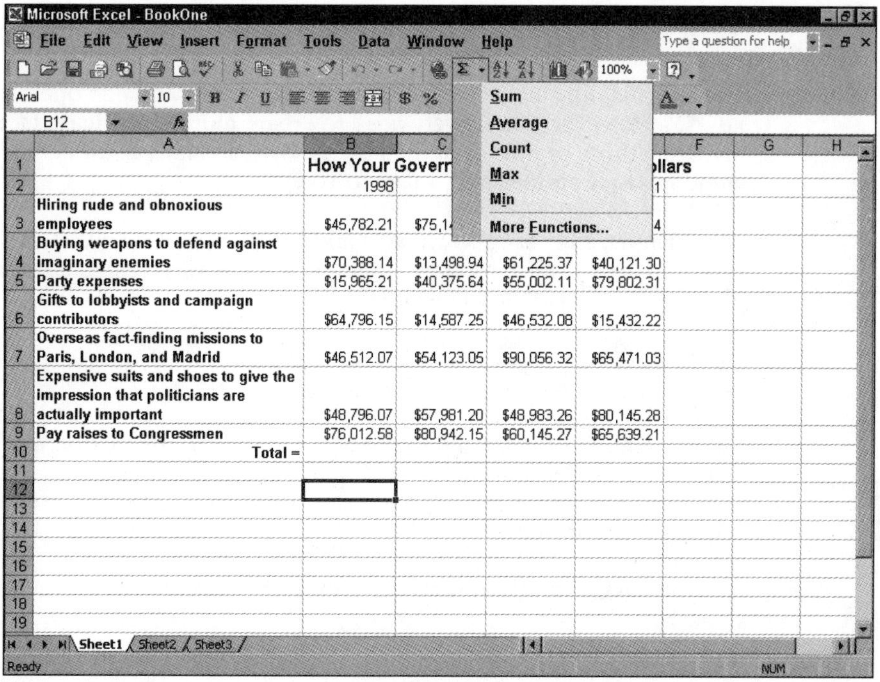

Figure 9-2:
By clicking
the
AutoSum
button, you
can choose
from a
variety of
common
functions.

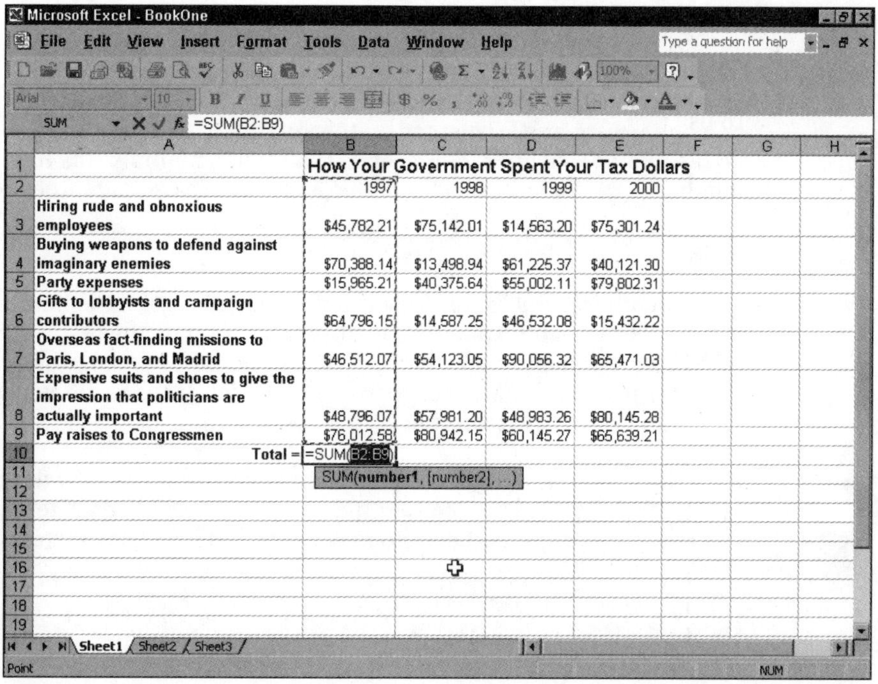

Figure 9-3:
Using the
AutoSum
button to
sum up a
column of
numbers
quickly.

The magic of parentheses

The simplest formulas can use two cell references and one operator, such as =B4*C4. However, you'll likely need to create more complicated formulas, involving three or more cell references. With so many cell references, you should use parentheses to organize everything.

For example, suppose you want to add the numbers in cells D3, D4, and D5 and then multiply the total by a number in cell D6. To calculate this result, you may try to use the following formula:

```
=D3+D4+D5*D6
```

Unfortunately, Excel interprets this formula to mean, "Multiply the number in D5 by the number in D6 and then add this result to the numbers in D3 and D4." The reason has to do with *order of operations* — Excel searches a formula for certain operators (such as *) and calculates those results before calculating the rest of the formula.

Say you have the following values stored in the cells:

D3	$45.95
D4	$199.90
D5	$15.95
D6	7.75%

The formula =D3+D4+D5*D6 calculates the number $247.09, which isn't the result you want at all (trust me on this one). What you really want is to add all the numbers in cells D3, D4, and D5 and then multiply this total by the number in D6. To tell Excel to do this, you have to use parentheses:

```
=(D3+D4+D5)*D6
```

The parentheses tell Excel, "Hey, stupid! First add up all the numbers stored in cells D3, D4, and D5 and *then* multiply this total by the number stored in D6." Using the same values for D3, D4, D5, and D6 as in the example without parentheses, Excel now calculates $20.29, which is the result you wanted. (How did I know? Just psychic . . .)

If you figure out nothing else from this section (or get a scary flashback to high school algebra), remember that you must always organize multiple cell references in parentheses to make sure that Excel calculates them in the right order.

Referencing two or more cells

Sometimes you may need to reference two or more cells. A group of multiple cells is called a *range*. The two types of cell ranges are

- Contiguous ranges (cells next to each other), such as D3+D4+D5
- Noncontiguous ranges (cells that are not next to each other), such as D3+T44+Z89

Specifying a contiguous range

A *contiguous range* of cells is nothing more than a bunch of cells touching each other, such as cells stacked one over the other or side by side. You can specify contiguous cells by using the colon. For example, typing **A2:A5** tells Excel to use the cells A2, A3, A4, and A5.

You can also specify adjacent cells that span two or more columns or rows. For example, typing **D2:E5** tells Excel to use the cells D2, D3, D4, D5 and the cells E2, E3, E4, and E5. This particular contiguous range spans four columns *and* two rows.

Contiguous ranges are handiest when you're using Excel's *functions* — built-in mathematical formulas that act as shortcuts — such as =SUM(D2:D6), which adds together all the numbers stored in cells D2 through D6. Some functions that work with contiguous ranges include AVERAGE, MAX, MIN, and COUNT. To use a function, all you do is pick a cell for the function to live in and then choose a function from the box that appears when you choose Insert⇨Function. You can find out more about functions in the "Picking a Function to Use" section, later in this chapter.

Suppose you want to use the following formula:

```
=(D3+D4+D5)*D6
```

Cells D3, D4, and D5 are a contiguous range of cells, so you can simplify the formula by just typing the following:

```
=SUM(D3:D5)*D6
```

The D3:D5 reference tells Excel, "Hey, dunderhead! Take all the numbers stored in cells D3 through D5 and sum (add) them all together; then multiply this result by the number in D6."

To specify a contiguous range in a formula, follow these steps:

1. **Click the cell in which you want the results of the formula to appear.**

2. **Type = (the equal sign).**

3. **Type the built-in function that you want to apply to your contiguous range — such as** SUM **or** AVERAGE **and then type the left parenthesis, which looks like this: (.**

4. **Click the cell that contains the first number that you want to use in your formula (for example, cell D3).**

5. **Hold down the left mouse button and drag the mouse to select the entire cell range that you want to include.**

   Excel highlights your selected cell range with a dotted line, as shown in Figure 9-4.

6. **Let go of the mouse button and type the right parenthesis, which looks like this:).**

7. **Type the rest of your formula (if necessary) and press Enter.**

Specifying a noncontiguous range

If you want to include certain numbers in a formula, but they're stored in cells that don't touch each other, you can create a *noncontiguous range* (tech-speak for "a range that includes cells that don't touch each other"). For example, consider the following formula:

```
=SUM(D3,G5,X7)
```

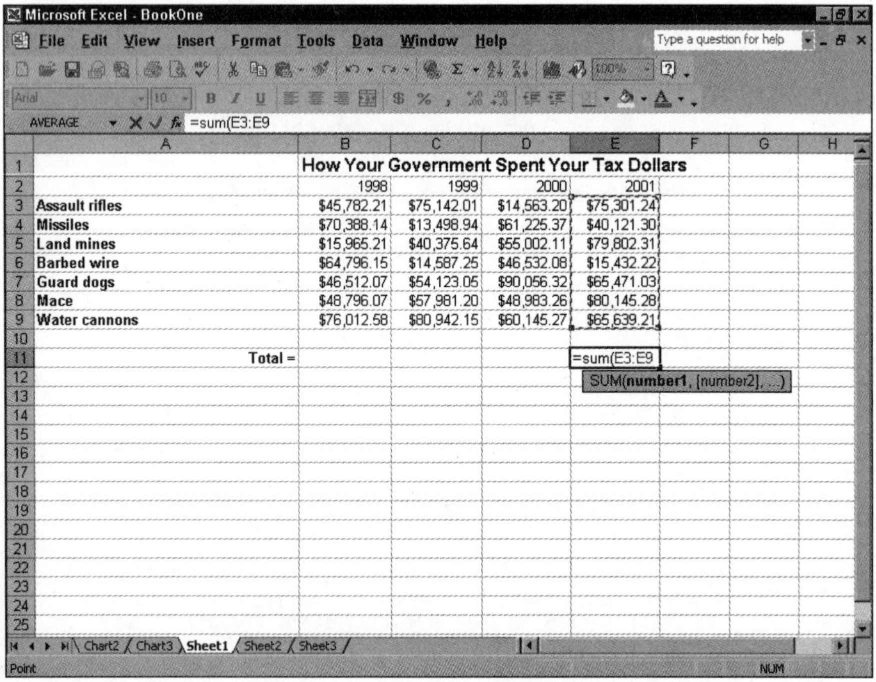

Figure 9-4:
Selecting a contiguous range of cells.

This formula tells Excel, "Take the number stored in cell D3, add it to the number stored in cell G5, and add the result to the number stored in cell X7." Excel salutes smartly and gets to work.

To specify a noncontiguous range in a formula, here's the drill:

1. **Click the cell where you want the results of the formula to appear.**

2. **Type = (the equal sign).**

3. **Type the built-in function that you want to apply to your noncontiguous range, such as SUM or AVERAGE, and then type the left parenthesis, which looks like this: (.**

4. **Click the cell containing the first number that you want to use in your formula (such as cell D3). (Or just type the cell reference you want to use, such as** D3.)

5. **Type , (a comma).**

6. **Click the cell containing the next number that you want to use in your formula (such as cell D7). (Or just type the cell reference you want to use, such as** D7.)

7. **Repeat Steps 5 and 6 as often as necessary.**

8. **Type a right parenthesis, which looks like this:), and press Enter when you're finished building your formula.**

Copying formulas

Just as school was a lot easier when you copied someone else's homework, creating formulas in Excel is much easier if you just copy an existing formula — no one will flunk you for doing it. Excel changes the formula cell references automatically for each row or column of numbers.

For example, if you need to add the first five numbers in column A together and want to do the same thing in columns B and C, your formula in cell A6 may look like this:

```
=SUM(A1:A5)
```

When you copy and paste this formula into cells B6 and C6, Excel automatically changes the formula in cell B6 to read

```
=SUM(B1:B5)
```

and changes the formula in cell C6 to read

```
=SUM(C1:C5)
```

TIP

Copying an existing formula is especially useful when you have rows or columns of numbers that use the exact same type of formula, such as three columns of numbers that all display a total at the bottom, as shown in Figure 9-5.

To copy a formula and paste it for other rows or columns to use, follow these steps:

1. **Type the formula you want to copy.**

   You can skip this step if the formula you want to copy already exists.

2. **Highlight the cell containing the formula you want to copy.**

3. **Press Ctrl+C or click the Copy button on the Standard toolbar.**

   Excel displays a dotted line around the cell that you highlighted in Step 2.

4. **Highlight the cell or range of cells where you want to paste the formula.**

5. **Press Ctrl+V or click the Paste button on the Standard toolbar.**

   Excel displays the results of the formula in your chosen cell or range of cells.

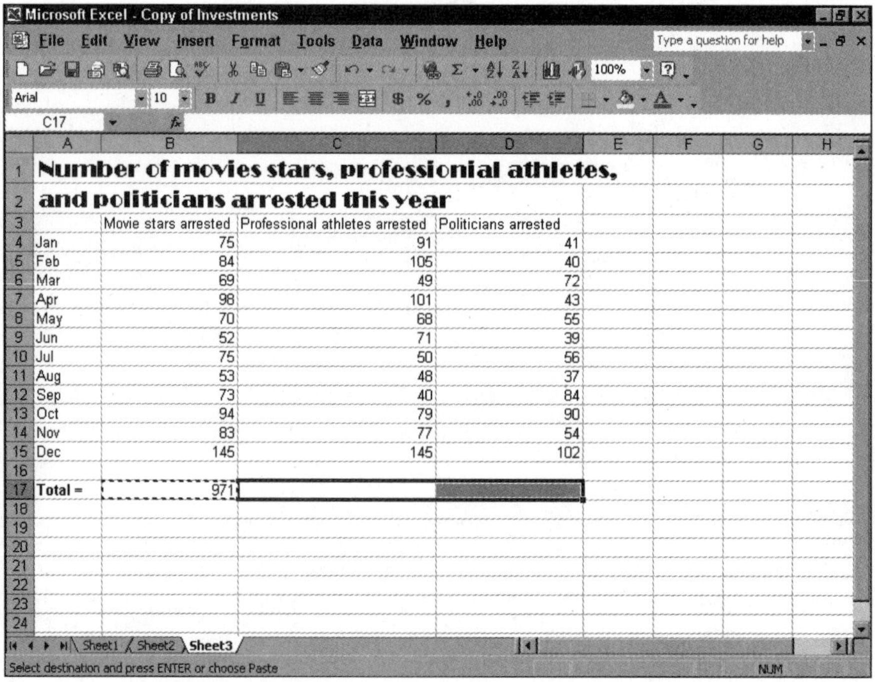

Figure 9-5:
Copying and
pasting a
formula
makes
calculating
easier.

	A	B	C	D
1	**Number of movies stars, professional athletes,**			
2	**and politicians arrested this year**			
3		Movie stars arrested	Professional athletes arrested	Politicians arrested
4	Jan	75	91	41
5	Feb	84	105	40
6	Mar	69	49	72
7	Apr	98	101	43
8	May	70	68	55
9	Jun	52	71	39
10	Jul	75	50	56
11	Aug	53	48	37
12	Sep	73	40	84
13	Oct	94	79	90
14	Nov	83	77	54
15	Dec	145	145	102
16				
17	Total =	971		

For a faster way of copying a formula, click the formula so a tiny black box appears in the lower right-hand corner of that cell. Move the mouse pointer over this tiny box so the mouse pointer turns into a crosshair, and then drag the mouse to highlight neighboring cells. Excel magically copies your formulas into those cells.

Editing Your Formulas

After you type a formula into a cell, you can always go back and edit it later. This capability comes in handy when you type a formula incorrectly (such as when you forget to use parentheses).

Displaying formulas

Before you can edit a formula, you have to find it. (Hey, obvious things need love too.) A cell with a formula in it looks exactly like a cell with just a regular number in it. That's because a cell with a formula shows the *results* of the formula, not the formula itself — so you may have trouble distinguishing between cells that contain plain old numbers and cells containing formulas.

To display all your formulas in a worksheet, just press Ctrl+` (yep, it's a reverse accent mark). That odd little mark, which you type while holding down the Ctrl key, normally appears on the same key as the tilde symbol (~).

If you have to hunt for your reverse accent (`) key, try looking just to the left of the 1 key on the top row. On some other keyboards, this key appears at the bottom, near the spacebar.

When you press Ctrl+`, Excel displays all the formulas currently hanging out in the worksheet, as shown in Figure 9-6. If you press Ctrl+` a second time, Excel hides the formulas. (As an alternative to pressing Ctrl+`, you can also choose Tools⇨Formula Auditing⇨Formula Auditing Mode.)

Wiping out a formula

The quickest way to edit a formula is to wipe it out completely and start all over again. When you want to exercise your destructive urges and delete a formula for good, follow these steps:

1. **Click the cell containing the formula that you want to delete.**

2. **Press Delete or Backspace.**

   Excel wipes out your formula (and doesn't leave too big a crater).

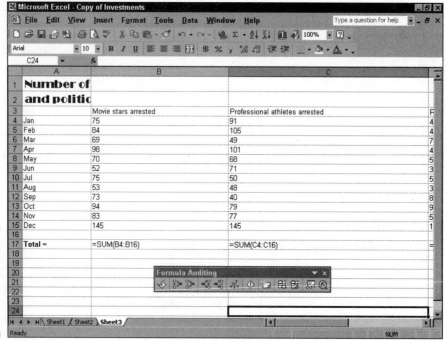

Figure 9-6:
Revealing
the formulas
hidden
behind
numbers.

These steps work for deleting the contents of any cell. If you delete something by mistake, you can recover it by immediately pressing Ctrl+Z or clicking the Undo button.

Changing a formula

If you want to edit a formula by making a minor change — say, typing a paren-thesis or adding another cell reference — you can use the Formula Bar, shown in Figure 9-7. Each time you click a cell containing a formula, the Formula Bar displays the formula you're using so you can view the whole thing and edit it.

To edit a formula:

1. Click the cell containing the formula that you want to edit.

Excel dutifully displays that formula on the Formula Bar (see Figure 9-7).

2. Click in the Formula Bar so that a cursor appears in it.

Excel highlights all the cells that your chosen formula uses to calculate its result.

Microsoft Excel - Copy of Investments

File   Edit   View   Insert   Format   Tools   Data   Window   Help   Type a question for help

SUM   =SUM(C4:C16)

	A	B	C	D	E	F	G	H
1	**Number of movies stars, professionial athletes,**							
2	**and politicians arrested this year**							
3		Movie stars arrested	Professional athletes arrested	Politicians arrested				
4	Jan	75	91	41				
5	Feb	84	105	40				
6	Mar	69	49	72				
7	Apr	98	101	43				
8	May	70	68	55				
9	Jun	52	71	39				
10	Jul	75	50	56				
11	Aug	53	48	37				
12	Sep	73	40	84				
13	Oct	94	79	90				
14	Nov	83	77	54				
15	Dec	145	145	102				
16								
17	Total =	971	=SUM(C4:C16)	713				
18								

Sheet1 / Sheet2 \ Sheet3

Edit   NUM

Figure 9-7:
Editing a
formula in
the Formula
Bar.

3. **Edit your formula as you please.**

   Press Backspace or Delete to erase part of your formula. Use the → and
   ← keys to move the cursor around; type any corrections.

4. **Press Enter.**

   Excel calculates a new result for that cell, based on your modified formula.

For a faster way to edit a formula in a cell, double-click that cell and type or
edit the formula directly in the cell.

Picking a Function to Use

Quick! Write out the formula for calculating the depreciation of an asset for
a specified period, using the fixed-declining-balance method. If you have
absolutely no idea what the previous sentence means, you're not alone. Of
course, even if you *do* know what that sentence means, you may still have
no idea how to create a formula to calculate this result.

Well, don't worry. It won't be on the final exam. Instead of making you rack
your brain to create cumbersome and complicated formulas on your own,
Excel provides you with predefined formulas called *functions*.

The main difference between a function and a formula is that a function already has a formula built in. A function just asks you what cell references (numbers) to use; a formula you have to build piece by piece, choosing cell references and telling Excel whether to add, subtract, multiply, or divide. For simple calculations, you can create your own formulas, but for really complicated calculations, you may want to use a built-in function instead.

Just in case you're wondering, you can use functions within any formulas you create. For example, the following formula uses the SUM function but also uses the multiplication operator:

```
=SUM(D4:D5)*D7
```

To help you choose the right function, Excel comes with the Paste Function feature, which guides you step-by-step as you choose a function and fill it with cell references. Relax — you don't have to do it all yourself.

To use the Paste Function feature:

1. **Click the cell where you want to use a function.**

2. **Click the downward-pointing arrow on the AutoSum button and choose More Functions, choose Insert⇨Function, or click the Insert Function button. (It's the one sporting the fx logo.)**

   The Insert Function dialog box appears, as shown in Figure 9-8.

Figure 9-8: The Insert Function dialog box provides a variety of functions you can use to calculate different results.

Insert Function	? X
Search for a function:	
Type a brief description of what you want to do and then click Go	Go
Or select a category: Most Recently Used	
Select a function:	
HYPERLINK COUNT MAX SIN SUMIF PMT STDEV	
PMT(rate,nper,pv,fv,type)	
Calculates the payment for a loan based on constant payments and a constant interest rate.	
Help on this function	OK Cancel

3. **In the Select a Category drop-down list box, click the category that contains the type of function you want to use (Financial, Statistical, and so on).**

4. **Click the function that you want to use in the Select a Function box.**

   Each time you click a function, Excel displays a brief explanation of that function at the bottom of the dialog box.

5. Click OK.

Excel displays a Function Arguments dialog box, asking for specific cell references, as shown in Figure 9-9.

Depending on the function you chose in Step 4, the dialog box that appears after Step 5 may look slightly different.

Shrink Dialog Box button

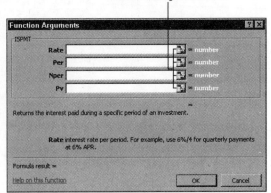

Figure 9-9:
The
Function
Arguments
dialog box
allows you
to specify
the type of
data for
your chosen
function.

6. Click the cells containing the numbers that you want to use (such as cell E3) or type the cell reference yourself.

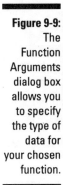

If you click the Shrink Dialog Box button, the dialog box shrinks so you can see the rest of your worksheet. You may still need to move the dialog box to get it out of the way.

7. Click OK.

Excel calculates a value based on the function that you chose and the numbers that you told it to use in Step 6.

Checking Your Formulas for Accuracy

Computers aren't perfect (although they may have fewer faults than some of the people you have to work with). Therefore, even if Excel appears to be calculating correctly, you may want to recheck your calculations just to make sure. Some common errors that can mess up your calculations include these little gems:

✔ **Missing data:** The formula isn't using all the data necessary to calculate the proper result.

✔ **Incorrect data:** The formula is getting data from the wrong cell.

✔ **Incorrect calculation:** Your formula is incorrectly calculating a result.

Common Excel functions

Although Excel contains several hundred different functions, you may never have to use all of them in your lifetime. Here's a short list of the players on the all-star function team; use it as a reference the next time you want to use a common function:

Function Name	What It Does
AVERAGE	Calculates the average value of numbers stored in two or more cells
COUNT	Counts how many cells contain a number instead of text

MAX	Finds the largest number stored in two or more cells
MIN	Finds the smallest number stored in two or more cells
ROUND	Rounds a decimal number to a specified number of digits
SQRT	(No, it isn't what you do with a water pistol.) Returns the square root of a number
SUM	Adds the values stored in two or more cells

How can you find errors in your worksheets? Well, you could manually check every formula and type in different numbers, just to make sure the formulas are calculating the correct results. But worksheets can contain dozens of formulas (any of which may be interrelated with others) — checking them all manually is impractical unless you've got about a century to spend. As an alternative, Excel comes with built-in *auditing* features for checking your formulas. Using these features, you can

- ✔ Make sure your formulas are using data from the correct cells.

- ✔ Find out instantly whether a formula could go haywire if you change a cell reference.

Finding where a formula gets its data

Even the greatest whiz-bang formula is no help if it calculates its results using data from the wrong cells. *Tracing* a formula shows you which cells a formula is retrieving data from.

Any cell that supplies data to a formula is called a *precedent*.

To trace a formula:

1. **Choose View➪Toolbars➪Formula Auditing.**

   The Formula Auditing toolbar appears as shown in Figure 9-10.

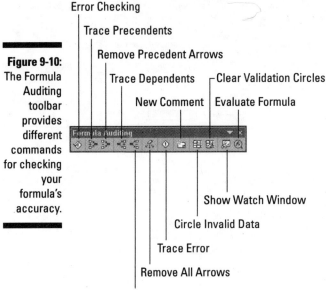

Figure 9-10:
The Formula Auditing toolbar provides different commands for checking your formula's accuracy.

Error Checking

Trace Precedents

Remove Precedent Arrows

Trace Dependents — Clear Validation Circles

New Comment — Evaluate Formula

Show Watch Window

Circle Invalid Data

Trace Error

Remove All Arrows

Remove Dependent Arrows

2. **Click the cell containing the formula that you want to check.**

3. **Click Trace Precedents on the Formula Auditing toolbar.**

Excel displays a line showing all the cells that feed data into the formula you chose in Step 2, as shown in Figure 9-11.

If a cell supplies data to a formula, Excel displays a dot over that cell. If a formula doesn't use data from a cell, no dot appears, even if the arrow appears over that particular cell.

4. **Click the Remove Precedent Arrows or Remove All Arrows button on the formula Auditing toolbar when you want to make the arrows go away.**

Finding which formula(s) a cell can change

Sometimes you may be curious how a particular cell might affect a formula stored in your worksheet. Although you could just type a new value in that cell and look for any changes, an easier (and more accurate) way is to use the Formula Auditing toolbar.

Any formula that receives data is called a *dependent*.

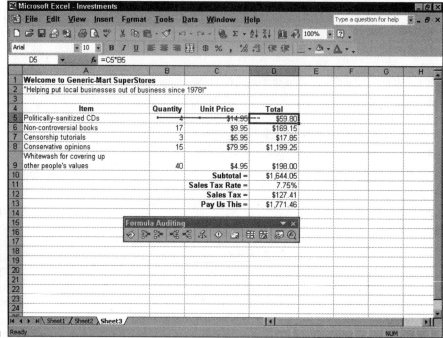

Figure 9-11:
Tracing
precedent
cells that
feed data
into a
formula.

To find one or more formulas that changing a single cell can affect:

1. **Choose View➪Toolbars➪Formula Auditing.**

   The Formula Auditing toolbar appears (refer to Figure 9-10).

2. **Click the cell that you want to examine.**

3. **Click the Trace Dependents button on the Formula Auditding toolbar.**

   Excel draws a line showing you the cell containing a formula that depends on the cell that you chose in Step 1, as shown in Figure 9-12.

4. **Click the Remove Precedent Arrows or Remove All Arrows button on the Formula Auditing toolbar when you want to make the arrows go away.**

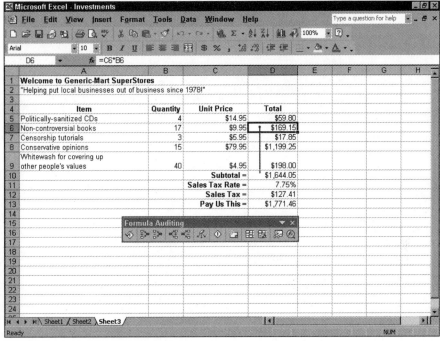

Figure 9-12:
Tracing
dependent
cells shows
you which
formulas a
single cell
can change.

Chapter 10

Charting Your Numbers

· ·

· ·

A picture may be worth a thousand words, but unless your picture makes sense, the only words it's likely to evoke are four-letter ones. Granted, most Excel worksheets consist of nothing but rows and columns full of numbers that utterly flummox most people. But you may want to make your data easier to understand by turning your numbers into charts that show trends, quantities, or patterns at a glance.

Understanding the Parts of a Chart

Excel can create gorgeous (or ugly) charts that graphically represent the numbers in your worksheets. Of course, to provide maximum flexibility, Excel offers numerous graphing options that may overwhelm you.

But take heart — after you enter your data in a worksheet, creating a chart is just a matter of letting Excel know which information you want to use, what type of chart you want, and where you want to put it. Although you don't need to know much charting lingo to create charts, you should understand a few terms that are confusing at first.

Most charts contain at least one data series. A *data series* is just a set of numbers for a particular category. For example, one data series may be sales results for one particular product sold during January, February, and March. Another data series may be the combined sales of five different products over the same period.

Charts also have an x-axis and a y-axis. The *x-axis* is the horizontal plane (that's left to right), and the *y-axis* is the vertical plane (that's top to bottom).

To help you understand your numbers, a chart may also include a chart title (such as Chart of Our 2001 Losses) and a legend. A *legend* identifies what the different parts of a chart represent, as shown in Figure 10-1.

Some of the more common types of charts include the following, which are shown in Figure 10-2:

- **Line chart:** One or more lines where each line represents a single item being tracked, such as hot dog buns or transmission failures. You can use a line chart to show trends over time in your data, such as whether sales of different products have been rising (or declining) over a five-year period.

- **Area chart:** Identical to a line chart except it provides shading underneath each line to emphasize the values being displayed. If you plan to plot more than four items, an area chart can become cluttered and difficult to read.

- **Column chart:** Compares two or more items over time (such as sales of white bread versus wheat bread over a six-month period). Columns that represent different items show up side by side, displaying not only how each product is selling month by month, but also how each product sells in comparison to other products.

- **Bar chart:** Essentially a column chart tipped on its side, a bar chart displays bars of different lengths from left to right. Bar charts are most useful for comparing two or more items or amounts over time. For example, a bar chart may use five different bars to represent a five different products; the length of each bar can represent the profit made from each product.

- **Pie chart:** Compares how separate parts make up a whole, such as determining how much money each sales region contributes to (or takes away from) a company's profits each year.

Many charts are also available in 3-D, which gives the chart a different look. Some people find 3-D charts easier to read; others think that 3-D makes the chart look more complicated than it needs to be. (Know your audience.)

Creating a Chart with the Chart Wizard

To help you create charts (almost) automatically, Excel offers the Chart Wizard, which kindly guides you through the process of creating charts from your data.

Creating Excel charts is easiest when your data is set up in a table format using adjacent rows and columns.

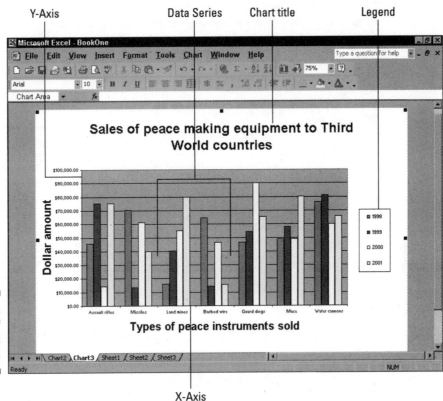

Figure 10-1:
The parts of
a typical
Excel chart.

To create a chart with the Chart Wizard, follow these steps:

1. **Select all the cells, including the column and row headings, containing the data that you want to chart.**

   Excel uses column headings for the x-axis title and row headings for the chart legend. (You can always change the headings used in your chart later.)

2. **Click the Chart Wizard button on the Standard toolbar or choose Insert⇨Chart.**

   The Chart Wizard dialog box appears, as shown in Figure 10-3.

3. **In the Chart Type list box, click the type of chart you want (such as Line, Pie, or Stock).**

4. **In the Chart Sub-type group, click the variation of the chart you want.**

5. **Click Next.**

   The second Chart Wizard dialog box appears, showing you what your chart looks like, as shown in Figure 10-4.

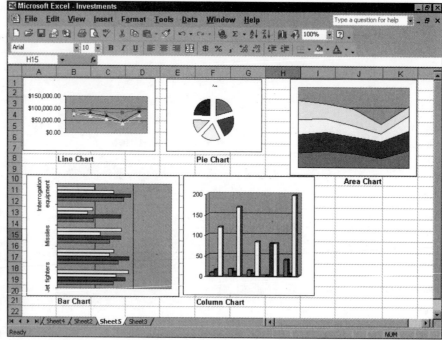

Figure 10-2:
Common
types of
Excel charts
you can use
to plot your
data.

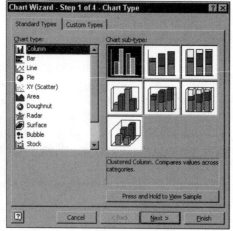

Figure 10-3:
The Chart
Wizard
dialog box
guides you
through the
process of
creating
a chart.

6. Click either the Rows or Columns option button to change the way Excel uses your data to create a chart.

Choosing the Rows option button means that Excel uses your row labels (if any) to appear on the x-axis of your chart. Choosing the Columns option button means that Excel uses your column labels (if any) to appear on the x-axis of your chart.

Collapse Dialog Box button

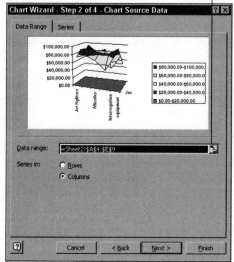

Figure 10-4:
The Chart
Wizard
dialog box
shows you
what your
chart looks
like so you
can accept
or modify it.

7. **Click the Collapse Dialog Box button.**

   The Chart Wizard shrinks to a tiny floating window.

8. **Select the labels and data you want to chart. (You can skip this step if you don't want to change the labels and data you chose in Step 1.)**

   Excel highlights your chosen data with a dotted line.

9. **Click the Expand Dialog Box button (formerly the Collapse Dialog Box button) and then click Next.**

   The third Chart Wizard dialog box appears, letting you choose a chart title as well as titles for the x-axis and y-axis (see Figure 10-5).

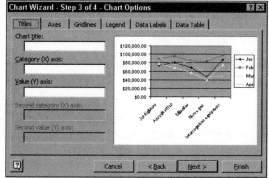

Figure 10-5:
The Chart
Wizard
dialog box.

10. **Type any titles that you want to add to your chart; then click Next.**

    The fourth Chart Wizard dialog box appears, as shown in Figure 10-6, asking whether you want to place your chart on the same worksheet as your data or on a separate sheet. Sometimes you may prefer keeping the chart on the same worksheet as the data used to create it. Other times, you may want to put the chart on a separate worksheet, especially if the chart is as big as your entire computer screen.

Figure 10-6: Choosing whether to place your chart on a separate sheet or on an existing sheet.

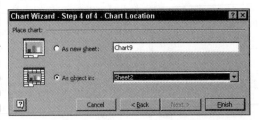

11. **Select either the As New Sheet or the As Object In option button and choose the worksheet where you want to place the chart.**

12. **Click the Finish button.**

    Excel draws your chart for you and places it on your chosen worksheet.

Editing Your Charts

The Chart Wizard helps you create a chart quickly, but afterwards, you may decide to go back and modify your chart a little to make it prettier, move it around, or resize it. Just remember that you can always change any chart you create, so don't be afraid of experimenting and letting your imagination go wild.

Moving, resizing, and deleting an entire chart

Sometimes you may not like where Excel puts your chart. So rather than suffer under the tyrannical rule of Excel, take matters into your own hands and change the chart's position and size yourself.

To move, resize, or delete an entire chart, follow these steps:

1. **Click the chart that you want to move, resize, or delete.**

   After you select a chart, little black rectangles, called *handles,* appear on the corners and the sides of the chart's border.

2. **Choose one of the following:**

   Note: You can move or resize a chart only if you chose the As Object In option button in Step 11 in the section "Creating a Chart with the Chart Wizard."

   • **To move a chart to a new location without changing the size of the chart, click the edge of the chart to select your entire chart.**

   After selecting the chart, place the mouse cursor inside the chart (not on one of the handles) and hold down and move the left mouse button so the mouse cursor turns into a four-headed arrow. Drag the mouse and notice how Excel shows you an outline of where your chart will appear if you release the mouse button at that point. When you're satisfied with the location, release the left mouse button.

   • **To change the size of a chart, click the edge of the chart and drag a handle.**

   Place the mouse cursor directly over a handle and hold down the left mouse button so the mouse cursor turns into a two-headed arrow. Drag the mouse and notice how Excel shows you an outline of how your chart looks if you release the mouse button at that point. When you're satisfied with the size, release the left mouse button.

   Note: Middle handles change the location of only one side of the chart; corner handles control two sides at once. If you drag the top-middle handle, for example, you can move the top side of the chart to make the chart taller or shorter (the bottom side stays where it is). If you drag the top-right corner handle, you move both the top side and the right side at the same time.

   • **To delete a chart, press Delete.**

Editing the parts of a chart

In addition to moving, resizing, or deleting the parts of a chart, you can also modify them as well. For example, if you misspell a chart title, suddenly decide you really want an x-axis title, or don't like the colors in your chart legend, then you can change whatever you don't like. You can change any part of a chart at any time, so be bold and experiment as much as you want, especially if you're being paid to goof around with Excel.

An Excel chart consists of several objects that you can modify. Most charts include these common parts:

- **Chart area:** The entire box that contains the plot area plus the legend
- **Plot area:** The actual chart (pie, bar, line, and so on) and its x- and y-axis labels
- **Legend:** A small box that defines what each color represents on the chart
- **Chart title:** Text that describes the chart's purpose

Changing text on your chart

After you create a chart, you may find that you want to modify any text that appears, such as the axis labels, legend entries, or chart title. To edit text, follow these steps:

1. **Click the text that you want to edit.**

   A gray box appears around your text.

2. **Click anywhere inside the text that you want to edit (such as the chart title) so the I-beam cursor appears.**

3. **Type any changes you want to make (or delete the text altogether, if you want).**

   You can use the arrow keys, the backspace key, and delete key to edit your title.

Formatting text

In addition to (or instead of) changing text, you may just want to change the formatting style used to display the text. To change the formatting of text, follow these steps:

1. **Click the text that you want to format.**

   Handles appear around your chosen text. (If you want to edit a particular legend entry, you have to click twice on that particular legend entry.)

2. **Right-click the text that you want to modify.**

   A pop-up menu appears.

3. **Click the Format command (such as Format Legend or Format Chart Title).**

   A Format dialog box appears.

4. **Choose the font, font style, size, color, and any other formatting options you want to apply to your legend entry.**

5. **Click OK.**

Picking a different type of chart

Some charts look better than others, so if you first pick a chart type (bar, for example) that doesn't visually make your data any easier to understand, try picking a different chart type, such as a pie, line, or scatter chart. To change your chart type, follow these steps:

1. **Click the edge of the chart that you want to change.**

   Handles appear around the chart and a pop-up menu appears.

2. **Right-click and choose Chart Type.**

   The Chart Type dialog box appears.

3. **Click a chart type that you want to use; then click OK.**

Changing the chart type can change the entire look of your chart, possibly messing up its appearance. If the chart looks really messed up after you change its type, press Ctrl+Z right away to undo your last action.

Using the Chart toolbar

If you're going to modify charts often, you may want to display the Chart toolbar, which provides several icons that you can click to view and modify the appearance of your chart.

To display (or hide) the Chart toolbar, choose View⇨Toolbars⇨Chart. The Chart toolbar appears, as shown in Figure 10-7, offering commands for modifying your chart.

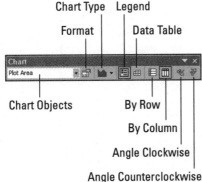

Figure 10-7:
The Chart
toolbar.

Chart Type   Legend

Format   Data Table

Chart Objects   By Row

By Column

Angle Clockwise

Angle Counterclockwise

The Chart toolbar comes packed with the following features:

- **Chart Objects:** Allows you to select part of your chart, such as the legend or category axis, without having to click it
- **Format:** Allows you to change the colors, borders, or font of the object you clicked or chose in the Chart Objects list box
- **Chart Type:** Allows you to quickly choose a different chart type for plotting your data, for example, by switching from a column chart to a pie chart
- **Legend:** Hides or displays a legend on your chart
- **Data Table:** Displays the actual data used to create the chart
- **By Row:** Uses row headings to define your chart
- **By Column:** Uses column headings to define your chart
- **Angle Clockwise:** Changes the appearance of text clockwise at an angle
- **Angle Counterclockwise:** Changes the appearance of text counterclockwise at an angle

Part IV
Making Presentations with PowerPoint

The 5th Wave   By Rich Tennant

"NIFTY CHART, FRANK, BUT NOT ENTIRELY NECESSARY."

In this part . . .

The fear of public speaking is the number one fear of most people — with the fear of death running a distant second. Although Microsoft Office XP can't help you overcome your fear of death, it can help you overcome your fear of public speaking and giving presentations with the help of Microsoft PowerPoint, which can help you organize and design a presentation that can keep others so amused that they won't even bother looking in your direction.

When you use PowerPoint to create a presentation, you won't need to rely on mere words, pointless hand gestures, or crudely drawn diagrams scribbled on a white board. With PowerPoint, you can give flawless presentations consisting of text, graphics, and even sound effects that people will remember.

The next time you need to dazzle an audience (with facts, rumors, or blatant lies dressed up to look like facts), flip through this part of the book and see how PowerPoint can help you create dazzling slide show presentations and handouts that can clarify, emphasize, or entertainingly distort topics for your audience until you have a chance to sneak out of the room.

Chapter 11

Creating Slide Show Presentations

In This Chapter

▶ Making a presentation

▶ Adding text to a slide

▶ Viewing a presentation

▶ Printing a presentation

*T*he number one fear of many people is speaking in public. (The number two fear is wasting time sitting through a boring presentation.) Giving a speech can be terrifying, but displaying a presentation along with your speech can provide an important crutch — visuals. Visuals can take the form of handouts, 35mm slides, black-and-white or color overhead transparencies, or computer images displayed on a monitor or projected on a screen.

Visuals can help structure your presentation so you don't have to memorize everything yourself. Instead, you can display pretty charts and talk about each one without having the entire audience staring at you all the time.

To help you create presentation slide shows on your computer, Microsoft Office XP includes a presentation program called PowerPoint. By using PowerPoint, you can show presentations on your computer or print them out as nifty handouts.

PowerPoint can help you make visually interesting presentations, but all the special visual effects in the world can't save a worthless presentation. Before rushing to create a PowerPoint slide show presentation, take some time to decide what's important to your audience and what you want to accomplish with your presentation (sell a product, explain why dumping oil into the ocean is harmless to the environment, raise support to sell weapons to unstable Third World countries just for the money, and so on).

Creating a Presentation

When you want to create a PowerPoint presentation, you have four choices:

- ✔ Create the presentation from scratch, which can be tedious and time-consuming as well as boring and mind deadening. (When you first start PowerPoint, the program creates a blank presentation for you.)
- ✔ Use the PowerPoint AutoContent Wizard to guide you through the steps of creating a presentation.
- ✔ Use one of the PowerPoint presentation templates so all you have to do is type in your own information.
- ✔ Create a presentation based on the style of an existing presentation.

Although you can create a presentation from scratch, letting PowerPoint create most of a presentation for you is so much easier. If you create a presentation with the AutoContent Wizard or use a template, you can always modify the presentation later if you feel extra creative.

Presenting the AutoContent Wizard

To help you create a presentation that demands attention, PowerPoint offers the AutoContent Wizard, which lets you put together a presentation almost without thinking, which is the way most people prefer to work anyway. The AutoContent Wizard can create a presentation in minutes, so all you have to do is go back and type in your own text.

To use the AutoContent Wizard, follow these steps:

1. **Choose File⇨New.**

   The New Presentation pane appears.

2. **Click From AutoContent Wizard under the New category.**

   An AutoContent Wizard dialog box appears to let you know that it's about to help you create a presentation.

3. **Click Next.**

   Another AutoContent Wizard dialog box appears, asking for the type of presentation you want to give (such as Communicating Bad News or Recommending a Strategy).

4. **Click the desired type of presentation (such as Brainstorming Session or Communicating Bad News) and then click Next.**

Another AutoContent Wizard dialog box appears, asking how you want to use your presentation.

5. **Click a radio button (such as On-screen presentation or Web presentation) and then click _N_ext.**

   Yet another AutoContent Wizard dialog box appears, asking you to name your presentation and type a footer that you want to appear on all your slides.

6. **Type your title and any footer information in the appropriate text boxes and then click _N_ext.**

   The final AutoContent Wizard dialog box appears, letting you know that you're finished answering questions.

7. **Click _F_inish.**

   PowerPoint displays your first slide along with an outline for your entire presentation, as shown in Figure 11-1.

After you create a presentation with the AutoContent Wizard, you can always modify and edit it later.

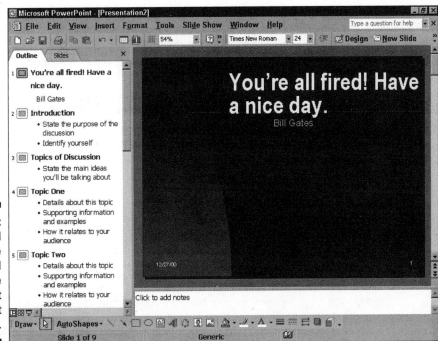

Figure 11-1:
An initial slide created by the PowerPoint AutoContent Wizard.

Filling in the blanks with a PowerPoint template

As an alternative to using the AutoContent Wizard, you can pick a predesigned PowerPoint template and just type in your text. By creating a presentation based on a template, you can make a presentation quickly without much effort, thought, or time.

The main difference between the AutoContent Wizard and PowerPoint templates is that the AutoContent Wizard guides you through the creation of your presentation. A PowerPoint template simply contains a predesigned style and layout for your slide that you can modify (just as long as you know what you're doing).

To create a presentation with a PowerPoint template, follow these steps:

1. **Choose File⇨New.**

   The New Presentation pane appears.

2. **Click General Templates under the New from Template category.**

   A Templates dialog box appears, as shown in Figure 11-2, providing a list of templates on the Design Templates tab. (You can choose from different visual styles.) The templates on the Presentations tab offer slides based on specific tasks, such as Company Handbook or Communicating Bad News.

3. **Click a template that best describes the kind of presentation you want (you can pick any template from the General, Presentation, or Design Templates tab) and then click OK.**

   PowerPoint displays the first slide of the template, ready for you to edit and customize for your own needs, as explained later in the "Using the Presentation Outline pane" section.

Creating a presentation from an existing presentation

Although templates can make creating a new presentation quick and easy, you may want to save time by basing your new presentation on an existing one instead. For example, if you (or someone else) already created a visually stunning presentation, you may just want to copy that existing file to modify for creating your new presentation.

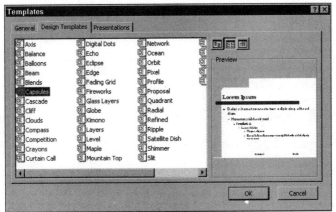

Figure 11-2:
The
Templates
dialog box.

To copy an existing presentation, follow these steps:

1. **Choose File⇨New.**

   The New Presentation pane appears.

2. **Click Choose Presentation under the New from Existing Presentation category.**

   A New from Existing Presentation dialog box appears. You may have to switch drives or folders to find the PowerPoint presentation file that you want to use as the basis for your new presentation.

3. **Click the presentation file that you want to copy and then click Create New.**

   PowerPoint creates a copy of your chosen presentation. All you need to do now is edit this presentation and save it under a new name, which is explained later in the "Saving your file under a new name" section.

Hefting PowerPoint's Toolbars

PowerPoint provides two toolbars that contain the most commonly used commands. These two toolbars, the Standard toolbar and the Formatting toolbar, automatically appear when you first install and start PowerPoint. You can hide them later or move them around the screen if you want.

Exploring the Standard toolbar

The Standard toolbar offers access to the program's most frequently used commands, arranged from left to right in roughly the order of their frequency of use, as shown in Figure 11-3.

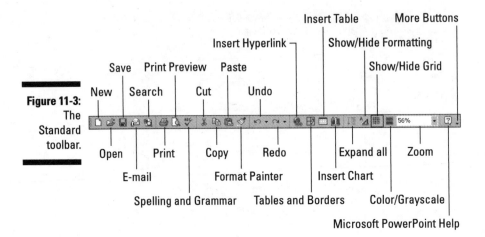

Figure 11-3: The Standard toolbar.

To find out quickly what each button on the Standard toolbar does, point the mouse over a button and then wait a second or two until the ScreenTip — a brief explanation of the button — appears.

Using the Formatting toolbar to change the way presentations look

The Formatting toolbar contains commands to make your text look pretty with different fonts, type sizes, and typefaces (such as bold, italics, and underline). The buttons on the Formatting toolbar appear in the following order from left to right, as shown in Figure 11-4.

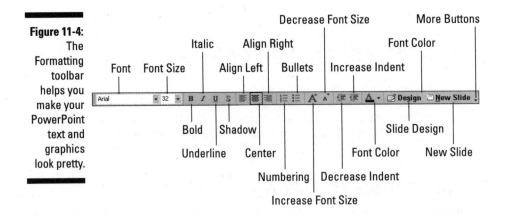

Figure 11-4: The Formatting toolbar helps you make your PowerPoint text and graphics look pretty.

PowerPoint offers more toolbars than just the Standard and Formatting toolbars, but these two toolbars contain the most common commands that you need.

Understanding the PowerPoint Interface

When you create a presentation, PowerPoint displays three window panes, as shown in Figure 11-5.

The PowerPoint user interface includes the following:

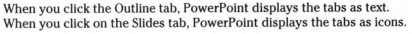

✓ **The Presentation Outline pane:** Displays two tabs: an Outline tab and a Slides tab. The Outline tab displays the text of each slide in an outline, for easy viewing and editing. The Slides tab displays a thumbnail view of each slide.

When you click the Outline tab, PowerPoint displays the tabs as text. When you click on the Slides tab, PowerPoint displays the tabs as icons.

✓ **The Slide pane:** Displays the text and graphics of the current slide (explained in more detail in Chapter 12).

✓ **The Notes pane:** Displays any notes you want to include for each slide. Notes are additional text, stored in your presentation for your own reference. They do not show up on any slide when you give your presentation. If you want, however, you can choose to print them out as handouts for your audience.

Using the Presentation Outline pane

The Presentation Outline pane is useful for organizing your entire presentation. With the Presentation Outline pane, you can

✓ View and edit slide titles

✓ Add, delete, or edit text that appears on each slide

✓ Add, delete, or rearrange your slides

The purpose of the Presentation Outline pane is to show you the overall design of your PowerPoint presentation without worrying about the actual appearance or formatting of your presentation.

Adding subtitles and text boxes to a slide

Most slides display text to make a point or list items. Each slide can consist of exactly one title, zero or more subtitles, and zero or more text boxes.

Presentation Outline pane   Slide pane

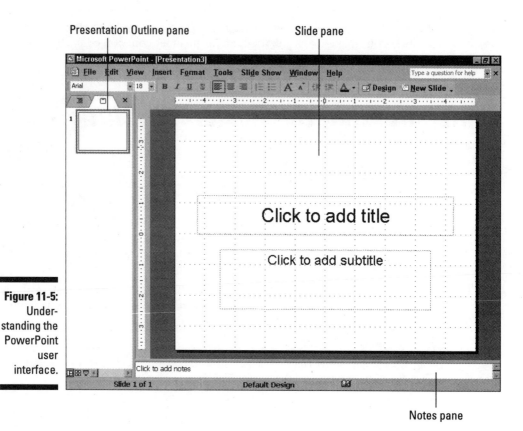

Figure 11-5:
Under-
standing the
PowerPoint
user
interface.

Notes pane

Descriptive titles, such as Ways to Cut Losses or People We Will Fire Tomorrow, help identify the purpose of the slide. Each slide can have only one title.

Subtitles provide additional explanations or lists of text for viewers to read. The Presentation Outline pane displays subtitles as subheading text and is indented and displayed in a smaller font size than title text. (Refer to Figure 11-1.)

Text boxes are blocked-off areas that you can add to the slide for entering blocks of text. They do not appear in the Presentation Outline pane but only on the slide itself.

To add subtitles to a slide, follow these steps:

1. **Click in the Presentation Outline pane to display the slide to which you want to add a subtitle.**

   You can click the Outline or Slides tab in the Presentation Outline pane to display the slide you want.

2. **Click to the far right of the slide's title or any existing subtitles that already appear on the slide.**

3. **Press Enter and type the subtitle you want for your slide.**

To add a text box to a slide, follow these steps:

1. **Click in the Presentation Outline pane to display the slide to which you want to add text.**

   You can click the Outline or Slides tab in the Presentation Outline pane to display the slide you want.

2. **Choose Insert⇨Text Box.**

   The mouse pointer turns into a downward-pointing arrow.

3. **Move the mouse pointer over the slide where you want to draw one corner of your text box, hold down the left mouse button, and drag the mouse.**

   PowerPoint draws your text box on the slide.

4. **Release the left mouse button.**

   PowerPoint displays your text box on the slide with a blinking cursor inside.

5. **Type any text that you want.**

Text that appears in text boxes does not appear in the Presentation Outline pane.

Viewing and editing text on your slides

The Outline tab in the Presentation Outline pane displays all your slide titles as outline headings and all text that appears on each slide as a subheading. If you have many slides in your presentation, you can collapse your outline so that it displays only slide titles and not any text that appears on any slides.

To collapse all the slide titles in your outline, click the (not aptly named) Expand All button on the Standard toolbar. Clicking the Expand All button again (now aptly named) expands all the slide titles.

To collapse just one slide title, double-click the icon that appears to the left of the outline heading that you want to collapse. PowerPoint underlines collapsed slide titles, as shown in Figure 11-6, which shows the Alternatives Considered outline heading collapsed. If you double-click the icon of a collapsed slide title, PowerPoint expands it.

A collapsed outline heading   Expand All button

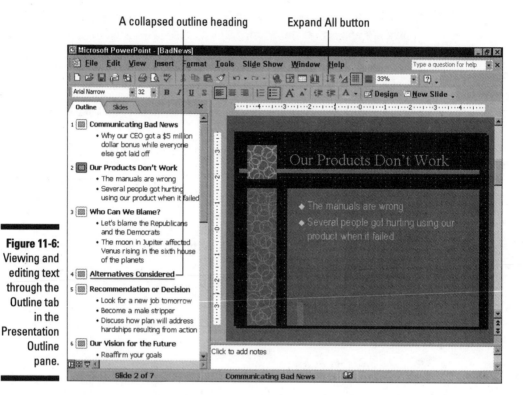

Figure 11-6:
Viewing and
editing text
through the
Outline tab
in the
Presentation
Outline
pane.

To edit text that appears on a slide using the Presentation Outline pane, follow these steps:

1. **Choose View⇨Normal.**

   PowerPoint displays the Presentation Outline pane on the left-hand side of the screen.

2. **Click the Outline tab.**

   PowerPoint displays the titles of your slides as outline headings. (Refer to Figure 11-6.)

3. **Click any text that you want to edit. You can use the Backspace, Delete, or arrow keys to edit your slide title.**

You can also edit slide text by clicking directly on the text that appears on a slide.

To create new text on a slide, follow these steps:

1. **Choose View⇨Normal.**

   PowerPoint displays the Presentation Outline pane on the left-hand side of the screen.

2. **Click the Outline tab.**

   PowerPoint displays the titles of your slides as outline headings. (Refer to Figure 11-6.)

3. **Click to the far right of the slide title where you want to add text and then press Enter.**

   PowerPoint displays a new slide icon directly underneath the slide title you chose.

4. **Click the Increase Indent button on the Formatting toolbar.**

   PowerPoint displays a bullet under the slide title you chose in Step 3.

5. **Type the text that you want to appear on the slide.**

   As you type your text, PowerPoint magically displays your text on the slide so you can see how it looks.

If a slide already contains text, click to the far right of that text in the Presentation Outline pane, press Enter, and then type the text you want to add.

Indenting text

You can indent text on a slide up to four times to the right (or left). Each time you indent text, it appears on the slide further to the right (or left) and in a slightly smaller (or larger) font size. To indent text, follow these steps:

1. **Choose View⟶Normal.**

   PowerPoint displays the Presentation Outline pane on the left-hand side of the screen.

2. **Click the Outline tab.**

   PowerPoint displays the titles of your slides as outline headings. (Refer to Figure 11-6.)

3. **Click anywhere in the text that you want to indent.**

   A cursor appears in your chosen text.

4. **Click the Decrease Indent or Increase Indent button on the Formatting toolbar.**

   PowerPoint indents your chosen text to the right (if you clicked the Increase Indent button) or to the left (if you clicked the Decrease Indent button).

Adding a new slide

Each outline heading in the Presentation Outline pane represents one slide. To add a new slide, follow these steps:

1. **Choose View⇨Normal.**

   PowerPoint displays the Presentation Outline pane on the left-hand side of the screen.

2. **Click the Outline tab.**

   PowerPoint displays the titles of your slides as outline headings. (Refer to Figure 11-6.)

3. **Click the mouse pointer to the far left of an outline heading (to the left of the outline text but to the right of the slide icon) in the Presentation Outline pane and press Enter to create a new slide.**

   A new outline heading (slide) appears above the outline heading (slide) you chose.

4. **Press the up arrow key to move the cursor to the newly created outline heading.**

   PowerPoint displays a blank slide.

5. **Type an outline heading in the Presentation Outline pane.**

   As you type, PowerPoint automatically displays your outline heading in both the Presentation Outline pane and in the Slide pane.

To add a new slide and choose the slide's layout for displaying text and graphics at the same time, follow these steps:

1. **Choose View⇨Normal.**

   PowerPoint displays the Presentation Outline pane on the left-hand side of the screen.

2. **Click the Outline tab.**

   PowerPoint displays the titles of your slides as outline headings. (Refer to Figure 11-6.)

3. **Click the mouse pointer to the far left of an outline heading (to the left of the outline text but to the right of the slide icon).**

   If you click in the middle or to the right of an outline heading, PowerPoint creates your new slide after the current slide.

4. **Choose Insert⇨New Slide, press Ctrl+M, or click the New Slide button on the Formatting toolbar.**

   A Slide Layout pane appears, as shown in Figure 11-7.

5. **Type the heading you want to appear on your slide.**

   If you press Enter and click the Increase Indent button, you can create additional text on your new slide as well.

6. **Click the slide design that you want to use.**

   PowerPoint shows you how your chosen layout will look.

7. **Click the Close box of the Slide Layout pane to make it go away.**

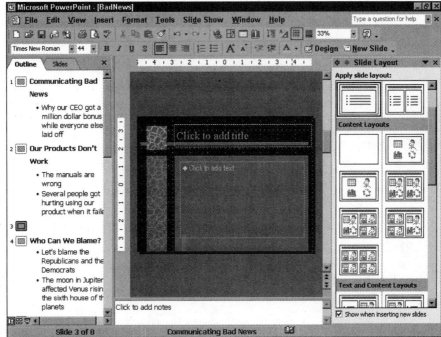

Figure 11-7:
The Slide
Layout pane
allows you
to pick a
design for
your new
slide.

Deleting a slide

Sometimes you may want to delete a slide that you no longer need. To delete
a slide, follow these steps:

1. **Choose View⇨Normal.**

   PowerPoint displays the Presentation Outline pane on the left-hand side
   of the screen.

2. **Click the Outline tab.**

   PowerPoint displays the titles of your slides as outline headings. (Refer
   to Figure 11-6.)

3. **Click the slide icon of the slide that you want to delete.**

   PowerPoint highlights the outline heading along with any subheadings
   that appear underneath.

4. **Press Delete.**

   PowerPoint deletes your chosen slide.

If you made a mistake and deleted the wrong slide, press Ctrl+Z or click the
Undo button to recover the slide you just wiped out.

Rearranging your slides

To help you rearrange your slides, the Presentation Outline pane can display your slides in an outline view (so you can see the text that appears) or in thumbnail view (so you can see the appearance of your slides). By using both the outline and thumbnail views, you can rearrange slides at any time.

If you have a large number of slides, you may want to collapse your outline headings to make it easier to see your actual slide titles. To collapse your outline headings, Microsoft provides the oddly named Expand All button that you can click on the Standard toolbar.

To rearrange your slides in outline view, follow these steps:

1. **Choose View⇨Normal.**

   PowerPoint displays the Presentation Outline pane on the left-hand side of the screen.

2. **Click the Outline tab.**

   PowerPoint displays the titles of your slides as outline headings. (Refer to Figure 11-6.)

3. **Move the mouse pointer over the slide icon of the outline heading (slide title) that you want to move and hold down the left mouse button.**

   PowerPoint highlights your outline heading and any subheadings underneath it.

4. **Drag the mouse up or down.**

   PowerPoint displays a horizontal line at the slide's new location and turns the mouse pointer into a double-pointing arrow.

5. **Release the left mouse button when the line is where you want your slide to be.**

Using the Presentation Outline pane to rearrange your slides is fine, but you can't see how all your slides look in relation to one another. If you prefer to rearrange your slides visually, follow these steps:

1. **Choose View⇨Normal.**

   PowerPoint displays the Presentation Outline pane on the left-hand side of the screen.

2. **Click the Slides tab.**

   PowerPoint displays thumbnail views of all your slides, as shown in Figure 11-8.

3. **Move the mouse pointer over the slide that you want to move and hold down the left mouse button.**

   PowerPoint highlights the slide with a black border.

Outline tab

Slides tab

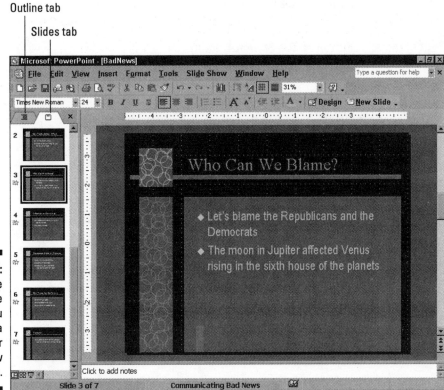

Figure 11-8:
The Slide
Layout pane
allows you
to pick a
design for
your new
slide.

4. **Drag the mouse pointer to where you want to move the slide.**

   PowerPoint displays a horizontal line where your slide will move when you release the left mouse button.

5. **Release the left mouse button when the line is where you want your slide.**

   PowerPoint moves your slide to its new location.

Converting outline headings into subheadings (and vice versa)

An outline heading appears as a slide title and outline subheadings appear as text on a slide. Through the wonders of modern technology, PowerPoint lets you turn outline headings into subheadings and subheadings into outline headings.

✔ **To turn an outline heading into a subheading:** In the Presentation Outline pane, click anywhere inside the outline heading that you want to convert into a subheading and then click the Decrease Indent button on the Standard toolbar.

> ✔ **To turn a subheading into an outline heading:** In the Presentation Outline pane, click anywhere inside the subheading that you want to convert into an outline heading and then click the Increase Indent button on the Standard toolbar.

Adding notes to a slide

The Notes pane lets you type notes to go along with each slide. You can refer to these notes during your presentation or pass them out as handouts so your audience has a handy reference during and after your presentation. (The section "Printing Your Presentation" explains how to print your notes with your slides.)

Text that you type on the Notes portion of a slide doesn't appear on the slide itself. Notes are just a way to keep related text together with your slides.

To type a note for a slide, follow these steps:

1. **Click in the Notes pane.**

   PowerPoint displays each slide with a text box at the bottom where you can type notes. (Refer to Figure 11-5.)

2. **Type any text that you want.**

Saving Your Presentations

Unless you enjoy creating everything from scratch over and over again, you should save your work. For extra protection, you should periodically save your work while you're modifying your presentation, as well.

Saving your presentation

To save a presentation, click the Save button (the picture of a disk) on the Standard toolbar, press Ctrl+S, or choose File⇨Save. Feel free to choose the Save command as often as possible. That way if the power goes out or your computer suddenly crashes, you won't lose your valuable data.

If you haven't saved the file before, the Save As dialog box appears, asking you to choose a file name and a directory to store your file in.

Saving your file under a new name

One easy way to create a presentation quickly is to open an existing presentation file, then save the file under a new name. This way, you can just modify an existing presentation rather than create everything all over again.

To save an older file under a different name, choose File⇨Save As and type in a new name for the file.

PowerPoint presentations are compatible with PowerPoint 2000 files, but not with older versions of PowerPoint, such as those created by PowerPoint 97 or PowerPoint 4.0. To save a PowerPoint presentation so someone else can edit it using an older version of PowerPoint, choose the Save As command and then choose the appropriate version of PowerPoint, such as PowerPoint 4.0, in the Save as Type list box of the Save As dialog box.

Saving PowerPoint presentations to go

Many people create PowerPoint presentations on their desktop computer where they can fine-tune and modify their presentation. Then they pack up their presentation and store it on a laptop computer that they take to another location.

To make this process easier, PowerPoint includes a special Pack and Go feature that crams all the files you need in one location. That way, you minimize the chances of forgetting an important file 3,000 miles away from your desktop computer.

To use PowerPoint's Pack and Go feature, load the PowerPoint presentation that you want to transfer and follow these steps:

1. **Choose File⇨Pack and Go.**

   The Pack and Go Wizard dialog box appears.

2. **Click Next.**

   The Pack and Go dialog box asks which presentation you want to pack up, as shown in Figure 11-9.

3. **Click the Active Presentation check box to choose the presentation that you're currently viewing. Then click Next.**

   The Pack and Go dialog box asks where you want to store your presentation.

4. **Click in the appropriate option button, such as A:\ drive and then click Next.**

   The Pack and Go dialog box displays two check boxes: Include linked files and Embed TrueType fonts.

Figure 11-9:
The Pack
and Go
Wizard
dialog box
guides you
through the
steps of
packing
your
presentation
for another
computer.

The Include linked files option saves your presentation as two or more separate files. So if you chose to save your files on drive A:, this option stores all the files on drive A:. If you accidentally erase one of these files, your presentation won't be able to run on another computer.

The Embed TrueType fonts option creates one fat PowerPoint presentation file, which can be inconvenient for transferring to another computer. If you chose some really weird fonts, you may want to choose the Embed TrueType Fonts check box just to make sure that you can display those fonts on another computer that may not have those fonts installed.

5. **Click in the appropriate check boxes (such as Include Linked Files) and then click Next.**

The Pack and Go dialog box asks whether you want to include the PowerPoint viewer if you'll be running the presentation on a computer that doesn't have PowerPoint installed.

The PowerPoint viewer is a special version of PowerPoint that can display and print PowerPoint files, but cannot edit them.

6. **Click in the appropriate radio button (such as Don't Include the Viewer) and then click Next.**

If you choose to copy your presentation to a floppy disk, get a stack of blank floppy disks ready in case your presentation takes up multiple floppy disks.

7. **Click Finish.**

After you package a PowerPoint presentation on a removable disk, such as a floppy or Zip drive, your entire presentation appears compressed in a file called PNGSETUP. You have to run this file before you can see the actual slides that make up your presentation. To run the PNGSETUP file, click the Start button on the Windows taskbar, choose Run, click Browse, and search for the folder containing the PNGSETUP file. Then click OK in the Run dialog box.

Printing a Presentation

After you get your presentation in the shape that you want it in, you can print out your hard work so that you can create handouts or wallpaper your office with your wonderfully creative presentations. To print a presentation, follow these steps:

1. **Choose File⇨Print.**

   The Print dialog box appears.

2. **Click the Print What list box and choose one of the following:**

   - **Slides:** Prints one slide per page so you can see all the text and graphics on each slide

   - **Handouts:** Prints one or more miniature versions of your slides on a page that audience members can take home and study later

   - **Notes Pages:** Prints only your notes for each slide, which you can either hand out to your audience or keep for your own reference

   - **Outline View:** Prints your Presentation Outline so you can see the overall structure of your presentation without graphics getting in the way

   You can also limit the print job to specific slide numbers by clicking the Current Slide option button or filling in the Slides text box in the Print Range area with the slide numbers you want to print.

3. **Click OK.**

If you click the Preview button, you can see what your presentation will look like before you actually start printing.

Chapter 12

Adding Color and Pictures to PowerPoint

. . . .

In This Chapter

▶ Coloring your slides

▶ Picking a design template

▶ Adding pictures

. . . .

*A*t the simplest level, a PowerPoint presentation can consist of nothing but text. Although functional, such a presentation looks boring. To spice up your presentation, PowerPoint gives you the option of adding colors and pictures on your slides so people will think your presentation is visually interesting, even if the content may be dry and dull.

Color and pictures may look nice, but use them to enhance your presentation and not as substitutes for a well thought out, clearly organized presentation. If people really want to look at fancy colors or pictures, they can just watch TV instead.

Changing Colors on Your Slides

Color can make your slides look extra special (or extra stupid if you're not careful). The two main parts of your slide that you can color are

  ✔ Any text that appears on your slide, including your slide title

  ✔ The background of your slides

Changing the color of text

Text normally appears in black, but you may want to emphasize your text in red, yellow, or any other color you choose. To change color of text:

1. **Click the text that you want to modify.**

   PowerPoint draws a gray border around your chosen text.

2. **Highlight the text that you want to change.**

   PowerPoint highlights your chosen text.

   The Font Color button displays the last color you chose. If you want to use that color shown on the Font Color button, just click the Font Color button and not on the downward-pointing arrow that appears on its right.

3. **Click the downward-pointing arrow next to the Font Color button on the Formatting toolbar.**

   A drop-down menu appears.

   Instead of clicking the Font Color button on the Formatting toolbar, you can choose Format⇨Font to display a Font dialog box and then click the Color list box. Besides allowing you to change colors, the Font dialog box also allows you to choose font style, font size, and special effects, such as subscript or superscript, for your text.

4. **Click <u>M</u>ore Colors.**

   A Colors dialog box appears, showing you the entire spectrum of colors available, as shown in Figure 12-1.

5. **Click the color you want for your text and click OK.**

   PowerPoint displays your highlighted text in your chosen color.

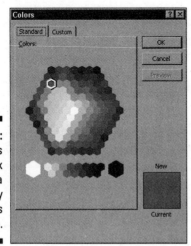

Figure 12-1:
The Colors dialog box offers a wide variety of colors to choose.

Coloring your background

A plain white background for your slides may give your presentation a generic look. So to add a little personality to your presentation, color your background.

If you color your text and your background, make sure the colors compliment each other. Trying to read bright yellow text against a bright yellow background will definitely make your presentation harder to read and understand.

To color the background of your presentation:

1. Display the slide whose background you want to change.

You may need to select the slide you want to modify by clicking the slide in the Presentation Outline pane. You can skip this step if you want to change the background of your entire presenatation and not just one slide.

If you hold down the Ctrl key and click on each slide in the Presentation Outline pane that you want to modify, you can change the background on two or more slides rather than just one slide or all your slides.

2. Choose Format⇨Background, or right-click and choose Background.

A Background dialog box appears, as shown in Figure 12-2.

Figure 12-2:
The Background dialog box can change the background color of the currently displayed slide or your entire presentation.

Background Fill list box

3. Click in the Background Fill list box.

A drop-down menu appears.

   4. **Click <u>M</u>ore Colors.**

   A Colors dialog box appears (refer to Figure 12-1).

   5. **Click a color you want to use for your background and click OK.**

   PowerPoint displays your chosen color on the background of the
   Background dialog box.

   6. **Click <u>A</u>pply (to apply your chosen color to the currently displayed
   slide) or Apply <u>t</u>o All (to apply your chosen color to all slides in your
   presentation).**

   PowerPoint displays your chosen color on the background of your slide
   or presentation.

If the background color you chose looks hideous, press Ctrl+Z (or click the
Undo button) right away to de-hideous the vicinity.

Using a color scheme

If wading through individual colors to find a suitable background color sounds
too tedious and time-consuming, PowerPoint provides a variety of color
schemes that offer colors already chosen for their suitability as a background.

To pick a color scheme

   1. **Display the slide whose background you want to change.**

   You may need to select the slide you want to modify by clicking the slide in
   the Presentation Outline pane. You can skip this step if you want to change
   the background of your entire presenatation and not just one slide.

   If you hold down the Ctrl key and click on each slide in the Presentation
   Outline pane that you want to modify, you can modify the color scheme
   on each slide that you selected.

   2. **Choose <u>F</u>ormat⇨Slide <u>D</u>esign, or right-click and choose Slide <u>D</u>esign.**

   The Fill Effects dialog box appears, offering a Slide Design pane (as
   shown in Figure 12-3) with a range of backgrounds.

   3. **Click Color Schemes.**

   The Slide Design pane displays a list of different color schemes.

   4. **Move the mouse pointer over the color scheme you want to use.**

   A downward-pointing arrow appears to the right of your chosen color
   scheme.

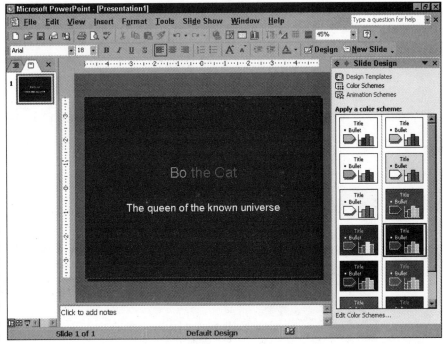

Figure 12-3:
The Slide
Design pane
of the Fill
Effects
dialog box.

5. **Click the downward-pointing arrow.**

   A drop-down menu appears.

6. **Choose Apply to All Slides or Apply to Selected Slides.**

   PowerPoint uses your color scheme to color your slides.

Picking a background pattern

Besides coloring your slides with a solid color, PowerPoint also gives you the option of choosing color gradients or different patterns, such as marble, wood, or striped patterns.

To choose a background pattern

1. **Display the slide whose background you want to change.**

   You may need to select the slide you want to modify by clicking the slide in the Presenatation Outline pane. You can skip this step if you want to change the background of your entire presenatation and not just one slide.

   If you hold down the Ctrl key and click on each slide in the Presentation Outline pane that you want to modify, you can selectively modify the background pattern on the slides you picked.

2. **Choose Format▷Background, or right-click and choose Background.**

   A Background dialog box appears (refer to Figure 12-2).

3. **Click in the Background Fill list box.**

   A drop-down menu appears.

4. **Click Fill Effects.**

   A Fill Effects dialog box appears, as shown in Figure 12-4.

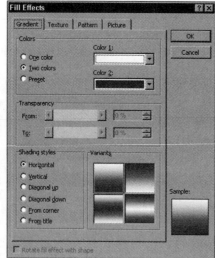

Figure 12-4:
The Fill
Effects
dialog box
can provide
different
back-
grounds for
your slides.

5. **Click one of the following tabs:**

   • **Gradient:** choose one or more colors that gradually fade away to one side of your slide

   • **Texture:** choose patterns that resemble marble or wood

   • **Pattern:** choose striped, brick, or checkerboard patterns

   • **Picture:** allows you to use a graphics file of your choice for your background

6. **Click the choices you want and then click OK.**

   PowerPoint displays your chosen background in the Background dialog box.

7. **Click Apply (to apply your chosen color to the currently displayed slide) or Apply To All.**

   PowerPoint displays your chosen background on your slide or presentation.

If your newly created background looks hopelessly unsnazzy, press Ctrl+Z or click the Undo button right away to remove the background and start over.

Using a Design Template

If you don't want to nitpick patterns and colors for your background, use a *design template* — a pre-designed slide — instead. You can modify it to suit your needs.

To use a design template, follow these steps:

1. **Display the slide you want to change.**

   You may need to select the slide by clicking it in the Presenatation Outline pane. (Skip this step if you want to change your entire presentation.)

   If you hold down the Ctrl key and click on each slide in the Presentation Outline pane that you want to modify, you can modify the design on each slide that you've selected.

2. **Choose Format⇨Slide Design, right-click and choose Slide Design, or click the Design button on the Formatting toolbar.**

   A Slide Design pane appears on the right-hand side of the screen.

3. **Click Design Templates.**

   The Slide Design pane offers a range of design templates, as shown in Figure 12-5.

4. **Move the mouse pointer over the design template you want to use.**

   A downward-pointing arrow appears to the right of your chosen design template.

5. **Click the downward-pointing arrow.**

   A drop-down menu appears.

6. **Choose Apply To All Slides or Apply To Selected Slides.**

   PowerPoint uses your design template to modify your slides.

Putting Pictures on Your Slides

Because pictures are worth a thousand words (and nobody wants to read a thousand words on a slide), you may want to add pictures on your slides, such as pictures captured through a digital camera or drawn yourself.

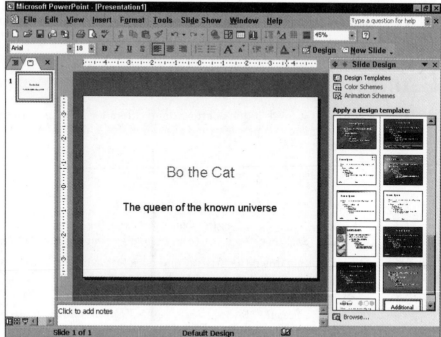

Adding your own pictures to a slide

If you have any graphic images on your hard disk that you want to include on your slide, you can insert a picture by doing the following:

1. **Choose Insert⇨Picture⇨From File.**

   An Insert Picture dialog box appears.

2. **Click the picture you want to use and click Insert.**

   You may have to switch folders or drives to find the pictures you want to use. PowerPoint displays your chosen picture on the slide, along with the Picture toolbar (as shown in Figure 12-6) so you can tweak the image.

To move your picture, move the mouse pointer directly over your picture until the mouse pointer turns into a four-way pointing arrow. Then drag the mouse to move your picture. To resize your picture, move the pointer over a resize handle; then click, hold, and drag. To rotate your picture, move the mouse pointer over the rotate handle and then drag in the direction you want the image to rotate.

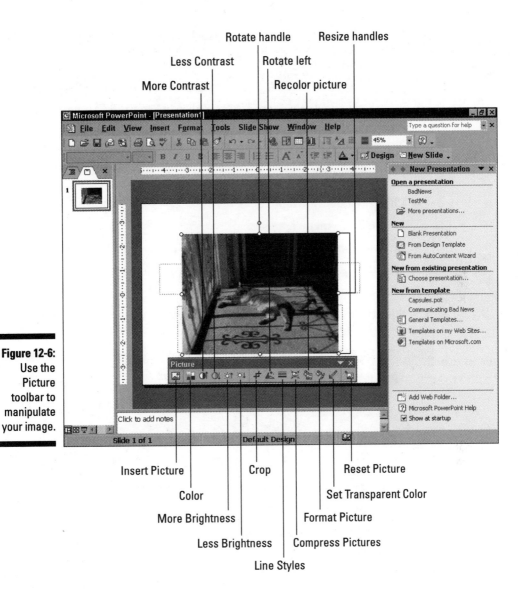

Figure 12-6:
Use the
Picture
toolbar to
manipulate
your image.

Adding a chart

To impress people, you may want to add a bar chart to your slide to give
your presentation an official business appearance (even if nobody under-
stands what the chart is trying to tell them). To add a chart

1. Display the slide to which you want to add a chart.

To select a slide to modify, click the slide in the Presenatation Outline
pane. (Skip this step if you want to change your entire presentation.)

If you hold down the Ctrl key and click on each slide in the Presentation Outline pane that you want to modify, you can add charts on each slide that you've selected.

2. **Choose Format⇨Slide Layout, or right-click and choose Slide Layout.**

   The Slide Layout pane appears (as shown in Figure 12-7), offering possible layouts.

3. **Move the mouse pointer over the design layout you want to use.**

   A downward-pointing arrow appears to the right of your chosen design layout.

4. **Click the downward-pointing arrow.**

   A drop-down menu appears.

5. **Choose Apply to Selected Slides or Apply Layout.**

   A box of six icons appears on your slide, as shown in Figure 12-8.

6. **Click the Insert Chart button.**

   PowerPoint displays a chart and a datasheet, as shown in Figure 12-9.

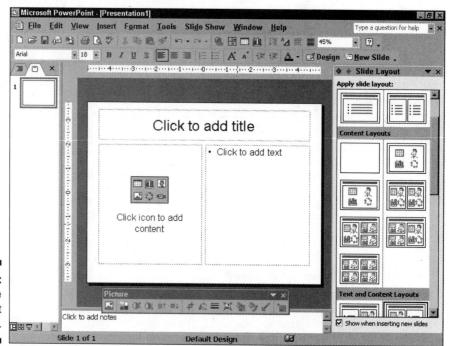

Figure 12-7:
The Slide
Layout
pane.

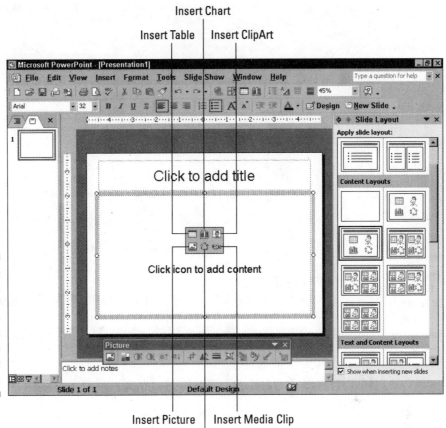

Insert Chart

Insert Table   Insert ClipArt

Insert Picture   Insert Media Clip

Insert Diagram or Organizational Chart

Figure 12-8:
You can pick
the type of
graphic
images
you want to
add to
your slide.

7. **Type any numbers and labels that you want to use in the datasheet.**

   As you change numbers and labels, PowerPoint redraws your bar chart.

8. **Click in the close box of the datasheet window.**

   The datasheet window disappears and shows you your bar chart on
   the slide.

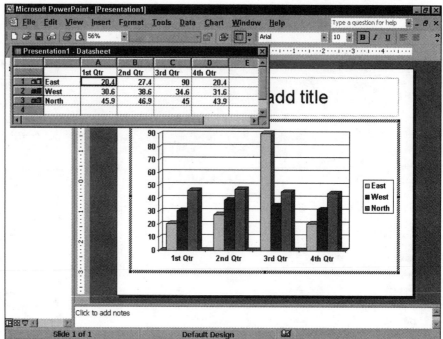

Figure 12-9:
Drawing a
chart on
your slide.

Making your pictures look prettier

After you put a picture or bar chart on your slide, you may want to add a border or modify the appearance of the images on your slide. If so, follow these steps:

1. **Click the picture or bar chart that you want to modify.**

   PowerPoint displays handles around your chosen picture.

2. **Choose Format⇨Object, or right-click and choose Format Object.**

   A Format Object dialog box appears, as shown in Figure 12-10.

3. **Click one of the following tabs:**

   - **Colors and Lines:** adds borders and background colors

   - **Size:** specifies the width and height of your picture

   - **Position:** specifies the location of your picture on your slide

   - **Picture:** adjusts the brightness or contrast of your picture

4. **Make any changes you want to your picture and click OK.**

   PowerPoint displays your picture with the options you chose.

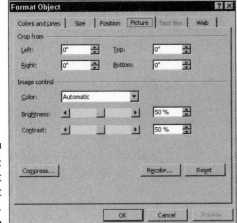

Figure 12-10:
The Format
Object
dialog box.

Deleting a picture

If you decide to get rid of a picture on your slide, you can always delete it:

1. **Click the picture or bar chart that you want to delete.**

   PowerPoint displays handles around your chosen picture.

2. **Press Delete.**

   PowerPoint deletes your chosen picture.

Press Ctrl+Z (or click the Undo button) to retrieve any picture in case you decide you don't want to delete it after all.

Chapter 13

Showing Off Your PowerPoint Presentations

. . . .

. . . .

After you create a slide show with Microsoft PowerPoint, don't be sur-prised if you want to show it off so that other people can ooh and ahh over it. Because the appearance of your presentation is often more important than substance (which may explain why your boss gets paid more than you do), Microsoft PowerPoint provides all sorts of ways to spice up your slide show. Some of these ways include Hollywood-style transitions from slide to slide, sound effects to accompany each slide, and scrolling text that makes your slides more entertaining to watch.

Just remember that old saying about too much of a good thing. If you go too far with special effects, you can make your slide show memorable for being obnoxious. Choose your slide show presentation features carefully.

Making Nifty Transitions

Almost everyone has been held captive watching a boring slide show in a classroom, a living room, or a conference room. One slide appears, and everyone yawns. A new slide appears, and everyone yawns again and secretly checks the time.

On the other hand, almost everyone has also been captivated by an informa-tive, inspiring, or just plain interesting slide show that makes the whole audi-ence pay attention and almost regret that the time has passed so quickly.

Which of these two options describes the way you want your presentations to go over? (Wait a minute. Is this a trick question?)

To help keep your slide show interesting, PowerPoint lets you create special transitions between your slides. Your slides can dissolve into one another on-screen, wipe themselves away from left to right, slide up from the bottom of the screen to cover the previous slide, or split in half to reveal a new slide underneath.

PowerPoint gives you two types of transitions to create for your slides:

- ✔ **Visual transitions:** Determine how your slide looks when it first appears
- ✔ **Text transitions:** Determine how the text on your slide appears

Creating visual transitions for your slides

A *visual transition* determines how your slide shows itself on-screen (for example, sliding across the screen or popping up right away). To create the visual transition for each slide in your presentation, follow these steps:

1. **Display the slide you want to change.**

   You may need to select the slide you want to modify by clicking on the slide in the Presentation Outline pane. (Skip this step if you want to change the background of your entire presentation.)

   If you hold down the Ctrl key, you can click on two or more slides in the Presentation Outline pane that you want to change.

2. **Choose Slide Show⇨Slide Transition.**

   The Slide Transition pane appears, as shown in Figure 13-1.

3. **Click the Apply to Selected Slides list box and choose an effect, such as Cut, Dissolve, or Wipe Right.**

   PowerPoint shows you the effect in the picture box.

4. **Click on the Speed list box and choose the speed of the transition, such as Slow, Medium, or Fast.**

   PowerPoint shows you the effect of the chosen speed.

5. **Click in the Sound list box and choose a sound.**

   Select the Loop until Next Sound check box if you want your chosen sound to keep playing continuously until the presentation comes to another slide with a different sound assigned to it.

   Use the Loop until Next Sound option sparingly: Having sound playing continuously may eventually annoy your audience.

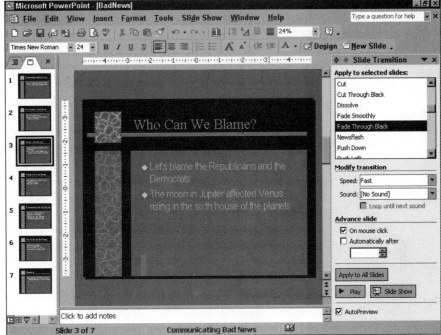

Figure 13-1:
The Slide
Transition
pane is
where you
can create
visual
effects for
your slides.

6. **In the Advance Slide group, choose how the current slide advances to the next.**

   Select the On Mouse Click check box if you want to advance this slide by clicking the mouse. Select the Automatically After check box and, in the Seconds box, type the number of seconds PowerPoint must wait before advancing to the next slide so your presentation can proceed automatically.

7. **Click the Apply to All Slides button if you want to apply your transition to every slide in your presentation. (Skip this step if you selected multiple slides by holding down the Ctrl key in Step 1.)**

   Click the Play button to review how your slide transition looks.

8. **Click the Close box of the Slide Transition pane to make it go away.**

Creating text transitions for your slides

The whole idea behind *text transitions* is to make your slide appear without any text at first (or with only a part of its text revealed), and then have each click of the mouse bring a new chunk of text sliding into view. Such dramatics can keep your audience interested in watching your slides, if only to see what unusual and amusing effects you cooked up when you were supposed to be doing some actual work. (Oh well. You can always *pretend* it wasn't fun.)

Text transitions affect an entire text box, whether it contains one word or several paragraphs. If you want different transitions for each word, line, or paragraph, you have to create separate text boxes, as explained in Chapter 11.

To create a transition for the text on a slide, follow these steps for each slide that you want to add a transition to:

1. **Display the slide containing the text you want to change.**

   You may need to select the slide you want to modify by clicking the slide in the Presentation Outline pane.

2. **Click on the text box that you want to modify.**

   PowerPoint highlights your chosen text box with a border and handles.

3. **Choose Slide Show➪Custom Animation.**

   The Custom Animation pane appears (as shown in Figure 13-2), offering options that you can use to modify the way your text appears on a slide.

4. **Click the Add Effect button.**

   A pop-up menu appears.

5. **Choose one of the following:**

   - **Entrance:** Defines how text first appears on the slide.

   - **Emphasis:** Defines the appearance of text, such as increasing or decreasing the font size.

   - **Exit:** Defines how text disappears off the slide.

   - **Motion Paths:** Defines the direction that text moves when appearing or disappearing off a slide.

6. **Choose the option you want for your text.**

   PowerPoint shows you how your text appears with your chosen transition. As you add transitions, PowerPoint displays numbers near your text and puts the transitions you chose in the Custom Animation pane (as shown in Figure 13-3).

7. **Repeat Steps 4 through 6 until you're done picking transition effects for your text.**

8. **Click the Play button.**

   PowerPoint shows you how the different transitions appear on your slide.

9. **Click in the Close box of the Custom Animation pane to make it go away.**

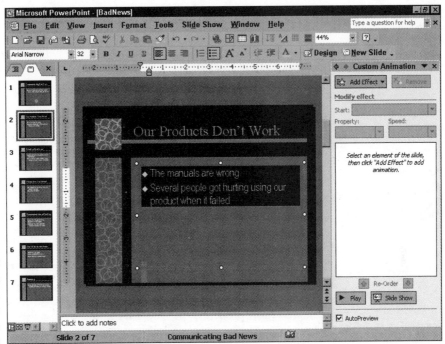

Figure 13-2:
The Custom
Animation
pane.

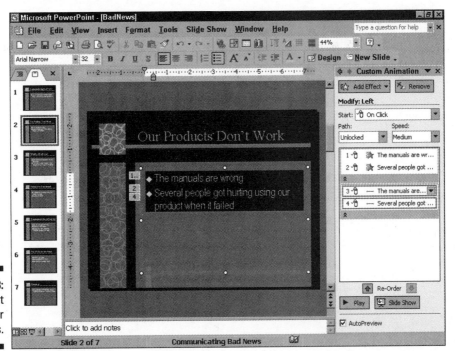

Figure 13-3:
PowerPoint
labels your
transitions.

Removing transitions

Transitions may be nice, but you may also get tired of seeing the same slides and text whirling around the screen.

To remove a slide transition, follow these steps:

1. **Display the slide that you want to change.**

   You may need to select the slide that you want to modify by clicking the slide in the Presentation Outline pane.

   If you hold down the Ctrl key, you can click on two or more slides in the Presentation Outline pane that you want to change.

2. **Choose Slide Show⇨Slide Transition.**

   The Slide Transition pane appears (refer to Figure 13-1).

3. **Choose No Transition in the Apply To Selected Slides list box.**

4. **Click the Apply To All Slides button. (Skip this step if you want to remove a transition from the currently displayed slide or if you selected multiple slides in Step 1 by holding down the Ctrl key.)**

5. **Click the close box of the Slide Transition pane to make it go away.**

To remove text transition from a slide, follow these steps:

1. **Display the slide that contains the text transition you want to change.**

   You may need to select the slide you want to modify by clicking on the slide in the Presenatation Outline pane.

2. **Choose Slide Show⇨Custom Animation.**

   The Custom Animation pane appears (refer to Figure 13-2). PowerPoint displays a number on the slide next to each text box that contains a transition.

3. **Click on the text containing the transition you want to remove.**

   PowerPoint displays a border around your chosen text box.

4. **Click the Remove button.**

   PowerPoint removes any transitions from your chosen text box.

5. **Click the Close box of the Custom Animation pane.**

   The Custom Animation pane disappears.

Preparing Your Presentation for the Public

After your slide show is perfectly organized, complete, and ready to go — you can reveal it to the unsuspecting public. For maximum flexibility, PowerPoint lets you add different elements to your presentation to help you progress through the presentation manually or display it as a self-running presentation for others to view themselves.

Adding buttons

Most presentations display slides one after another in the same boring order. Keeping a single order is fine sometimes, especially if you're giving the presentation, but it can be too confining if others are going to watch your presentation without your supervision.

Instead of forcing someone to view your slides one after another, you can put buttons on your slides. Clicking a button can display any slide, whether it's the first, last, next, previous, or sixth slide from the last.

Adding buttons (which PowerPoint calls hyperlinks) gives your audience the chance to jump from one slide to another. That way, you (or the people controlling your presentation) have greater freedom and flexibility in delivering your presentation.

Creating a hyperlink to another slide

To create a button or hyperlink on a slide, follow these steps:

1. **Display the slide where you want to add hyperlink buttons.**

   You may need to select the slide you want to modify by clicking on the slide in the Presentation Outline pane.

2. **Choose Slide Show➪Action Buttons.**

   A menu of different buttons appears, as shown in Figure 13-4.

   If you move the mouse pointer over the top of the pop-up menu, the pointer turns into a four-way pointing arrow. Then if you drag the mouse, you can detach the pop-up menu so it appears on the screen at all times.

3. **Click a button from the menu.**

   The mouse cursor turns into a crosshair.

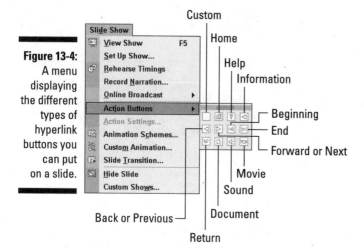

Figure 13-4:
A menu
displaying
the different
types of
hyperlink
buttons you
can put
on a slide.

4. **Place the mouse where you want to draw the button, hold down the left mouse button, drag the mouse to draw your button, and then release the left mouse button.**

   The Action Settings dialog box appears (as shown in Figure 13-5), offering ways to define how your hyperlink button works.

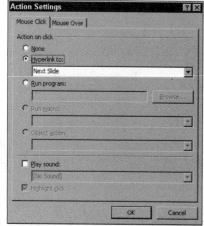

Figure 13-5:
The Action
Settings
dialog box.

5. **Select the Hyperlink To radio button, click the list box, and then choose a slide such as Next Slide or Last Slide Viewed.**

   When choosing an option in Step 5, such as Next Slide, make sure your option corresponds to the visual appearance of the button that you clicked in Step 3.

6. **Click OK.**

   To test your button, choose View⇨Slide Show.

After you create a hyperlink button, you may want to change the slide that the button jumps to when it's clicked. Click the button that you want to change, click the right mouse button, and choose Edit Hyperlink to summon the Action Settings dialog box, where you can choose the new destination slide.

Deleting a hyperlink button

One day you may want to remove a certain hyperlink button from your presentation. You can delete a hyperlink button at any time by following these steps:

1. **Display the slide containing the hyperlink buttons you want to delete.**

   You may need to select the slide you want to modify by clicking the slide in the Presentation Outline pane.

2. **Click the hyperlink button that you want to delete.**

   PowerPoint highlights your chosen hyperlink button.

3. **Press Delete or choose Edit⇨Clear.**

   PowerPoint wipes out your chosen hyperlink button.

Defining how to present your slide show

Many people use PowerPoint to create presentations that they can show like slide shows or lectures — but you can also create self-running presentations for someone else to control. For example, a museum can put a computer in the lobby on which visitors can view a PowerPoint presentation that shows them the main attractions.

To define how to display your presentation, follow these steps:

1. **Choose Slide Show⇨Set Up Show.**

   The Set Up Show dialog box appears.

2. **Click one of the following option buttons:**

   - **Presented by a speaker (full screen):** Slides take up the full screen. You can navigate them with a mouse or keyboard.

   - **Browsed by an individual (window):** Slides appear in a window with the PowerPoint menus and toolbars fully visible. You can navigate slides with a mouse or keyboard.

   - **Browsed at a kiosk (full screen):** Slides take up the full screen, but you can only navigate them with a mouse. (To make this option work properly, be sure to put hyperlink buttons on your slides.)

3. **Select one or more of the following check boxes:**

- **Loop continuous until 'Esc':** Keeps repeating your entire presentation until someone presses the Esc key.

- **Show without <u>n</u>arration:** Eliminates any narration that you may have recorded using the Sli<u>d</u>e Show⇨Record <u>N</u>arration command. (The Record Narration feature lets you add your own voice or other sounds through a microphone. To find out more about this feature, look at *PowerPoint 2002 For Dummies* by Doug Lowe, published by Hungry Minds, Inc.)

- **<u>S</u>how without animation:** Eliminates all the fancy text and slide transitions you may have painstakingly created.

4. **In the Advance Slides group, click either the <u>M</u>anually or <u>U</u>sing Timings If Present radio button.**

5. **Click OK.**

If you click the Browsed At A Kiosk option button in Step 2 and Using Timings If Present option button in Step 3, choose Sli<u>d</u>e Show⇨Slide <u>T</u>ransition and make sure that all your slides have the Automatically After check box chosen. Otherwise you won't be able to advance through your slide show presentation.

Testing your slide show

Before showing your presentation during that crucial business meeting, you should test your slide show. That way, if you find any mistakes or annoying visual effects, you can edit them out, and they won't detract from your presentation.

Besides making sure that your text and slide transitions work, make doubly sure that your spelling and grammar are correct. Nothing can make you look dumber than spelling your own company's name wrong. (How do I know? I'll take the Fifth on that one.)

To test your slide show, follow these steps:

1. **Choose Sli<u>d</u>e Show⇨<u>V</u>iew Show, or press F5.**

   PowerPoint displays your first slide.

2. **To see the next slide, press any key or click the left mouse button.**

3. **Press Esc to end the slide show at any time.**

Part V
Getting Organized with Outlook

The 5th Wave   By Rich Tennant

"The new technology has really helped me get organized. I keep my project reports under the PC, budgets under my laptop, and memos under my pager."

In this part . . .

After a few days on the job, most people's desks disappear under a pile of memos, reports, and papers. If you want to actually use the top of your desk as a writing surface rather than a filing cabinet or garbage bin, you may need the help of Microsoft Outlook to save the day — a combination e-mail program and a personal information organizer.

In addition to helping you create, send, receive, and sort through your e-mail, Outlook also organizes your appointments, tasks, and important contacts. With the help of Outlook, you can track meetings and appointments you'd rather avoid, store the names of people you might forget, and organize e-mail in a single location so that you don't have to search frantically all over your hard drive for an important message that could determine the future of your career or your business.

Outlook can handle all your personal information so you can focus on doing the work that really needs to get done. Who knows? If Outlook makes you productive enough at work, you just may find that you have enough time to relax and take that extended lunch break you've needed for so long.

Chapter 14

Scheduling Your Time

*T*o help you keep track of pressing appointments, pending tasks, and important names and addresses, Microsoft Office XP includes a personal information organizer called *Microsoft Outlook 2002.*

Microsoft Outlook acts like an electronic version of a day planner. By tracking your appointments, tasks, and contacts on your computer, you are always sure to remember your daily, weekly, monthly, and even yearly tasks. Unless, of course, you forget to turn on your computer.

The first time you start Outlook, you'll be forced to wade through the Outlook Startup Wizard, which configures Outlook. If you aren't sure of any of the settings, just use the default settings and keep clicking the Next button until the Startup Wizard goes away.

Making an Appointment

If you're not careful, you can overload yourself with so many appointments that you never have time to do any work, which may not be so bad if you don't like your job anyway. So to help you sort out your appointments and keep them handy, Outlook keeps track of your busy and free time.

Making a new appointment

Outlook lets you schedule appointments for tomorrow or (if you prefer the long view) decades in advance. To make an appointment in Outlook, follow these steps:

1. **Switch to Calendar view by doing one of the following:**

   • Choose View⇨Go to⇨Calendar.

   • Click the Outlook Shortcuts button in the Outlook Bar and then click the Calendar icon.

   The Calendar view appears (as shown in Figure 14-1), showing the current and next month along with an appointment list and a to-do list.

2. **Click the day on which you want to schedule an appointment.**

   Outlook highlights the current day in a box. If you click another day (such as tomorrow or a day three weeks from today), Outlook highlights your newly chosen day in gray but displays a box around the current day.

3. **Click the time on the Appointment list that you want your appointment to begin, such as 11:00 or 3:00.**

   If you want to set an appointment in the morning, make sure you click on the time slots between 12 am and 12 pm.

   Outlook highlights your chosen time.

4. **Type a short description for your appointment, such as** Lunch with mistress **or** Dinner at Boring Office Banquet.

   Outlook displays your text in the Appointment list and highlights it with a border.

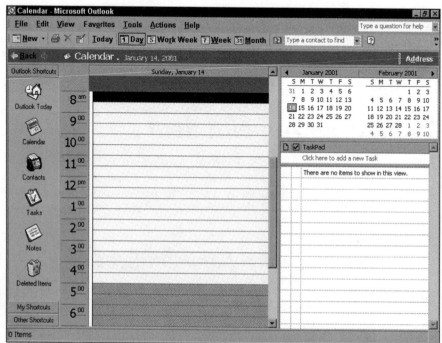

Figure 14-1:
The Calendar view in Outlook.

5. **Move the mouse pointer over the bottom edge of the border surrounding your appointment.**

   The mouse pointer turns into a double-pointing arrow.

6. **Hold down the left mouse button and drag the mouse down to the time when you hope the appointment will end, such as 12:30.**

   Congratulations! You just stored an appointment in Outlook.

Editing an appointment

After you create an appointment, you may want to edit it to specify the appointment location, the appointment subject, the exact starting and ending times, and whether Outlook should beep a reminder before you risk missing the appointment altogether.

To edit an appointment in Outlook:

1. **Switch to Calendar view by using one of the following techniques:**

   • Choose View➪Go to➪Calendar.

   • Click the Outlook Shortcuts button in the Outlook Bar and then click the Calendar icon.

   The Calendar view appears. (Refer to Figure 14-1.)

2. **Click the calendar day that contains the appointment you want to edit.**

3. **Open the appointment by doing one of the following:**

   • Double-click the appointment.

   • Click the appointment and press Ctrl+O.

   • Right-click the appointment and click Open.

   The Appointment dialog box appears, as shown in Figure 14-2.

4. **Click in the Subject text box and put in a description of your appointment.**

   For example, type **Turn in two-week notice, flee job, streak parking lot.**

5. **Click in the Location text box and type the location of your appointment.**

   If you have typed locations for other appointments, you can click the downward-pointing arrow and click a location you've used before (such as a specific meeting room, restaurant, convention center, or secret headquarters).

6. **Click in the Start Time: list boxes to specify the date and time when the appointment begins.**

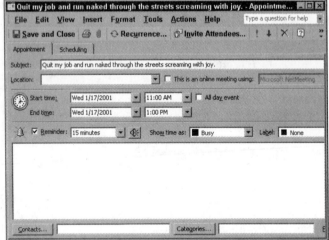

Figure 14-2:
The
Appointment
dialog box.

7. **Click in the End Time: list boxes to specify the date and time when the appointment ends.**

8. **If you want Outlook to remind you of your appointment, select the Reminder check box to put a check mark in it.**

   The Reminder list box tells Outlook to remind you when your appointment is coming up (such as 15 minutes or one hour beforehand). As long as Outlook is running on your computer (even if minimized or hidden), it can remind you of an appointment — no matter what other program you're using at the time.

9. **Click the Show Time As list box and choose Free, Tentative, Busy, or Out of Office.**

   If you're on a network, you can signal co-workers to let them know whether they can bother you during your appointment. Choosing Out of Office, for example, sends a pretty clear I-am-not-here-so-don't-bug-me message.

10. **Click the Save and Close button near the top of the dialog box.**

    Outlook displays your appointment on-screen.

When you set a reminder for an appointment, that appointment appears on the Appointment list with an alarm bell icon next to it. When the time comes to remind you of an upcoming appointment, Outlook displays the Reminder box, as shown in Figure 14-3. To have Outlook repeat the reminder in a little while, click the Snooze To Be Reminded Again In list box, specify how long Outlook must wait to remind you again, and then click the Snooze button.

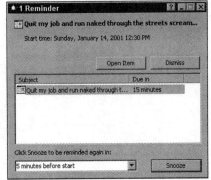

Figure 14-3:
Outlook
reminds you
of upcoming
appoint-
ments.

The Reminder feature works only when Outlook is running (you can minimize the program so it doesn't clutter your screen). If you want to be reminded of appointments, make sure that you don't exit Outlook. If it's shut down, it can't do *anything* for you.

Seeing the big picture of your appointments

To help you organize your life, Outlook offers five ways to display your appointments:

- ✔ **Day:** Shows a single day, hour by hour (refer to Figure 14-1), so you can see what appointments you may have already missed today.

- ✔ **Outlook Today:** Shows all appointments and tasks scheduled for today. (See Figure 14-4.)

- ✔ **Work Week:** Shows all appointments for a single week (see Figure 14-5) except Sundays and Saturdays.

- ✔ **Week:** Shows all appointments for a single week, including weekends (see Figure 14-6) so you won't forget that Saturday golf game.

- ✔ **Month:** Shows all appointments for a calendar month (see Figure 14-7) so you can keep track of really crucial pending appointments for several weeks.

To switch to a particular view in Outlook, here's the drill:

- ✔ **Day view:** Choose View➪Day or click the Day button on the Standard toolbar.

- ✔ **Outlook Today view:** Click the Outlook Shortcuts button in the Outlook Bar and then click the Today icon.

✔ **Work Week view:** Choose <u>V</u>iew⇨Wo<u>r</u>k Week or click the Work Week button on the Standard toolbar.

✔ **Week view:** Choose <u>V</u>iew⇨Wee<u>k</u> or click the Week button on the Standard toolbar.

✔ **Month view:** Choose <u>V</u>iew⇨<u>M</u>onth or click the Month button on the Standard toolbar.

Changing an appointment

Because appointments can always change or get cancelled, you may need to edit an appointment by following these steps:

1. **Click the appointment that you want to edit.**

2. **Press Ctrl+O or double-click the appointment that you want to modify.**

   The Appointment dialog box appears. (Refer to Figure 14-2.)

3. **Make your changes to the appointment.**

   For example, click the Start Time or End Time list box and type a new time to change the start or end time or date for your appointment.

4. **Click the <u>S</u>ave and Close button.**

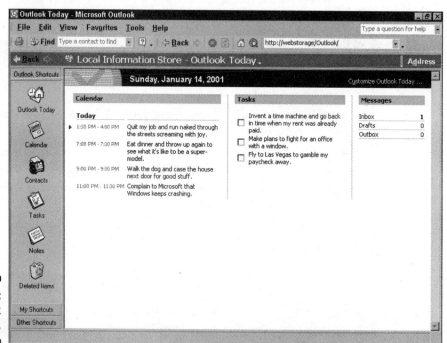

Figure 14-4:
The Outlook Today view.

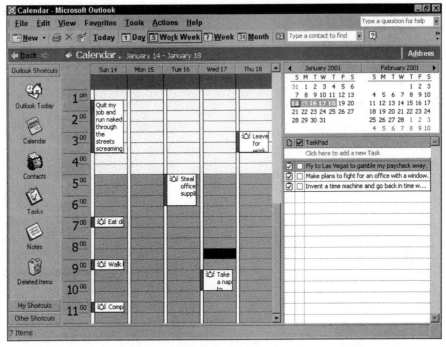

Figure 14-5:
The Outlook
Work Week
view:
Monday
through
Friday.

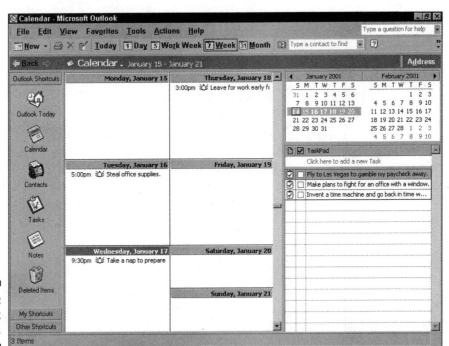

Figure 14-6:
The Outlook
Week view.

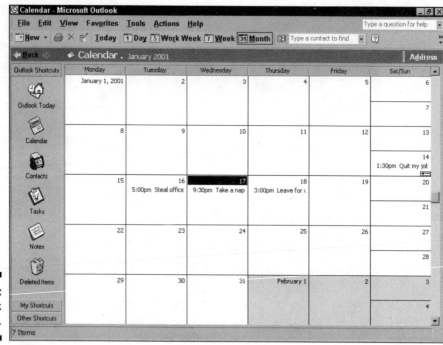

Figure 14-7:
The Outlook
Month view.

Deleting an appointment

After an appointment has passed or been canceled, you can delete it to make room for other appointments. To delete an appointment, follow these steps:

1. **Click the appointment that you want to delete.**

   If you are in the Outlook Today view, Outlook displays the Appointment dialog box. (Refer to Figure 14-2.) If you are in any other view, Outlook just highlights your chosen appointment.

2. **Press Ctrl+D.**

If you delete an appointment by mistake, press Ctrl+Z to recover it again.

If you delete an appointment from within the Outlook Today view, pressing Ctrl+Z will never recover it again, so make sure you really want to delete an appointment before you do so.

Defining a recurring appointment

You may have an appointment that occurs every day, week, month, or year (such as going to lunch with the boss on the first Monday of the month or that Feng Shui-for-cubicles class every Friday evening). Instead of typing in recurring appointments again and again, you can enter them once and then define how often they occur. Outlook automatically schedules those appointments unless you specifically tell it otherwise.

Creating a new recurring appointment

If you are currently in the Outlook Today view, switch to the Day, Work Week, Week, or Month view first.

To define a recurring appointment in the Day, Work Week, Week, or Month view:

1. **Choose Actions⇨New Recurring Appointment.**

   The Appointment Recurrence dialog box appears, as shown in Figure 14-8.

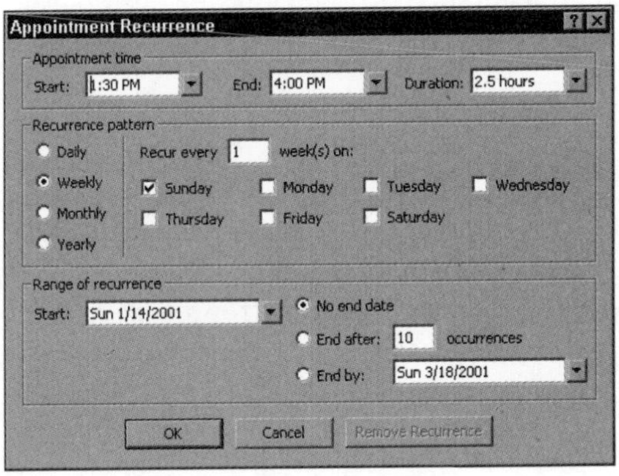

Figure 14-8:
The
Appointment
Recurrence
dialog box is
where you
specify how
often an
appointment
occurs.

2. **In the Appointment Time group, click the Start list box and enter the start time for your recurring appointment by clicking the down-pointing arrow until the right time shows up.**

   You can also type a time, such as **8:13 AM**, in the Start list box.

3. **Click the End list box and enter the end time for your recurring appointment.**

4. **Click the Duration list box and enter the length of your appointment.**

5. **Select one of the following radio buttons to specify the frequency of the appointment: Daily, Weekly, Monthly, or Yearly (or choose a specific day, such as Sunday or Tuesday).**

6. **In the Range of Recurrence area, click the Start list box and click the date that corresponds to the first instance of your recurring appointment.**

7. **Select one of the radio buttons in the Range of Recurrence area to define when you want the appointments to stop recurring.**

   You can specify a number of occurrences (End After), an end date (End By), or no ending at all (No End Date).

8. **Click OK.**

   The Appointment dialog box appears for you to define your recurring appointment.

9. **Type your appointment in the Subject box (for example,** leave early from work**).**

10. **Type the location of your appointment in the Location box.**

11. **Click the Reminder check box if you want Outlook to flash you a reminder message.**

    Click the Reminder list box to specify when you want Outlook to remind you of your appointment (such as 15 minutes or one hour beforehand).

12. **Click the Show Time As list box and choose Free, Tentative, Busy, or Out of Office.**

    See Step 9 in the "Editing an appointment" section for more information about these options.

13. **Click the Save and Close button.**

    Outlook displays your appointment on-screen, as shown in Figure 14-9. Recurring appointments show revolving arrows next to the appointment descriptions.

You can make any existing appointment recur by double-clicking it and then clicking the Recurrence button. (Logical, isn't it?)

Editing a recurring appointment

To edit a recurring appointment from the Day, Work Week, Week, or Month view:

1. **Click the recurring appointment that you want to edit.**

2. **Press Ctrl+O or double-click the appointment.**

   The Open Recurring Item dialog box appears.

3. **Click one of the following option buttons:**

   • **Open This Occurrence:** You can edit just this specific appointment (for example, just the instance that occurs on October 18).

   • **Open the Series:** You can edit the entire series of recurring appointments (for example, all your "leave work early on Friday" appointments).

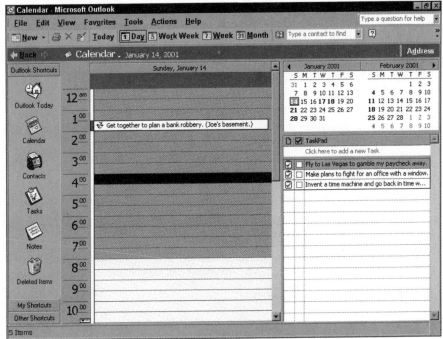

Figure 14-9:
A recurring
appointment
is
character-
ized by its
circular
indicator.

Outlook displays the Appointment Recurrence dialog box. (Refer to Figure 14-8.)

4. **Make any changes to your recurring appointment (such as changing start time, end time, or day of occurrence), and then click the Save and Close button.**

Printing Your Schedule

Unless you carry a laptop computer around all day, you may occasionally need to print your appointment schedule on paper so you can look at it without using electricity or copy it for all your fans and relatives. To print your appointments from the Day, Work Week, Week, or Month view, follow these steps:

1. **Switch to Calendar view by doing one of the following:**

   • Choose View⇔Go To⇔Calendar.

   • Click the Outlook Shortcuts button in the Outlook Bar and then click the Calendar icon.

   The Calendar view appears. (Refer to Figure 14-1.)

2. Choose one of the following:

  - Choose File⇨Print.

  - Press Ctrl+P.

  - Click the Print icon on the Standard toolbar.

The Print dialog box appears, as shown in Figure 14-10. (*Note:* If you click the Print icon on the Standard toolbar, Outlook prints your entire appointment schedule without giving you a chance to go through Steps 3 through 5.)

3. Click a style in the Print Style box (such as Weekly Style or Monthly Style).

This is where you can define the time frame for printing your schedule.

4. Click the Preview button to see what your schedule will look like when it's printed.

To specify a printout size to fit your day planner, you can click the Page Setup button, click the Paper tab, and choose an option in the Size list box — booklet, a Day-Timer page, a Day-Runner page, or a Franklin Day Planner page.

5. Click the Print button to start printing.

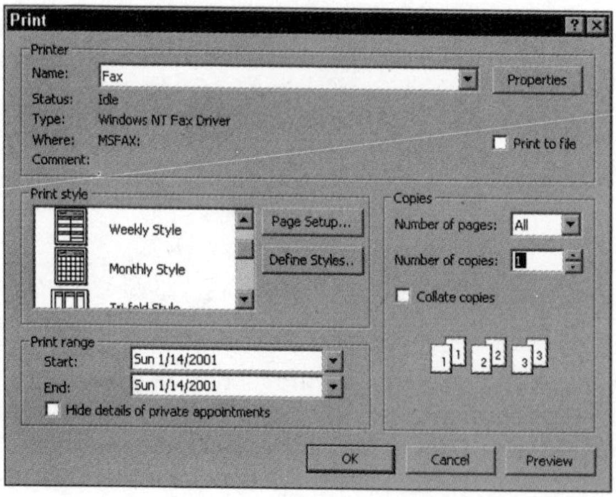

Figure 14-10:
The Print
dialog box.

Chapter 15

Setting Tasks and Making Contacts

· ·

In This Chapter

▶ Storing names and addresses

▶ Organizing names by categories

▶ Creating a to-do list

· ·

*B*esides letting you make and break appointments, Microsoft Outlook lets you create your own to-do lists (so you don't have to waste money buying special paper labeled "Things to do today"), as well as store valuable names, addresses, phone numbers, and other important information about people who may be able to further your career.

For more information about using Outlook's wonderful features, pick up a copy of *Outlook 2002 For Dummies,* by Bill Dyszel (published by Hungry Minds, Inc.).

Organizing Contact Information

Most folks have business cards that they can hand out to people who may be useful to them in the future. People stuck in the Dark Ages store their business card collection in a Rolodex file, but you can progress to the twenty-first century by storing names and addresses in Outlook instead. By using Outlook, you can quickly copy your valuable business contacts and share them with others or just get rid of your cumbersome Rolodex file and put a much more cumbersome computer on your desk instead.

Storing contact information

To store information about a contact in Outlook, start Outlook and then follow these steps:

1. **Switch to Contacts view by using one of the following methods:**

   - Choose View➪Go To➪Contacts.

   - Click the Outlook Shortcuts button in the Outlook Bar and then click the Contacts icon.

   The Contacts view appears, as shown in Figure 15-1.

2. **Choose Actions➪New Contact or press Ctrl+N.**

   The Contact dialog box appears, as shown in Figure 15-2.

3. **Type the name, address, phone number, and any other information you want to store about the contact in the appropriate boxes.**

   If you type a company name, make sure you type it consistently. Don't type it as "Hungry Minds Books" one time and just "Hungry Minds" another time, or Outlook won't consider those names to mean the same company.

   - If you click the Full Name button, a Check Full Name dialog box appears. In it, you can specify a title (such as Dr. or Ms.); first, middle, and last name; and a suffix (such as Jr. or III).

   - If you click the Address button, a Check Address dialog box appears. Here, you can specify a street name, city, state or province, postal code, and country.

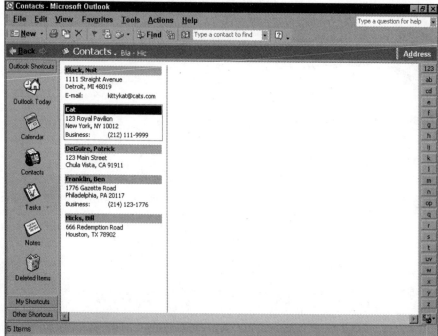

Figure 15-1:
Outlook can list your contacts on the screen.

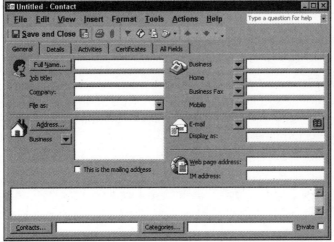

Figure 15-2:
The Contact dialog box is where you can type information for a new contact.

- If you click the list box that appears directly below the Address button, you can specify two or more addresses for each person, such as a business address and a home address.

- The This is the Mailing Address check box lets you specify which address to use when sending postal mail.

- The button that looks like an open book that appears to the right of the E-mail list box displays a list of e-mail addresses that you have previously stored for all your contacts.

4. **After you finish entering the information, click $\underline{S}$ave and Close.**

You don't have to fill in every single box. For example, you may just want to store someone's name and phone number. In this case, you don't need to type in the address or any other irrelevant information.

Changing your point of view

The real power of your computer and Outlook comes into play in sorting and displaying different views of your information to help you find just the information you need. You have seven ways to display your contacts in Outlook:

✔ **Address Cards:** Displays names (sorted alphabetically by last name), addresses, phone numbers, and e-mail addresses.

✔ **Detailed Address Cards:** Displays every piece of information about a person, such as company name, fax number, and job title.

✔ **Phone List:** Displays names and phone numbers (including business, home, fax, and mobile phone numbers) in row-and-column format for easy viewing.

✔ **By Category:** Displays information according to categories such as Business, Hot Contacts, Key Customer, and Suppliers. (You can learn how to organize your contacts into categories in the "Categorizing your contacts" section, later in this chapter.)

✔ **By Company:** Displays names grouped according to company name. (Useful for finding multiple names belonging to the same company.)

✔ **By Location:** Displays information by country, city, and state/province.

✔ **By Follow-Up Flag:** Displays contacts identified with a follow-up flag, which you can add to a contact by pressing Ctrl+Shift+G or by choosing Actions➪Flag for Follow-Up.

To choose a different view to display your contact information, make sure you're in the Contacts view and then follow these steps:

1. **Choose View➪Current View.**

   A pop-up menu appears.

2. **Choose the desired view (such as Detailed Address Cards or Phone List).**

   Outlook displays your contact information in your chosen view.

Searching your contacts

After you start using Microsoft Outlook, you may wind up storing globs of information that you may have trouble finding again. So to help you search for a specific contact stored in Outlook, make sure you're in Contacts view and then follow these steps:

1. **Choose Tools➪Find, press Ctrl+F, or click the Find button on the toolbar.**

   The Find Items in Contacts bar appears at the top of the Contacts view, as shown in Figure 15-3.

2. **Click in the Look For box and type the phrase (first name, last name, and so on) that you want to find.**

   To make the search faster, type as much of the phrase that you want to find. For example, instead of typing **F** to search for everyone with a first name that begins with F, make it more specific and type as much of the name as possible, such as **FRAN**.

3. **Click Find Now.**

   Outlook displays the contacts that match your search criteria. You can double-click the contact that you want to view.

Find button   Close box

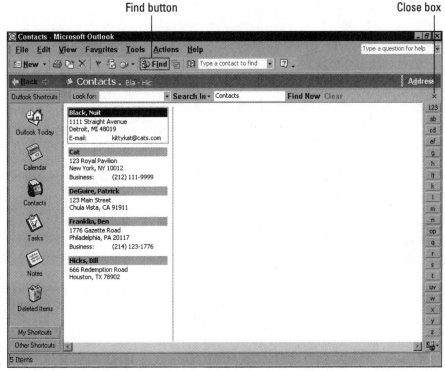

Figure 15-3:
The Find
Items
Contacts
bar allows
you to
search
through
your
contacts.

4. **Click the Close box of the Find Items in Contacts bar.**

   Outlook displays all your contacts again when you close the Find Items
   in Contacts window.

For a more sophisticated way to find specific contacts, choose
Tools➪Advanced Find or press Ctrl+Shift+F. The Advanced Find dialog box
appears and gives you more options for searching your list of contacts.

Categorizing your contacts

If you're a busy person (or just a pack rat who can't resist storing every possible name and address that you find), you may find your Outlook contact list
so full of names that trying to find any single name is cumbersome.

To solve this problem, you can organize your contacts into categories, such
as personal or customer contacts. When you want to see information for just
a particular group of contacts, you can tell Outlook to sort your contact list
by the appropriate category.

Defining a category for a contact

Before you can ask Outlook to organize your contacts by category, you need to define which contacts belong in the category. To define a category for each contact, make sure you're in the Contacts view and then follow these steps:

1. **Click a contact that you want to categorize.**

2. **Choose Edit➪Categories.**

   The Categories dialog box appears, as shown in Figure 15-4.

Figure 15-4: The Categories dialog box allows you to group your contacts.

Categories	? X
Item(s) belong to these categories:	
	Add to List
Available categories:	

Business
Competition
Favorites
Gifts
Goals/Objectives
Holiday
Holiday Cards
Hot Contacts
Ideas
International
Key Customer
Miscellaneous
Personal
Phone Calls

OK   Cancel   Master Category List...

3. **Click the check box for each category that your contact belongs in.**

   Many contacts may logically belong in multiple categories, such as under the Business, Hot Contacts, and Key Customer categories.

4. **Click OK.**

TIP

As a faster method for categorizing your contacts, right-click a contact and click Categories from the pop-up menu. Then follow Steps 3 and 4.

In case you want another way to define a category for a contact, or if you want to organize multiple contacts into a category, follow these steps:

1. **Click the Organize button on the toolbar.**

   The Ways to Organize Contacts window appears, as shown in Figure 15-5.

2. **Click the contacts you want to add to a category.**

   You can choose multiple contacts by holding down the Ctrl key and clicking on the contacts you want to include.

Organize button

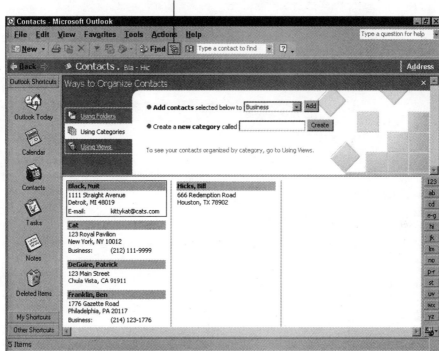

Figure 15-5:
The Ways
to Organize
Contacts
window
helps you
organize
multiple
contacts
into
categories.

3. **Click in the Add Contacts list box, choose a category (such as Business or Hot Contacts) and click the Add button.**

   To create a new category, type the category name in the Create a New Category Called text box and click the Create button.

4. **Click the Close box of the Ways to Organize Contacts window.**

Sorting contacts by categories

After you assign your contacts to different categories, you can have Outlook show you only those contacts within a given category. That way, you can quickly find business-related contacts, personal contacts, or top secret contacts. To view your contacts by category, follow these steps:

1. **Choose View⇨Current View⇨By Category.**

   Outlook displays all the categories you checked, as shown in Figure 15-6.

2. **Click the plus sign next to the category that contains the contacts you want to view.**

   For example, if you want to see all Business contacts, click the plus sign next to the Categories: Business heading.

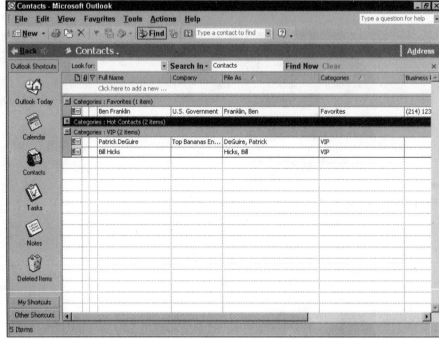

Figure 15-6:
Outlook can
organize
your
contacts
according to
categories.

3. **Double-click the contact that you want to view.**

   The Contact window appears, displaying all the information for your chosen contact.

4. **Click Save and Close when you're done viewing or editing the contact.**

Managing Your Tasks

To keep from wasting your days doing trivial tasks and forgetting all your important ones, you can create a daily to-do list in Outlook and check off your tasks as you complete them.

Creating tasks for a to-do list

To create a to-do list, follow these steps:

1. **Switch to Tasks view in one of the following ways:**

   • Choose View⇔Go To⇔Tasks.

• Click the Outlook Shortcuts button in the Outlook Bar and then
click the Tasks icon.

The Tasks view appears, as shown in Figure 15-7.

2. **Click the Click Here to Add a New Task text box and type a task.**

3. **Click the Due Date box. (Skip Steps 3 through 5 if you don't want to
choose a due date.)**

A downward-pointing arrow appears.

4. **Click the downward-pointing arrow.**

A calendar appears.

5. **Click a due date and press Enter.**

Outlook displays your task.

Editing a task

After you create a task, you can edit it later to set a reminder or track how
much of the task you've completed. To edit a task, follow these steps:

1. **Double-click a task (or click the task and then press Ctrl+O).**

The Task dialog box appears, as shown in Figure 15-8.

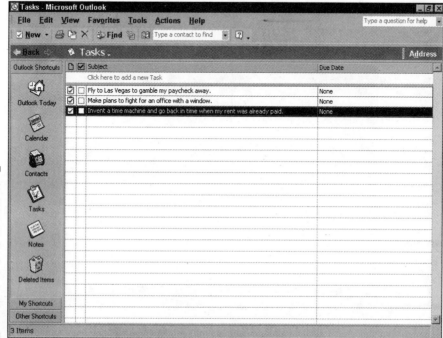

Figure 15-7:
The Tasks
view lists all
the tasks
you need to
accomplish
today (or
whenever
you get
around to it).

2. **Choose one or more of the following:**

   • **Click the Status list box and choose a status for your task, such as In Progress, Completed, or Waiting on Someone Else.**

   A task's status shows you how each task is progressing (or not progressing); this feature helps you manage time more effectively.

   • **Click the Priority list box and choose Low, Normal, or High.**

   Categorizing tasks by priority, you can identify the ones that really need to get done and the ones that you can safely ignore and hope they go away.

   • **Click the % Complete list box to specify how much of the task you've already completed.**

   • **Click the Reminder check box and specify a date and time for Outlook to remind you of this particular task.**

   If you click the Alarm button (it looks like a megaphone), you can specify a unique sound that Outlook plays to remind you of your task.

   • **Type your task in more detail in the big text box at the bottom of the Task dialog box.**

3. **Click Save and Close.**

You can view your task list and a calendar at the same time if you choose Calendar view and choose Outlook Today, Day, Work Week, or Week view. From any of these views, you can check off completed tasks just by clicking in each task's check box.

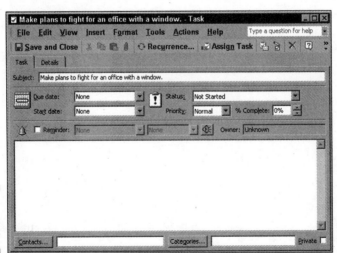

Figure 15-8:
The Task
dialog box.

Moving a task

Normally, Outlook organizes your tasks in the order that you created them. Because this order isn't always the most efficient way to organize tasks, take some time to move tasks around. To move a task, follow these steps:

1. **Click the task that you want to move.**

2. **Hold down the left mouse button.**

3. **Drag the mouse.**

   Outlook displays a red horizontal line showing you where it will move your task the moment you let go of the left mouse button.

4. **Release the left mouse button when the task appears where you want it.**

Finishing a task

Despite that natural tendency to procrastinate, many people actually do complete the tasks they set for themselves. To tell Outlook that you've joined this elite group, select the check box of the task you have actually completed. Outlook displays a check mark in the check box, dims the task, and draws a line through the task.

Outlook stores completed tasks so you can display all the tasks you've completed by choosing View⇨Current View⇨Completed Tasks. (It might just come in handy at review time.) To remove a task from Outlook's memory, you have to delete it specifically — details coming up.

Deleting a task

After you complete a task (or just decide to ignore it permanently), you may want to delete it from Outlook so it doesn't clutter up your screen. Here's how:

1. **Double-click the task that you want to delete.**

   A Task dialog box appears.

2. **Choose Edit⇨Delete, press Ctrl+D, or click the Delete icon on the task dialog box toolbar.**

   Outlook deletes your chosen task.

If you delete a task by mistake, press Ctrl+Z right away and Outlook kindly retrieves it for you.

Chapter 16

Organizing Your E-Mail

In This Chapter

▶ Setting up Outlook

▶ Making an address book

▶ Writing and sending e-mail

▶ Reading and replying to e-mail

*N*early everyone has an e-mail account nowadays — some people have several. If you're using multiple e-mail accounts, your messages may be scattered in different places, so you have a hard time sorting out who just sent what to whom.

Outlook can help you not only write, send, and read e-mail, but also funnel all your e-mail from your Internet accounts into a central mailbox. That way, when you want to read, write, or delete e-mail, you can do it all from within a single program.

Setting Up Outlook to Work with E-Mail

When you install Microsoft Office XP, Outlook digs through your computer and finds out what it needs to know to work with e-mail from an Internet account. However, you may later add or cancel an Internet account, so you need to know how to tell Outlook about these changes to your e-mail.

Defining an e-mail account for Outlook requires technical details, such as knowing your Internet's POP3 or SMTP information. If you don't have the faintest idea what this might be, call your Internet service provider for help or ask a knowledgeable friend to help you out.

Adding e-mail accounts to Outlook

To add an e-mail account to Outlook, follow these steps:

1. **Choose Tools⇨Options.**

   The Options dialog box appears.

2. **Click the Mail Setup tab.**

   The Mail Setup tab appears, as shown in Figure 16-1.

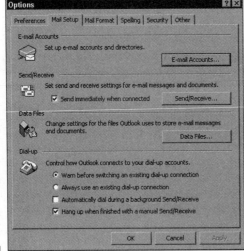

Figure 16-1:
The Mail
Setup tab in
the Options
dialog box is
where you
can specify
an e-mail
account to
use with
Outlook.

3. **Click the E-mail Accounts button.**

   The E-mail Accounts dialog box appears, as shown in Figure 16-2.

4. **Click the Add a New E-mail Account radio button and then click Next.**

   An E-mail Accounts dialog box asks for your server type, as shown in Figure 16-3.

   If you're connecting to an Internet account that forces you to dial through your phone line, click the POP3 radio button. If you want to connect to a Hotmail, Yahoo!, or another Web-based e-mail account, click the HTTP radio button. Talk to a computer expert (preferably someone nearby) to help you use the other options, which are often used to connect Outlook to a corporate e-mail account on a local area network.

Figure 16-2:
The E-mail
Accounts
dialog box
allows you
to add a
new e-mail
account or
modify an
existing one.

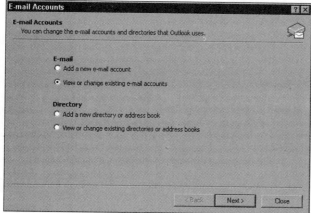

Figure 16-3:
To set up
an e-mail
account
with
Outlook, you
need to
know the
server type.

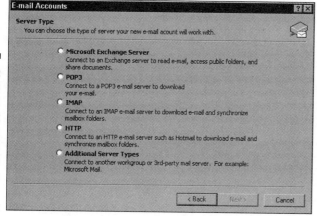

5. **Click a Server Type option (such as POP3) and click Next.**

   Depending on the option you chose, another dialog box appears, asking you to type in technical details about your e-mail account such as your mail server name.

6. **Type the information required in the User information text boxes.**

   Typical user information includes the following:

   • **Your Name:** Your name

   • **E-mail address:** Your actual e-mail address for example, yourname@isp.net.

- **Incoming mail server (POP3):** Your Internet service provider's POP3 information, for example pop.yourisp.net.

- **Outgoing mail server (SMTP):** Your Internet service provider's SMTP information, for example `smtp.yourisp.net`.

- **User Name:** The name of your Internet account, usually the first portion of your e-mail address, such as `Jsmith` if your e-mail address is `Jsmith@meISP.net`.

- **Password:** The password that magically lets you access your account

7. **Click Next.**

   Another dialog box appears, informing you that you have successfully created an e-mail account to work with Outlook.

8. **Click Finish.**

   The Options dialog box appears again.

9. **Click OK.**

Deleting e-mail accounts from Outlook

If you move to a different company or switch Internet service providers, your old e-mail account may no longer be valid. Rather than keep this obsolete information lodged in Outlook, delete it to keep Outlook from trying to send and retrieve e-mail from a dead e-mail account. To delete an e-mail account from Outlook, follow these steps:

1. **Choose Tools⇨Options.**

   The Options dialog box appears. (Refer to Figure 16-1.)

2. **Click the Mail Setup tab.**

3. **Click the E-mail Accounts button.**

   The E-mail Accounts dialog box appears. (Refer to Figure 16-2.)

4. **Click the View or Change Existing E-mail Accounts radio button and click Next.**

   A list of e-mail accounts appears, as shown in Figure 16-4.

5. **Click the Internet e-mail account that you want to delete and then click the Remove button.**

   A dialog box appears asking whether you're sure you want to delete your e-mail account.

6. **Click Yes.**

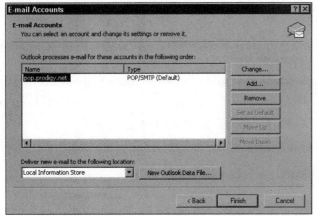

Figure 16-4:
Viewing
a list of
existing
e-mail
accounts in
Outlook.

7. **Click Finish.**

The Options dialog box appears again.

8. **Click OK.**

Storing e-mail addresses in Outlook

The trouble with e-mail addresses is that they look as cryptic as if a cat walked across your keyboard. Typical Internet addresses consist of letters separated by periods and that silly at-sign character (@), as in yourname@yourisp.net.

Type one character wrong and Outlook won't know how to send e-mail to the correct destination. In a desperate attempt to make computers less user-hostile, Outlook lets you store names and e-mail addresses in the Address Book. That way, you need only type the e-mail address right *once*. After that, you can just choose an address by clicking a name from the Address Book list.

Making an address book

To make a Personal Address Book, follow these steps:

1. **Choose Tools⇨Options.**

The Options dialog box appears. (Refer to Figure 16-1.)

2. **Click the Mail Setup tab.**

3. **Click the E-mail Accounts button.**

The E-mail Accounts dialog box appears. (Refer to Figure 16-2.)

4. **Click the Add a New Directory or Address Book radio button and click Next.**

   A dialog box appears, asking what type of directory or address book you want to create.

5. **Click the Additional Address Books radio button and click Next.**

   A dialog box appears, asking you to choose an address book type.

6. **Click Personal Address Book and click Next.**

   A Personal Address Book dialog box appears, as shown in Figure 16-5.

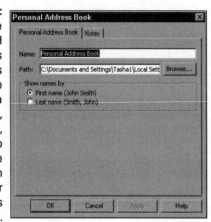

7. **Click in the Name text box and type a name for your address book, such as** List of Losers **or** Friends Who Owe Me Money.

8. **Click in the Path text box and type the path where you want to store your address book data.**

   You can click the Browse button to visually click and choose the folder where you want to store your address book data.

9. **Click in the First Name or Last Name radio button under the Show Names By group.**

   The First Name option displays names, such as John E. Doe, while the Last Name option displays names with the last name displayed first, such as Doe, John E. The option you choose is simply cosmetic and reflects the way you prefer looking at the names in your address book.

10. **Click OK.**

    A dialog box appears, informing you that you can't access your newly created address book until you restart Outlook.

11. Click OK twice.

Before you can use your Personal Address Book, you have to exit Outlook and restart it.

Stuffing addresses in your Personal Address Book

After you create a Personal Address Book, you can start storing names and addresses in it. To store a name and e-mail address in Outlook, follow these steps:

1. **Switch to the Contacts view by clicking on Contacts in the Outlook bar or by choosing View⇨Go To⇨Contacts.**

   The Contacts view appears.

2. **Choose Tools⇨Address Book or press Ctrl+Shift+B.**

   The Address Book window appears, as shown in Figure 16-6.

New Entry icon

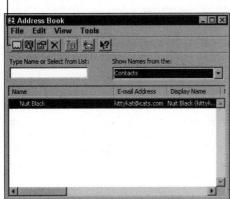

Figure 16-6:
The
Address
Book
window
displays
a list of
all your
contacts.

3. **Choose File⇨New Entry or click the New Entry icon.**

   The New Entry dialog box appears.

4. **Click the In The list box under the Put This Entry group and choose the name of the address book where you want to store your new entry, such as Personal Address Book or My List of Losers.**

5. **Click OK.**

   A New Other Address Properties dialog box appears, as shown in Figure 16-7.

Figure 16-7:
The New
Other
Address
Properties
dialog box is
where you
can type
names and
e-mail
addresses.

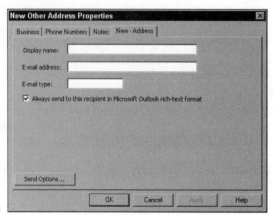

6. **Type the person's name and e-mail address in the appropriate text boxes.**

   The E-mail Type text box is where you can type a short description about the name and e-mail address you typed. Some sample descriptions might be "Friend" or "HotProspect."

7. **Click OK.**

   Outlook displays your entry in the Address Book window.

8. **To make the Address Book window go away, choose File➪Close or click the Close box (the X in the top right corner).**

When you type and save e-mail addresses in the Contact view (see Chapter 15 for more information about storing e-mail addresses in the Contact view), Outlook adds those e-mail addresses to your Address Book so you can click on the e-mail address you want to use without having to type it all over again.

Creating an E-Mail Message

You can write e-mail in Outlook when you're online (connected to the Internet) or when you're offline (not connected to the Internet).

You don't need to connect to the Internet to write e-mail, but you eventually have to connect to the Internet to send your e-mail.

To create an e-mail message, follow these steps:

1. **Choose View➪Go To➪Inbox, or press Crl+Shift+I.**

   The Inbox view appears.

2. **Click the New button on the toolbar, choose Actions⇨New Mail Message, or press Ctrl+N.**

   The Message dialog box appears, as shown in Figure 16-8.

3. **Click in the To text box and type the e-mail address where you want to send your message.**

Click the To button to display a Select Names dialog box and then double-click the name of the recipient. Then click OK. If the recipient isn't in your Address Book, type his or her e-mail address in the To box (for example, `myfriend@isp.net`).

To send the same e-mail to two or more people, click the To button and then double-click another name. In case you want to type an e-mail address in (because you didn't store that e-mail address in your Address Book), just type any additional e-mail addresses, separated by a semi-colon: `john@doe.com`; `jane@doe.com`.

To send a *carbon copy* (twentieth-century-speak for *identical message*) of the e-mail to other people, click the Cc button. Outlook displays a Select Names dialog box that lets you choose e-mail addresses for the people you want to send e-mail to. You can also type another e-mail address directly in the Cc box.

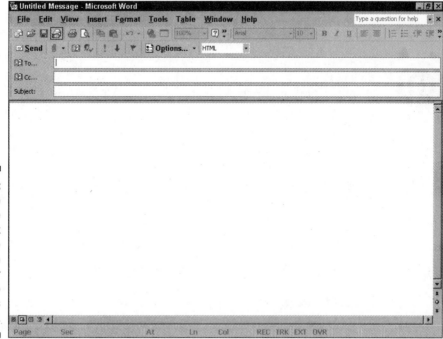

Figure 16-8:
The Message dialog box is where you can type your message to send as e-mail.

Although clicking the To and Cc buttons can send e-mail to two or more people, the Cc button is meant more to send e-mail to people so they can stay informed on your correspondence without necessarily having to respond to it.

4. **Click in the Subject box and type a subject for your message.**

   For example, type **Secret plans for eliminating gravity from the planet**.

5. **Click in the big text box at the bottom of the Message dialog box and type your message.**

   If you want to send a file along with your e-mail, don't follow Step 6 just yet. Instead, follow the instructions in the following section, "Attaching files to e-mail," and then return to Step 6.

   Choose Tools⇨Spelling or press F7 to check the spelling in your message.

6. **Click the Send button.**

   Outlook sends your e-mail right away if you're currently connected to the Internet. Otherwise, Outlook stores your message in the Outbox folder.

Attaching files to e-mail

Rather than just send plain text, you can also send pictures, programs, word processor documents, or any other type of file you care to send.

Try not to send massive files larger than one megabyte. The larger the file, the longer it will take for someone else to download it. To compress files, consider a file compression program, such as WinZip (www.winzip.com).

To attach a file to your e-mail, follow these steps:

1. **Create your e-mail following Steps 1 through 5 in the previous section, "Creating an E-Mail Message."**

2. **Choose Insert⇨File or click on the Insert File icon (it looks like a paperclip) on the toolbar.**

   An Insert File dialog box appears.

3. **Click on the file you want to send with your e-mail.**

   You may have to switch drives or folders to find the file you want to send.

4. **Click Insert.**

   Outlook displays an icon and your chosen file in an Attach text box directly underneath the Subject text box. At this point, you're ready to send your e-mail.

You can attach multiple files to an e-mail message. Just repeat Steps 2 through 4 for each additional file you want to attach.

5. Click the Send button.

Outlook sends your e-mail along with your attached file.

Using the Outbox folder

Until you connect to the Internet, Outlook stores any e-mail messages that you have not yet sent in the Outbox folder.

Viewing and editing messages in the Outbox folder

To view all the messages trapped temporarily in your Outbox folder, follow these steps:

1. **Choose View⇨Go To⇨Folder or press Ctrl+Y. (As a shortcut, click Outbox under the Messages heading in the Outlook Today view. Then skip to Step 3.)**

   A Go to Folder dialog box appears.

2. **Click the Outbox icon and click OK.**

   Outlook displays a list of e-mail messages waiting to be sent.

3. **Double-click the e-mail message you want to view.**

   You can edit your e-mail message.

4. **Click the Save button and choose File⇨Close to store your e-mail back in the Outbox folder.**

To send e-mail stored in your Outbox folder, follow the steps in the following section.

Sending e-mail from the Outbox folder

Messages stored in the Outbox folder remain there until one of two conditions occurs:

- ✔ You manually send them on their way.
- ✔ You configure Outlook to send all e-mail stored in the Outbox automatically the moment you connect to the Internet (or local area network).

To manually send e-mail from the Outbox folder, follow these steps:

1. **Choose View⇨Go To⇨Folder or press Ctrl+Y. (As a shortcut, click Outbox under the Messages heading in the Outlook Today view. Then skip to Step 3.)**

   A Go To Folder dialog box appears.

2. **Click the Outbox icon and click OK.**

   Outlook displays a list of e-mail messages that are waiting to be sent.

3. **Click the e-mail message you want to send.**

   To choose more than one e-mail message, hold down the Ctrl key and click each message you want to send. To select a continuous range of e-mail messages, click the first message you want to send, hold down the Shift key, and then click the last message you want to send.

4. **Click the Send/Receive button.**

   If you are not connected to the Internet, a dialog box appears, asking for the user name and password to your Internet account so Outlook can connect and send your e-mail.

In case manually sending e-mail from your Outbox seems troublesome, make Outlook send e-mail automatically instead. To configure Outlook to send e-mail automatically from your Outbox folder, follow these steps:

1. **Choose Tools⇨Options.**

   The Options dialog box appears. (Refer to Figure 16-1.)

2. **Click the Mail Setup tab.**

3. **Click the Send Immediately When Connected check box that appears under the Send/Receive category. (If a check mark already appears in the check box, skip this step.)**

4. **Click OK.**

   From now on, Outlook automatically sends all e-mail from your Outbox as soon as you connect to the Internet.

Retrieving and Reading E-Mail

With most Internet accounts, you can use Outlook to read and organize your e-mail.

If you're using America Online, you won't be able to use Outlook to read your e-mail.

Retrieving e-mail

To retrieve e-mail, follow these steps:

1. **Choose View⇨Go To⇨Inbox, press Ctrl+Shift+I, or click My Shortcuts in the Outlook bar and click the Inbox icon.**

   The Inbox view appears.

2. **Choose Tools⇨Send/Receive.**

   A pop-up menu appears, listing all the Internet accounts you've defined for Outlook.

3. **Click the Internet account you want to retrieve mail from.**

   If Outlook finds e-mail for you, it kindly stores your e-mail in the Inbox folder.

If you're already connected to your Internet account, you can retrieve your e-mail by just clicking the Send/Receive button on the toolbar.

Reading an e-mail message

To read an e-mail message, follow these steps:

1. **Choose View⇨Go To⇨Inbox, press Ctrl+Shift+I, or click Inbox under the Messages heading in the Outlook Today view.**

   The Inbox view appears.

2. **Click the e-mail message that you want to read.**

   The contents of your chosen message appear at the bottom of the screen.

3. **Choose File⇨Close or click the Close box of the message window.**

4. **After you finish reading the message, click another message.**

   If you want to reply to an e-mail message, skip Step 3 and follow the steps listed in the next section, "Replying to an e-mail message."

Replying to an e-mail message

You often need to reply to someone who has sent you an e-mail message, either out of courtesy or because you want something from them. Replying to e-mail is easy because Outlook automatically knows where to send your reply without making you retype that cryptic e-mail address. To reply to an e-mail message, follow these steps:

1. **Follow Steps 1 and 2 in the previous section, "Reading an e-mail message."**

2. **Choose Actions⇨Reply, press Ctrl+R, or click the Reply button on the toolbar.**

   If you want your reply to go to everyone who received the original message, choose Actions⇨Reply to All, press Ctrl+Shift+R, or click the Reply to All button on the toolbar.

   The Message dialog box appears with a copy of the original message in the message window and the recipient's e-mail address (or recipients' e-mail addresses) already typed for you.

3. **Type your reply and then click the Send button.**

Forwarding e-mail

Rather then reply to an e-mail, you may want to pass an e-mail message on to someone else, which can be an amusing way to distribute jokes while you are at work. Passing along an e-mail messages is known (in stuffier, more technical circles) as *forwarding* it. To (ahem) forward an e-mail message, follow these steps:

1. **Follow Steps 1 and 2 in the section, "Reading an e-mail message," earlier in this chapter.**

2. **Choose Actions⇨Forward, press Ctrl+F, or click the Forward button on the toolbar.**

   The Message dialog box appears with the original e-mail message already typed in for you.

3. **Type an address to whom you want to send the e-mail.**

   If you want to send e-mail to an address stored in your Address Book, click the To button and then click the recipient's name. If you want to send the message to someone who isn't in your Address Book, then you have to type the e-mail address in the To box.

4. **Type any additional message that you want to send along with the forwarded message.**

5. **Click the Send button.**

Deleting Old E-Mail

If you don't watch out, you may find your Inbox overflowing with ancient e-mail messages that you no longer need. Rather than waste valuable hard disk space storing useless e-mail messages, take some time periodically to clean out your Inbox.

Besides the Inbox, another folder that may get cluttered is the Sent Items folder, which contains copies of every e-mail message you've sent out. Although you may like to keep a record of these messages for future reference, you will probably want to wipe out at least some of your sent messages at some point.

Deleting e-mail

To delete an e-mail message in your Inbox or Sent Items folder, follow these steps:

1. **Choose View⇨Go To⇨Inbox, press Ctrl+Shift+I, or click My Shortcuts in the Outlook bar and click the Inbox icon.**

   If you want to delete old messages stored in the Sent Items folder, choose View⇨Go To⇨Folder, click the Sent Items icon, and then click OK to list all the messages in your Sent Items folder.

2. **Click the message that you want to delete.**

   If you want to delete multiple messages, hold down the Ctrl key and click each message you want to delete. If you want to delete a range of messages, hold down the Shift key, click the first message you want to delete, and then click the last message you want to delete.

3. **Choose Edit⇨Delete, press Ctrl+D, or click the Delete button on the toolbar.**

   Outlook deletes your chosen messages.

When you delete messages, Outlook stores them in the Deleted Items folder to give you one last chance to recover any e-mail messages that you want to save before you permanently delete them. (See "Recovering e-mail from Deleted Items," up next.)

Recovering e-mail from Deleted Items

If you delete a message from your Inbox or Sent Items folder and suddenly decide that you need it after all, you can still get it out of your Deleted Items folder. To recover e-mail from your Deleted Items folder, follow these steps:

1. **Click the Deleted Items icon on the Outlook bar.**

   Or choose View⇨Go To⇨Folder, click the Deleted Items icon, and then click OK to open the Deleted Items folder.

2. **Click the e-mail message that you want to recover.**

   If you want to recover a number of messages, you can select multiple messages by holding down the Ctrl key and clicking each message.

3. **Choose Edit⇨Move to Folder or press Ctrl+Shift+V.**

   The Move Items dialog box appears.

4. **Click the Inbox icon and then click OK.**

   The message appears in your Inbox in its original condition. (If you want, you can choose a folder other than Inbox.)

Deleting e-mail for good

Until you delete your e-mail messages from the Deleted Items folder, those messages can be retrieved and read by others. At the very least, your unwanted messages still just sit around and take up space on your hard disk until you get rid of them for good.

After you delete e-mail from the Deleted Items folder, you can never recover the message. So you'd better make sure you mean it.

To delete e-mail from your computer forever, follow these steps:

1. **Click the Deleted Items icon on the Outlook bar.**

   Or choose View⇨Go To⇨Folder, click the Deleted Items icon, and then click OK.

2. **Click the e-mail message that you want to delete.**

   If you want to delete a number of messages at one time, you can select multiple messages by holding down the Ctrl key and clicking each message.

3. **Choose Edit⇨Delete or press Ctrl+D.**

   A dialog box appears, warning you that you are about to permanently delete the e-mail messages.

4. **Click the Yes button.**

   Kiss your chosen e-mail messages good-bye. (It's quieter than a maniacal laugh.)

If you're in a hurry and want to dump all the e-mail stored in your Deleted Items folder, choose Tools⇨Empty "Deleted Items" Folder.

Part VI
Storing Stuff in Access

The 5th Wave   By Rich Tennant

"Did you click the 'HELP' menu bar recently? Mr. Gates is here and he wants to know if everything's alright."

In this part . . .

Personal computers provide an excellent tool for storing large chunks of information in databases so you don't have to store this same information in filing cabinets. Databases cannot only store huge amounts of data, but they can also sort and search through that data as well, which makes them particularly valuable to businesses that need to track their customers, inventories, or assets. So it's no surprise that the more advanced (and expensive) versions of Microsoft Office XP include a special database program called (what's in a name?) Access.

For those of you who enjoy deciphering computer terminology, Access is a relational database. For those of you who prefer English, the previous sentence means that Access lets you store lots of stuff in a variety of different ways so you can find it again — fast — when you need it.

This part of the book gets you started storing stuff in Access. The goal is to get you feeling comfortable enough to create databases with Access so you can store great huge stockpiles of useful information in your computer.

Chapter 17

Stuffing Information into a Database

In This Chapter

▶ Understanding database basics

▶ Entering your data

▶ Viewing your data

Despite the power of personal computers, many people still insist on storing important names, addresses, and phone numbers in Rolodex files, on index cards, or on sheets of paper stuffed into folders. Although sometimes convenient, paper is terrible for retrieving and analyzing information. Just look at a typical file cabinet and ask yourself how much time you need to find the names and phone numbers of every customer who lives in Missouri *and* ordered more than $5,000 worth of your products in the past six months. (Frightening isn't it?)

Instead of racking your memory or hunting for slips of paper, try using Microsoft Access to organize your information. Access enables you to store, retrieve, sort, manipulate, and analyze information — making trends or patterns in your data easier to spot (so you can tell whether your company is losing money and may be thinking about another downsizing). The more you know about your information, the better off you are when dealing with less knowledgeable (or even — *gasp* — computer-illiterate) competitors, co-workers, or supervisors.

For storing names and addresses, you may find Outlook much easier and faster than Access. (For more on Outlook, check out Part V.) If you need to store more complicated information, such as customer invoices or inventory part numbers, use Access.

Database 101

Access is a *programmable relational database,* which may sound intimidating (or stupid), but it boils down to a simple idea: Access is nothing more than a fancy virtual file cabinet — you dump information in and yank it back out again, almost instantly, without squashing your fingers. Before you can perform this feat, however, you have to tell the program what type of information you want to store. A typical Access file (stored on your hard disk with the funny file extension `.MDB`, which stands for *M*icrosoft *database*) consists of the following elements:

- **One or more fields:** A *field* contains one chunk of data, such as a name, fax number, or a telephone number.

- **One or more records:** A *record* contains two or more related fields; for example, an employee record could contain the person's name, address, phone number, and employee ID number.

- **One or more database tables:** A *database table* stores your information and displays it as one or more records in rows and columns, much like a spreadsheet. Database tables are convenient for viewing multiple records at one time, such as sorting all records alphabetically by last name.

- **One or more forms:** A *form* typically displays one record at a time, such as showing one person's name, address, and phone number. Forms provide a convenient way to enter and view data stored in a database table.

- **One or more reports:** A *report* contains predefined ways to display your data either on-screen or in print. Reports help you make sense of the data stored in your database such as printing out a list of employees who earn more than $50,000 a year and work in Iowa.

At the simplest level, you can use Access just for storing data, such as the names of your friends, their addresses, their mobile phone numbers, and their birthdays.

On a more complicated level, you can write miniature programs in Access to fit a specific purpose, such as managing inventory in an electronics company or creating a mailing list program for charities.

This book focuses mostly on the simpler uses for Access in storing data and getting it back out again. If you want to learn more about designing custom databases, pick up a copy of *Access 2002 For Dummies* by John Kaufeld, published by Hungry Minds, Inc.

Creating a new database file

Think of a database as a file cabinet devoted to holding one type of data — say information related to taxes or to tracking the inventory in your business. When you want to create a database, Access gives you two choices.

✔ **You can create an entire database from scratch,** defining the fields (such as name, phone number, part number, birth date, and so on) that describe the type of information you want the database to hold.

✔ **You can use the Access Database Wizard** to help speed you through the process of creating a database. When you create a database using the Access Database Wizard, Access creates a special window for your database called the *Main Switchboard window*. The Main Switchboard window provides a list of actions you can use with your database data (such as adding new data) so you don't have to use an Access form or table yourself.

Most of the time, the Access Database Wizard is the easier way to create a database. Remember, you can always modify a database after you create it with the wizard. Leave starting from scratch to those with too much time on their hands.

To create a new database file by using the Database Wizard, follow these steps:

1. **Start Microsoft Access.**

   The New File pane appears (as shown in Figure 17-1), giving you a choice of creating a new database or opening an existing one.

2. **Click General Templates under the New from Template category.**

   The Templates dialog box appears, as shown in Figure 17-2.

3. **Click the Databases tab.**

   Access shows you a list of predefined databases that you can customize.

4. **Click the type of database that you want to use (such as Asset Tracking, Inventory Control, or Contact Management) and then click OK.**

   Note: Depending on which database you choose, what Access shows you differs slightly from what you see in this book. The figures in this chapter show what happens when you choose the Contact Management Database Wizard.

   The File New Database dialog box appears.

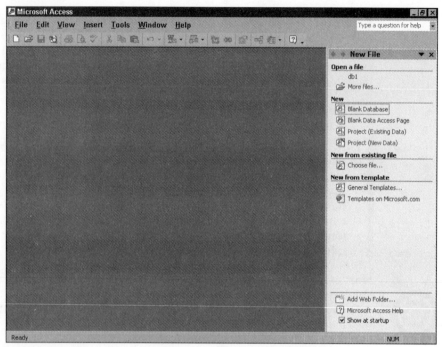

Figure 17-1:
The New
File pane.

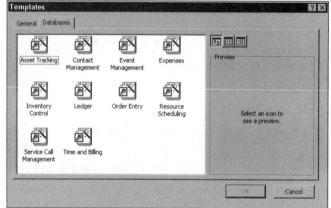

Figure 17-2:
The
Templates
dialog box.

5. **Type a name for your database in the File Name box and click the Create button.**

   If you want to store your database in a specific folder, click the Save In list box and choose the folder.

   After a few seconds, the Database Wizard dialog box appears, letting you know the type of information that the database will store.

6. Click Next.

Another Database Wizard dialog box appears, listing the tables and fields that it's ready to create. See Figure 17-3.

7. Click the check boxes of the additional fields that you want to store in your database, then click Next.

If your database consists of two or more tables, you may have to click on each table on the left side of the Database Wizard dialog box and then repeat Step 6 to choose any additional fields to add for each database table.

Still another Database Wizard dialog box appears, giving you the chance to select a background picture for your database forms, as shown in Figure 17-4.

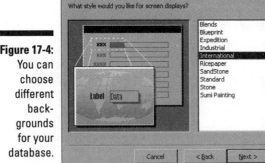

8. **Choose a screen display style (choose Standard if you don't like fancy backgrounds) and click Next.**

   Another Database Wizard dialog box appears, asking what style you want to use for printed reports, as shown in Figure 17-5. A *report* is a printed copy of your database information. A style makes your report look interesting (even if you have nothing important to say).

   To help you pick the style best suited to your needs, click several different styles, one at a time, and check out the left window to see what each style looks like.

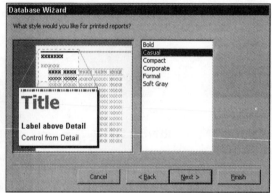

Figure 17-5:
Styles
make your
database
reports look
fancy.

9. **Choose a style and then click Next.**

   One more Database Wizard dialog box appears, asking you for a database title and if you want to add a picture on your reports. (Access displays the database title on the Main Switchboard window. The database title is purely decorative; it doesn't affect the design or organization of your database at all.)

10. **Type a title for your database (such as Valuable Names or People I Have to Deal With) and then click Next.**

    The last Database Wizard dialog box appears, letting you know that it's finished asking you annoying questions. If you want to start using your database right away, make sure the Yes, Start The Database check box is selected.

11. **Click Finish.**

    Access creates your database and displays the Main Switchboard window (a simple user interface for accessing your database), as shown in Figure 17-6.

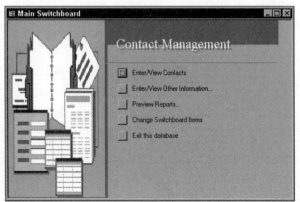

Figure 17-6:
The Main
Switch-
board in
Access.

Opening an existing database

To open a database file that you've created — to enter new information, view existing information, or edit or delete information — follow these steps:

1. **Start Microsoft Access.**

   Access displays the New File pane. (Refer to Figure 17-1.)

2. **Click on the database filename listed under the Open a File category.**

   If the file name you want to open doesn't appear, click the More Files link to display an Open dialog box so you can switch drives or folders to find the database file you want to open.

If Access is already running, and you want to open an existing database, follow these steps:

1. **Choose File⇨Open or press Ctrl+O.**

   The Open dialog box appears.

2. **Click the database name that you want to open, and then click Open.**

Looking at the parts of your database

When Access uses a wizard to create a database, the database actually consists of two separate windows:

✔ The Main Switchboard window
✔ The Database window

The Main Switchboard window provides a simple one-click method of using your database so you can view, edit, and print your database information. (Refer to Figure 17-6.)

If you create a database from scratch, your database won't have a Main Switchboard window.

The Database window shows all the separate parts (reports, modules, forms, tables, and macros) that make up your entire database, as shown in Figure 17-7.

A report allows you to print or view specific data from your database. Chapter 19 provides more information about creating and using reports. Modules store miniature programs, written in a programming language called Visual Basic for Applications (VBA) that is used to create custom databases. *Macros* store commonly used keystrokes so you can run repetitive commands at the touch of a button.

To switch between the Main Switchboard window and the Database window, choose <u>W</u>indow⇨Main Switchboard or <u>W</u>indow⇨Database.

The whole purpose of the Main Switchboard window is to hide the ugly details of managing a database. If you really want to get involved with creating, modifying, and programming Access, switch to the Database window. If you just want to use a database and couldn't care less about the fine details, use the Main Switchboard window instead.

Using toolbars in Access

Like most Office XP programs, Access offers toolbars that provide icons that represent some of the more common commands you need to do your work. Two of the toolbars you'll use most often are the Database toolbar and the Form View toolbar.

Figure 17-7:
The Database window shows the different parts that make up your Access database.

The Database toolbar appears when you open the Database window, as shown in Figure 17-8. The Database toolbar provides commands for opening or editing the structure of your database.

✔ **Open:** Displays part of your database, such as a form, table, or report, so you can view, add, and edit the information trapped inside your database.

✔ **Design:** Allows you to modify the structure and appearance of your database but doesn't affect the actual information trapped in your database.

✔ **Delete:** Allows you to delete part of your database, such as a form, table, or report.

✔ **Large Icons, Small icons, List, and Details:** Displays the parts of your database in different ways, such as representing them using big icons or displaying additional details about each part, such as the time and date it was last modified.

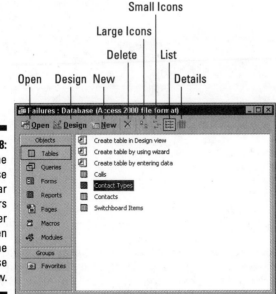

Figure 17-8: The Database toolbar appears whenever you open the Database window.

The Form View toolbar appears when you open a form to view, edit, or add information to your database, as shown in Figure 17-9. Although the Form View toolbar provides a bewildering number of icons, you only need to know a few icons to use Access effectively, including:

✔ **New Record:** Adds a new record to your database.

✔ **Delete Record:** Deletes the currently displayed record from your database.

New Record

Form View toolbar

Delete Record

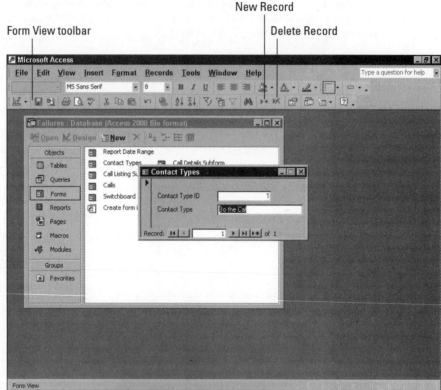

Using a Database

After Access creates a database, the new database is completely empty (and also completely useless) until you start stuffing your own information into it.

As you type data into a database, Access saves it to disk. (In other Office XP programs, such as Word or Excel, you have to manually save your data by pressing Ctrl+S.) That way if the power goes out or if Windows crashes, your data will (hopefully) still be stored on your hard disk.

Entering data through the Main Switchboard

The easiest way to stuff data into a new or existing database is from the Main Switchboard window. To use the Main Switchboard window to add new data, follow these steps:

1. **Open the database that you want to use and choose <u>W</u>indow⇨ Main Switchboard.**

   The Main Switchboard window appears. (Follow the instructions in the section "Opening an existing database" if you need help in opening an Access file.)

2. **Click one of the Enter/View buttons on the Main Switchboard window.**

   For example, if you want to add a new contact in the database displayed in Figure 17-6, click Enter/View Contacts.

   Access displays a form, showing the first record in your database and the fields where you can type information, as shown in Figure 17-10.

3. **Click the field where you want to add data (such as First Name or Address); then type the data.**

4. **To type data for the next record, choose <u>I</u>nsert⇨Ne<u>w</u> Record, click the New Record button that appears on the Form View toolbar, or click the Next Record button on the form.**

   Access displays a blank record.

5. **Repeat Steps 3 and 4 for each new record that you want to add to your database.**

6. **After you enter the data you want, click the Close box of the form window.**

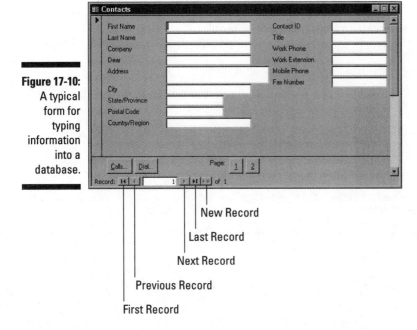

Figure 17-10:
A typical form for typing information into a database.

New Record

Last Record

Next Record

Previous Record

First Record

If you have several records in a database, you can view them by clicking one of the following buttons that appear on the database form:

- **First Record button:** Displays the first record of the database
- **Previous Record button:** Displays the record that comes before the one you're currently viewing
- **Next Record button:** Displays the record that comes after the one you're currently viewing
- **Last Record button:** Displays the last record of the database

Entering data through a table or form

If you don't use the Main Switchboard, you have to use the Database window and choose whether you want to enter data: through a table or through a form. Entering data in a table lets you see multiple records at once. Entering data in a form lets you see one record at a time.

Access doesn't care whether you enter data in a form or a table because forms and tables are just different ways of viewing the same data anyway.

Entering data into a form is equivalent to using the Main Switchboard to enter data.

To enter data in a table or form, follow these steps:

1. **Open an existing database.**

2. **Choose <u>W</u>indow⇨Database.**

   Access displays the Database window (refer to Figure 17-7).

3. **Click the Tables icon or Forms icon in the left panel of the Database window.**

4. **Double-click the table or form that you want to use to enter data.**

   Access displays your chosen table or form.

5. **Type your data in the appropriate fields.**

   To move from one field to another, use the mouse, press Tab, or press Shift+Tab.

6. **When you finish, click the Close box of the Table or Form window.**

Deleting data

Eventually, you may want to delete individual field data or even entire records. For example, you may have a record in your database containing information about someone that you never want to speak to again, such as a former spouse or roommate. Rather than have that person's name and address constantly haunt you by their existence in your database, you can delete that record and (figuratively) eliminate that person's name from the face of the earth — or at least the face of your computer.

Access provides two ways to delete data:

- ✔ Just delete the information stored in a field (useful for editing a single field, such as the address of someone who has moved).
- ✔ Delete all the information stored in an entire record (useful for wiping out all traces of a single record, which can be handy to completely obliterate all information about a person who no longer works for your company).

Deleting data in a field

To delete data stored in a field, follow these steps:

1. **Follow the steps in the "Entering data through the Main Switchboard" section or "Entering data through a table or form" section until you find the record containing data that you want to delete.**

2. **Click the field that contains the data that you want to delete.**

3. **Choose one of the following methods to delete the data:**

    - Press Delete or Backspace to delete one character at a time.

    - Drag the mouse to select the data; then press Delete or Backspace to delete the entire selected data.

Deleting an entire record

Deleting a single field or two can be useful for editing your records. But if you want to wipe out an entire record altogether, follow these steps:

1. **Follow the steps in the "Entering data through the Main Switchboard" section or "Entering data through a table or form" section until you find the record containing data that you want to delete.**

2. **Choose Edit⇨Select Record.**

    Access highlights your chosen record.

3. **Choose Edit⇨Delete or click the Delete Record button on the Form View toolbar.**

   A dialog box appears, warning that if you continue, your deleted record will be lost for good.

4. **Click the Yes button (but only if you're sure that you want to delete your chosen record forever). Otherwise click the No button.**

Make sure that you really want to delete the entire record — you won't be able to retrieve your deleted data afterwards.

Modifying the Structure of a Database

Although Access provides predefined databases that you can use, you may want to create a database from scratch or modify an existing database. The two most common parts of a database that you may need to add, delete, or modify are tables and forms.

Tables display data in row and column format, much like a spreadsheet. *Forms* display data like a paper form on the screen.

Adding a table

To add a table to an existing Access database file, follow these steps:

1. **Open an existing database.**

2. **Choose Window⇨Database.**

   Access displays the Database window (refer to Figure 17-7).

3. **Click the Tables icon in the left panel of the Database window.**

4. **Double-click the Create Table by Using Wizard icon.**

   The Table Wizard dialog box appears as shown in Figure 17-11.

5. **Select the Business or Personal radio button.**

   Access displays a list of common fields for Business or Personal databases.

6. **Click the Sample Tables list box and choose the table that most closely matches the table you want to create (such as Contacts or Mailing List).**

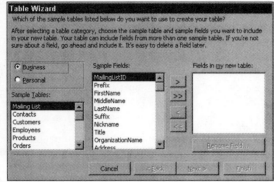

Figure 17-11:
The Table
Wizard
dialog box
can guide
you through
creating a
new table
for your
database
file.

7. **Click the Sample Fields list box and click the field that most closely matches the field you want to create (such as LastName or City).**

8. **Click the right arrow → button.**

   Access displays your chosen field in the Fields in My New Table list box. If you click the Rename Field button, you can (guess what?) rename a field.

9. **Repeat Steps 7 and 8 for each field you want to add.**

10. **Click Next.**

   Another Table Wizard dialog box appears.

11. **Type a name for your table and click Next.**

   Still another Table Wizard dialog box appears, asking you whether your new table contains records related to other tables stored in your database. Multiple tables can share the same fields, such as a Customer ID or a Company Name field.

12. **Click Next.**

   A final Table Wizard dialog box appears, asking whether you want to modify the design of your table or start entering data right away.

13. **Click one of the options (such as Enter Data Directly into the Table) and click Finish.**

What the heck is a relational database?

Sometimes people refer to Access as a "relational database." Essentially, this term means that one database table stores information that's identical to information stored in another database table.

The reason for doing this is partly out of laziness but mostly out of usefulness. For example, you might have one database table that stores employee ID numbers, names, addresses, and phone numbers. Then you might have a second database table that lists employee ID numbers along with the current salaries for each person. Obviously some of the same employee ID numbers need to be appear in each database table, so rather than force you to type this same information twice, the two database tables share this identical information between themselves, hence the term "relation" or "relational".

By sharing identical information between database tables, you can reduce typing identical information over and over again and store data separately so one database table doesn't have to list everything (such as cramming employee address information in the same database table as employee salary information).

If you select the `Enter Data into the Table Using a Form the Wizard Creates for Me` radio button, Access creates a plain-looking form where you can start typing in data.

Deleting a table

You may want to delete a table if you don't need to save the information stored in it.

Deleting a table wipes out any information, such as names and addresses, stored in that table. So make sure you really want to delete a table and all the data in it. If you delete a table, any forms you created to display that data will be useless. So if you're going to delete a table, you should also delete any forms that rely on that table.

To delete a table, follow these steps:

1. **Open an existing database.**

2. **Choose <u>W</u>indow⇨Database.**

    Access displays the Database window (refer to Figure 17-7).

3. **Click the Tables icon in the left panel of the Database window.**

4. **Click the table that you want to delete.**

5. **Choose Edit➪Delete, press Delete, or click the Delete icon in the Database toolbar.**

   A dialog box appears, asking whether you really want to delete your chosen table.

6. **Click Yes.**

Press Ctrl+Z if you suddenly decide you don't want to delete your table after all.

Modifying a table

After you create a table, you may want to modify the table (but not the data stored in the table). For example, you may have forgotten to create a field to store a person's employee ID, so you have to create a new field in a table to hold that information. Likewise, you may suddenly decide that you don't want to store people's phone numbers any more, so you can delete that field.

Adding a new field to a table

To add a field to a table, follow these steps:

1. **Open an existing database.**

2. **Choose Window➪Database.**

   Access displays the Database window (refer to Figure 17-7).

3. **Click the Tables icon in the left panel of the Database window.**

4. **Click the table where you want to add a new field.**

5. **Click the Design icon in the Database toolbar.**

   A Table window appears as shown in Figure 17-12.

6. **Click the row where you want to insert your new field.**

   Access doesn't care where you insert your new field. The location of a field is for your convenience, such as listing the First Name and Last Name fields next to each other.

7. **Choose Insert➪Rows, or click the Insert Rows icon on the Table Design toolbar.**

   Access inserts a blank row in your table.

8. **Type your field name under the Field Name column.**

9. **Click the Data Type column.**

   A downward-pointing arrow appears in the Data Type cell, and a Field Properties pane appears at the bottom of the screen.

Insert Rows

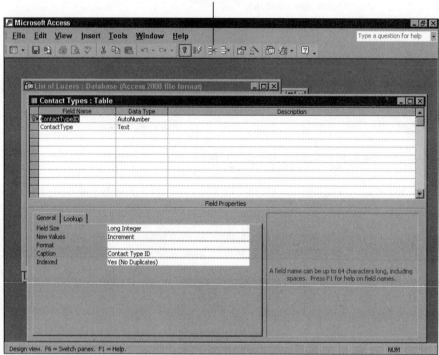

10. **Click the downward-pointing arrow in the Data Type column and choose the type of data you want to store, such as Text or Date/Time.**

    Depending on the data type you choose, you can modify the field properties by defining the maximum number of characters or the acceptable values the field can accept.

11. **Click the Close box of the Table window.**

    A dialog box appears, asking if you want to save the changes to your table.

12. **Click Yes.**

Modifying a field in a table

After you create a table, define various fields (such as Name, Phone, or Employee Nickname), and type actual data (such as Bob, 555-1234, or LoserBoss), you may suddenly realize that a particular field needs modification. For example, you may have initially defined a field so small that data appears cut off. Or if a field displays numbers, you may want to modify the appearance of those numbers as currency instead of in scientific notation.

To modify a field in a table, follow these steps:

1. **Open an existing database.**

2. **Choose <u>Window</u>⇨Database.**

   Access displays the Database window (refer to Figure 17-7).

3. **Click the Tables icon in the left panel of the Database window.**

4. **Click the table where you want to modify an existing field.**

5. **Click the <u>D</u>esign icon in the Database toolbar.**

   A Table window appears (refer to Figure 17-12).

6. **Click the field (row) that you want to modify and type or edit the field name.**

7. **Click the Data Type column.**

8. **Click the downward-pointing arrow in the Data Type column and choose the type of data you want to store, such as Text or Date/Time.**

   Depending on the data type you choose, you can modify the field properties by defining the maximum number of characters or the acceptable values the field can accept.

9. **Click the Close box of the Table window.**

   A dialog box appears, asking if you want to save the changes to your table.

10. **Click Yes.**

Deleting a field from a table

To delete a field from a table, follow these steps:

1. **Open an existing database.**

2. **Choose <u>Window</u>⇨Database.**

   Access displays the Database window (refer to Figure 17-7).

3. **Click the Tables icon in the left panel of the Database window.**

4. **Click the table where you want to delete an existing field.**

5. **Click the Design icon in the Database toolbar.**

   A Table window appears (refer to Figure 17-12).

6. **Click the gray box to the left of the field (row) that you want to delete.**

   Access highlights the entire row.

7. **Choose Edit⇨Delete, or press Delete.**

If the field contains data, a dialog box appears, asking whether you really want to delete the field and any data that may be stored in that field. If the field is empty, no dialog box appears, and you can skip to Step 9.

8. **Click Yes.**

9. **Click the Close box of the Table window.**

A dialog box appears, asking if you want to save the changes that you made to your table.

10. **Click Yes.**

Adding a form

A form mimics a paper form by providing an organized way to view and enter data. Because a form can display your data in different ways, you may later find that all your current forms display too much (or too little) data for certain uses. For example, you may need one form to display the names and medical insurance numbers of people, and a completely different form to display those same people's names, addresses, phone numbers, and contact information.

With multiple forms, you can customize the viewing and adding of data to your Access database for a variety of specific tasks. To add a new form to your database file, follow these steps:

1. **Open an existing database.**

2. **Choose Window⇨Database.**

Access displays the Database window (refer to Figure 17-7).

3. **Click the Forms icon in the left panel of the Database window.**

4. **Double-click the Create Form by Using Wizard icon.**

A Form Wizard dialog box appears (as shown in Figure 17-13), offering you a choice of which fields to display on your form.

5. **Click the Tables/Queries list box and choose a table containing the data you want to display on your form.**

6. **Click the Available Fields list box and choose the field you want to add to your form.**

You can choose fields from two or more database tables if you select a different database table in Step 5 and then choose fields from that database table in Step 6.

7. **Click the right arrow → button to add fields to the Selected Fields list.**

8. **Repeat Steps 6 and 7 for each field you want to display on your form.**

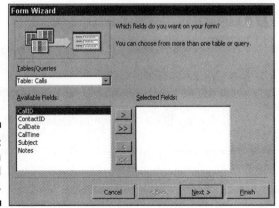

Figure 17-13:
The Form
Wizard
dialog box.

9. **Click Next.**

   A Form Wizard dialog box appears and asks how you want to view your data. (If you only chose fields in Step 6 from a single database table, you won't see this dialog box and you can skip to Step 11.)

10. **Click on one of the displayed options for displaying your data and click Next.**

    Another Form Wizard dialog box asks you to choose a layout for your form. If you chose to display fields from two or more database tables, the Form Wizard dialog box appears and asks how you want to view your data.

11. **Click one of the options (such as Tabular or Justified) and click Next.**

    Yet another Form Wizard dialog box asks you to choose a style for your form.

12. **Click a form style such as Blueprint or Sandstone and click Next.**

    A final Form Wizard dialog box asks for a title for your form.

13. **Type a name for your form and click Finish.**

    Access displays your form as shown in Figure 17-14.

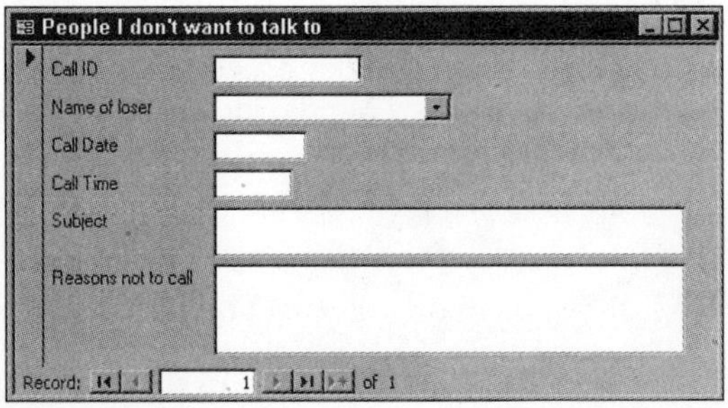

Figure 17-14:
A typical
form for
displaying
the contents
of your
database.

Deleting a form

If you delete a form, you can't recover it again. Make sure you really want to delete the form before you do so.

When you delete a form, you do not delete any data that the form displays. (If you want to delete the actual data stored in Access, you have to delete the table containing that data. Refer to the earlier section "Deleting data.")

In case you no longer need a particular form, you can get rid of it by following these steps:

1. **Open an existing database.**

2. **Choose Window⇨Database.**

    Access displays the Database window. (Refer to Figure 17-7.)

3. **Click the Forms icon in the left panel of the Database window.**

4. **Click the form that you want to delete.**

5. **Choose Edit⇨Delete, press Delete, or click the Delete icon in the Database toolbar.**

    A dialog box appears, asking whether you really want to delete your chosen table.

6. **Click Yes.**

Modifying a form

Forms just display data on the screen, making it easy for people to view or type in new information. The two most common items you will need to modify on a form are labels and text boxes.

Labels are purely decorative but are often used to describe what type of information appears in a text box, such as a name or phone number. *Text boxes* provide a blank box where actual data appears.

There are many ways to modify a form, but the most common way is to add or delete a new field that appears on a form. For more information on the different ways to modify a form, pick up a copy of *Access 2002 For Dummies,* by Michael MacDonald, published by Hungry Minds, Inc.

Adding a new field to a form

If you want to add a new field, you need to add a text box (to hold the actual data) and a label (to describe the type of information that appears in the text box). To add a text box (field) to a form, follow these steps:

1. **Open an existing database.**

2. **Choose <u>W</u>indow⇨Database.**

   Access displays the Database window (refer to Figure 17-7).

3. **Click the Forms icon in the left panel of the Database window.**

4. **Click the form that you want to modify.**

5. **Click the <u>D</u>esign icon on the Database toolbar.**

   Access displays your form along with a Form toolbox (as shown in Figure 17-15).

6. **Click the Text Box icon in the Form toolbox.**

   The mouse cursor changes into a crosshair with a Text Box icon attached to it.

7. **Move the mouse to the spot on the form where you want to draw your text box.**

8. **Hold down the left mouse button and drag the mouse to draw the text box.**

9. **Release the left mouse button when the text box is the size you want it.**

   Access draws the text box and automatically draws an accompanying label to go along with your newly drawn text box.

10. **Right-click the text box and choose <u>P</u>roperties.**

    A Text Box properties dialog box appears, as shown in Figure 17-16.

11. **Click the Control Source box.**

    A downward-pointing arrow appears.

12. **Click the downward-pointing arrow.**

    A list of fields stored in your database appears.

13. **Click a data source, such as FirstName or Address.**

    The data source you choose tells Access what type of data to display in your newly created text box.

14. **Click the Close box of the Text Box properties dialog box.**

Text Box icon

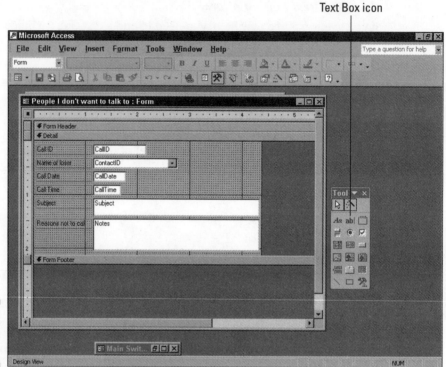

Figure 17-15:
Designing
a form.

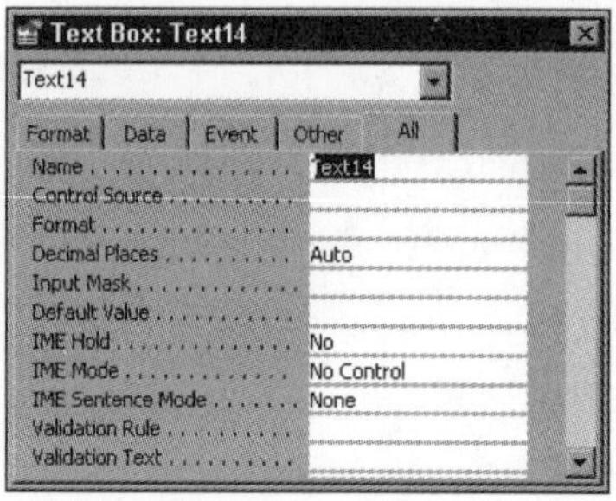

Figure 17-16:
The Text
Box
Properties
dialog box.

15. **Double-click the Field label.**

   A Label Properties dialog box appears.

16. **Click the Caption box and type a caption for your new field (such as Employee ID or Marital Status).**

   Whatever you type in the Caption box appears on your form.

17. **Click the Close box of the Label Properties dialog box.**

18. **Click the Close box of the Form window.**

    A dialog box appears, asking if you want to save changes to your form.

19. **Click Yes.**

Modifying a field on a form

After you create a field, you may need to resize or move the field so it looks nice and pretty on your form. To resize a field, follow these steps:

1. **Open an existing database.**

2. **Choose Window⇨Database.**

    Access displays the Database window (refer to Figure 17-7).

3. **Click the Forms icon in the left panel of the Database window.**

4. **Click the form that you want to modify.**

5. **Click the Design icon on the Database toolbar.**

    Access displays your form along with a Form toolbox.

6. **Click the field or its accompanying caption.**

    Access highlights the field or caption with black handles around its border.

7. **Move the mouse over a handle so the mouse cursor turns into a double-pointing arrow.**

8. **Hold down the left mouse button and drag the mouse to resize the field or caption.**

9. **Release the left mouse button when the field or caption is the size you want it.**

10. **Click the Close box of the Form window.**

    A dialog box appears, asking whether you want to save changes to your form.

11. **Click Yes.**

To move a field, follow these steps:

1. **Open an existing database.**

2. **Choose Window⇨Database.**

    Access displays the Database window (refer to Figure 17-7).

3. **Click the Forms icon in the left panel of the Database window.**

4. **Click the form that you want to modify.**

5. **Click the Design icon on the Database toolbar.**

   Access displays your form along with a Form toolbox.

6. **Click the field or its accompanying caption.**

   Access highlights the field or caption with black handles around its border. Notice that the biggest handle is in the upper-left corner.

7. **Move the mouse over the big handle in the upper-left corner, hold down the left mouse button, and drag the mouse.**

   Access shows you the outline of your field or caption as you move it.

8. **Release the left mouse button when the field or caption is in the location you want.**

9. **Click the Close box of the Form window.**

   A dialog box appears, asking if you want to save changes to your form.

10. **Click Yes.**

Deleting a field from a form

To delete a field from a form, follow these steps:

1. **Open an existing database.**

2. **Choose Window⇨Database.**

   Access displays the Database window (refer to Figure 17-7).

3. **Click the Forms icon in the left panel of the Database window.**

4. **Click the form that you want to modify.**

5. **Click the Design icon on the Database toolbar.**

   Access displays your form along with a Form toolbox.

6. **Click the field or its accompanying caption.**

   Access highlights the field or caption with black handles around its border.

7. **Press Delete.**

8. **Click the Close box of the Form window.**

   A dialog box appears, asking whether you want to save changes to your form.

9. **Click Yes.**

Saving Your Database

Access gives you two different ways to save your database:

> ✔ As an Access database file (recommended for most cases)
> ✔ As a foreign database file (good for sharing data stored in an Access database with people who use other database programs like Paradox or dBASE)

As you edit, delete, and add new data, Access automatically saves the data you type into your database file. However, if you add or delete fields or tables in your database, you must save the design of your database file, which includes any reports, forms, or tables you may have created and modified.

Saving your database as an Access file

To save changes to your database file as an Access file, you need to choose one of the following three methods:

> ✔ Choose File➪Save.
> ✔ Press Ctrl+S.
> ✔ Click the Save button on the Standard toolbar.

Exporting your database to a different file format

Despite Microsoft's best efforts to dominate the world without raising the ire of antitrust legislators, not everyone uses Access to store data. In the old days, many people used a slow, cumbersome program called dBASE. Some people eventually graduated to a faster cumbersome program called Paradox; others defected to rival cumbersome programs with odd names like FileMaker or FoxPro.

So if you have to share your data with people who still refuse to use Access, you have to export your data from an Access table into a file format that other programs (such as Paradox or FoxPro) can read.

Many people actually use their spreadsheets to store data, so Access can also save its databases as a Lotus 1-2-3 or Excel spreadsheet.

Almost every database program in the world can read dBASE III files because that used to be the database standard at one time. So if you want to share your files with other database programs such as FileMaker, FoxPro, or Approach, save your files to dBASE III format.

To export an Access database table into a different file format, follow these steps:

1. **Open an existing database.**

2. **Choose Window⇨Database.**

    The Database window appears.

3. **Click Tables in the left panel of the Database window.**

    Access displays a list of tables in your database.

4. **Click a database table.**

5. **Choose File⇨Export.**

    The Export Table To dialog box appears.

6. **Type a name for your file in the File Name text box.**

7. **Click the Save as Type list box and choose a file format to use such as dBASE III or Paradox 5.**

8. **Click Save.**

Whenever you have two copies of the same data stored in different files, you need to make sure that any changes you make to one copy of your data is also changed in the second copy of your data. Otherwise you could wind up with slightly different versions of the same data and then you won't know which copy of your data is the most current and reliable one to use.

Chapter 18

Searching, Sorting, and Making Queries

. . . .

. . . .

*T*he real power of a computer database comes from its superfast capability to perform tasks — such as searching, sorting, and retrieving information — that would be too tedious, boring, or frustrating to do with a paper database. Want to know which products are selling the fastest (and which ones deserve to be dropped like a lead anchor)? Access can tell you at the touch of a button. Need to know which of your salespeople are generating the most commissions (and business expenses)? Access can give you this information pronto, too. Knowledge may be power, but until you use the power of a computer database, your information may be out of reach.

Searching a Database

Typical paper databases, such as filing cabinets, Rolodex files, and paper folders, are designed for storing and retrieving information alphabetically. By contrast, Access can find and retrieve information any way you want: by area code, by ZIP code, alphabetically by last name or first name, by state, by date. . . . You get the idea.

Access provides two basic ways to search a database:

✔ You can search for a specific record.

✔ You can find one or more records by using a filter.

Access also provides a third way to search a database. You can ask it specific questions called *queries,* which you can find out about in the "Querying a Database" section, later in this chapter.

Finding a specific record

To find a specific record in a database file, you need to know part of the information you want. Because Access can't read your mind, you have to give it clues, such as "Find the name of the person whose fax number is 555-1904" or "Find the phone number of Bill Gates."

The more specific the data you already know, the faster Access can find the record you want. Asking Access to find the phone number of someone who lives in California takes longer (for example) than asking Access to find the phone number of someone whose last name is Bangladore and lives in California. You may have stored the names of several hundred people who live in California, but how many people in your database have the last name Bangladore?

To find a specific record in a database, follow these steps:

1. **Open the form that displays the information you want to search.**

   For example, if you want to find a customer's phone number, you must first open a form that displays customer phone numbers. You can open a form by clicking one of the Enter/View buttons on the Main Switchboard window, or by choosing Window⇨Database, clicking the Forms icon, and double-clicking the form that you want to display.

2. **Choose Edit⇨Find or press Ctrl+F.**

   The Find and Replace dialog box appears, as shown in Figure 18-1. If you haven't stored any information in your database, Access scolds you with a dialog box to let you know you can't use the Find command.

Figure 18-1:
The Find and Replace dialog box can help you search your database.

Find and Replace	? X
Find	Replace

Find What: [   ] Find Next

Cancel

Look In: First Name

Match: Whole Field

Search: All

☐ Match Case   ☑ Search Fields As Formatted

3. **In the Fi_n_d What text box, type the data that you want to find (such as Jefferson).**

4. **Click the _L_ook In list box and choose the field that you want to search (such as First Name or Phone Number).**

5. **Click the Matc_h_ list box and choose one of the following options:**

   - **Any Part of Field:** The text can appear anywhere in the field. (A search for *Ann* would find both Mary*ann*e and *Ann*Marie.)

   - **Whole Field:** The text must appear by itself, not as part of another word. (A search for *Ann* finds records containing just Ann by itself; it doesn't find Mary*ann*e or *Ann*Marie.)

   - **Start of Field:** The text appears at the beginning of the field. (A search for *Ann* finds *Ann*Marie and *Ann* but not Maryanne.)

6. **Click the Sea_r_ch list box and choose Up, Down, or All.**

   - **Up:** Searches your database starting with the currently displayed record up to the first record.

   - **Down:** Searches your database starting with the currently displayed record down to the last record.

   - **All:** Searches your entire database.

If you choose the Up or Down option in the Search list box and Access can't find the data you're looking for, that could mean either the data doesn't exist or that it's hiding out in part of the database that you didn't search. So if you chose the Up option and couldn't find your data, your data could be stored near the end of your database.

7. **Select the Match _C_ase check box if you want to choose this option.**

   The Match Case option tells Access to find only those records that exactly match the capitalization of what you typed in the Find What box. Choosing this option means that if you search for AnN, Access finds records containing AnN but not records containing Ann, ann, or aNN.

8. **Click the _F_ind Next button.**

   Access highlights the first record that contains your chosen data. You may have to move the Find and Replace dialog box so you can see the record that Access finds. If Access can't find a match, a dialog box pops up to inform you that the search item wasn't found in your database.

9. **Click Close to close the Find and Replace dialog box. (Or click _F_ind Next if you want to see the next record that contains your chosen data.)**

   Access shows you the record it found in Step 8 or searches for the next matching record.

Finding one or more records by using a filter

When you use a filter, Access displays only those records that contain the information you're looking for. That way, you can concentrate on viewing only the information you want to see without the rest of your database getting in your way.

Think of the difference between the Find command and a filter in this way: Suppose you want to find a matching pair of socks. The Find command forces you to look through an entire pile of laundry just to find a pair of purple and green socks. A filter simply separates all your socks from the rest of your laundry.

When you want to use a filter, use the Filter dialog box to specify several options:

- **Field:** Tells Access which fields you want to search. You can choose one or more fields.

- **Sort:** Tells Access to sort records in alphabetical order (ascending), to sort records in reverse alphabetical order (descending), or not to bother sorting at all (not sorted). We describe sorting records later in the section imaginatively titled "Sorting a Database."

- **Criteria:** Tells Access to look for specific criteria. Instead of simply listing addresses (for example), Access can find addresses of people who own homes in Oregon or California or those of people who own homes in both Oregon and California.

Sorting a database just reorganizes your data, but you can still see all the data stuffed in your database. Filtering by criteria only displays records that match specific criteria, which means some data may be hidden from view.

Filtering with a form

Forms can display one entire record on the screen. If a filter finds multiple records, the form displays the total number of records found (such as 1 of 6). To view all the records found by a filter, click the Next or Previous Record buttons on the form.

To find one or more records by using a filter, follow these steps:

1. **Open the form containing the information you want to search.**

2. **Choose Records⇨Filter⇨Filter by Form, or click the Filter by Form button on the Standard toolbar, as shown in Figure 18-2.**

   A Filter by Form dialog box appears, which looks strangely similar to the form you opened in Step 1.

Sort Ascending

Sort Descending

Filter by Selection

Filter by Form

Apply/Remove Filter

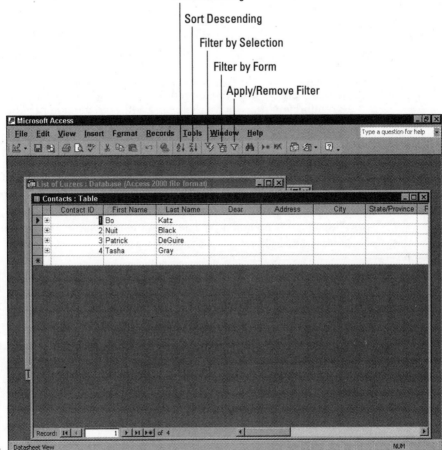

Figure 18-2:
The Filter by
Form and
Filter by
Selection
icons
appear
on the
Standard
toolbar.

3. Click the field that you want to use as your filter.

For example, if you want to find all the people who live in Illinois, click the State/Province field.

A downward-pointing arrow appears to the right of the field that you click.

4. Click the downward-pointing arrow.

A list appears, containing all the data (such as all the states stored in your database) available in that particular database field.

5. From this pull-down list, click the data that you want to find (such as IL to find Illinois).

6. Repeat Steps 3 through 5 for each field that you want to use for your filter.

The more filters you use, the narrower the search — which means you have fewer records to wade through before you find the ones you really want. You could end up filtering out and not seeing records that you actually want to include, so be selective when creating filters.

7. **Choose Filter⇨Apply Filter/Sort or click the Apply Filter icon on the toolbar.**

   Access displays only those records matching your search criteria. Just to remind you that you're looking at a filtered version of your database, Access politely displays the word (Filtered) near the bottom of the form. You may have to click the Next or Previous Record buttons to see other records that your filter found for you.

8. **When you're ready to see your whole database again (not just the results of the search), choose Records⇨Remove Filter/Sort, or click the Remove Filter button on the Standard toolbar.**

   Choosing this command displays all the information in your database once more.

After using a filter, make sure that you remove the filter by using the Remove Filter/Sort command; otherwise, Access displays only those records matching your last search, and you may think that the rest of your data is gone.

Filtering with a table

Rather than use a filter with a form, you may prefer using a filter with a table. The main advantage of using a filter is that a table can display multiple records at once, while a form can display only one record. To find one or more records by using a filter, follow these steps:

1. **Open the table containing the information you want to search.**

2. **Click the field that you want to use as your filter.**

   For example, if you want to find all people with the last name of Doe, click in any Last Name field that contains the name *Doe*.

3. **Choose Records⇨Filter⇨Filter by Selection, or click the Filter By Selection button on the Standard toolbar.**

   Access immediately displays only those records that meet your criteria.

   To select multiple criteria to filter your data, repeat Steps 2 and 3 as often as necessary.

4. **When you're ready to see your whole database again (and not just the results of the search), choose Records⇨Remove/Filter/Sort, or click the Remove Filter button on the Standard toolbar.**

Sorting a Database

To sort a database, you have to tell Access which field you want to sort by and how you want to sort it (in ascending or descending order).

For example, you can sort your database alphabetically by last name, country, or city. Unlike searching, which shows only part of your database, sorting simply shows your entire database with all your data rearranged.

When you sort a database, you can always restore the original order by choosing Records⇨Remove Filter/Sort.

To sort a database, follow these steps:

1. **Open the form or table containing the information you want to search.**

2. **Click the field that you want to sort by.**

   If you want to sort by last names, for example, click the field that contains last names.

3. **Choose Records⇨Sort⇨Sort Ascending (or Descending) or click the Sort Ascending or Sort Descending button on the Standard toolbar.**

   The Sort Ascending option sorts from A to Z (or 0 to 9). Sort Descending sorts in reverse, from Z to A (or 9 to 0).

   Access obediently sorts your records.

4. **When you're ready to restore the original order to your database, choose Records⇨Remove Filter/Sort.**

Because a table can display multiple records at once, you may find sorting a database through a table easier to see.

Querying a Database

Storing information in a database is okay, but the real fun comes when you use the data that you entered. After all, storing all the names and addresses of your customers is a waste if you don't use the information to help you make more money (which is what business is really all about).

To help you use your stored information effectively, Access provides different ways to analyze your data. When you store information on Rolodex cards, in address books, or on paper forms, the information is static. When you store data in Access, the data can be molded, shaped, and manipulated like Silly Putty.

Asking questions with queries

A *query* is a fancy term for a question that you ask Access. After you store information in a database, you can use queries to get the information back out again — and in different forms. A query can be as simple as finding the names and phone numbers of everyone who lives in Arkansas, or as sophisticated as making Access retrieve the names and quantities of all products your company sold between November 2 and December 29.

The secret to creating effective queries is to know what you want and to get the hang of telling Access how to find it.

What's the difference between a query and the Find command?

Both a query and the Find command tell Access to retrieve and display certain data from your database. Queries have an advantage, however: You can save them as part of your database file and use them over and over without having to define what you're looking for each time. (You always have to define what you want to look at each time you use the Find command.)

Think of a query as a way of storing filters that you can use over and over again to find specific information.

Use the Find command when you need to search through one or more fields only once and use queries when you need to search through one or more fields on a regular basis.

Creating a query

When you create a query, you must specify *search criteria,* attributes that tell Access the specific type of data you want to find.

Queries can get fairly complicated. For example, you can ask Access to find the names of all the people in your database who earn less than $75,000 a year, live in either Seattle or Detroit, have owned their own houses for over six years, work in sales jobs, own personal computers, and subscribe to more than three but fewer than six magazines a year.

Just remember that the quality of your answers depends heavily on the quality of your queries (questions). If you create a poorly designed query, Access probably won't find all the data you really need and may overlook important information that can affect your business or your job.

To create a query, follow these steps:

1. **Choose Window⇨Database.**

   The Database window appears.

2. **Click the Queries icon in the left panel.**

3. **Double-click the Create Query by Using Wizard icon.**

   The Simple Query Wizard dialog box appears, as shown in Figure 18-3.

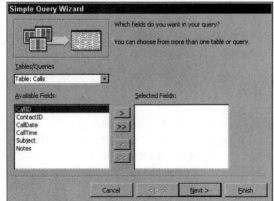

Figure 18-3: The Simple Query Wizard dialog box.

4. **Click the downward-pointing arrow to the right of the Tables/Queries list box and click the table that you want to search.**

A database table simply contains related information, such as names, addresses, and phone numbers of students. When you choose a database table, you're telling Access to search only in one particular table, not to search the entire database file, which may consist of one or more tables.

5. **Click the Available Fields list box and click a field that you want to display in the query result.**

   For example, if you want to display the FirstName and PhoneNumber fields, click one of them (then come back after Step 6 to click the other one).

6. **Click the single right arrow button that appears between the two big boxes.**

   Access displays your field in the Selected Fields box. Repeat Steps 5 and 6 for each field that you want to use in your query.

7. **Click Next.**

   Access asks what title you want to give your query.

8. **Type a name for your query in the What Title Do You Want for Your Query? text box.**

   Give your query a descriptive name, such as *Track low-selling products* or *List of employees I plan to fire.*

9. **Click Finish.**

   Access displays the result of your query in a Select Query window. Any time you need to use this query, just double-click the query name in the Database window.

10. **Click the close box of the Select Query window to make it go away.**

Using a query

After you create and save a query, you can use that query as many times as you want, no matter how much you add, delete, or modify the records in your database. Because some queries can be fairly complicated ("Find all the people in North Dakota who owe over $10,000 on their credit cards, own farms, and have sold their crops in the past thirty days"), saving and reusing queries saves you time, which is the purpose of computers in the first place.

Queries are most useful if you need to reuse the same query on a regular basis.

To use an existing query, open the database file containing your query and then follow these steps:

1. **Choose Window⇨Database.**

2. **Click the Queries icon in the left panel.**

   A list of your available queries appears.

3. **Double-click the query name that you want to use.**

   Access displays the results of your query in a window. At this point, you can view your information, or you can print it out by pressing Ctrl+P.

4. **Click the Close box to remove the window displaying your query result.**

Deleting a query

Eventually, a query may no longer serve its purpose as you add, delete, and modify the data in your database. To keep your database window from overflowing with queries, delete the ones you don't need.

Deleting a query doesn't delete data. When you delete a query, you're just deleting the criteria that you used to search your database with that query.

To delete a query, follow these steps:

1. **Choose Window⇨Database.**

2. **Click the Queries icon in the left panel.**

   A list of your available queries appears.

3. **Click the query that you want to delete.**

4. **Choose Edit⇨Delete or press Delete.**

   A dialog box appears, asking whether you really want to delete your chosen query.

5. **Click Yes.**

   Your query disappears from the Database window.

If you suddenly realize that you deleted a query by mistake, don't cringe in horror. Immediately choose Edit⇨Undo Delete or press Ctrl+Z. Access undoes your last command and restores your query to its original state.

Chapter 19

Reporting Your Access Data

In This Chapter
▶ Creating a database report
▶ Printing your reports
▶ Making your reports look beautiful in Word

*A*ccess can store gobs of useful (or useless) information within the sili-con brains of your computer. However, you may want to print your data once in a while so other people don't have to crowd around your computer screen to see your information.

Fortunately, you can print any data stored in an Access database file. But rather than just print a random jumble of names, addresses, and phone num-bers (or whatever data you have in the database), you can design reports so that other people can actually understand your data.

For example, you may use Access to keep track of all your customers. At the touch of a button (and with a little help from this chapter), you can create a report that prints out a list of your top ten customers. Touch another button, and Access can spit out a list of your top ten products. A report is simply a way for Access to print out and organize information so you can make sense of it.

Making a Report

A report can selectively display data and make it look so pretty that people forget that your data doesn't make any sense. To make a report from your database, follow these steps:

1. **Choose <u>Window</u>⇨Database.**

   The Database window appears.

2. **Click the Reports icon in the left panel.**

3. Double-click the Create Report by Using Wizard icon.

The Report Wizard dialog box appears, as shown in Figure 19-1.

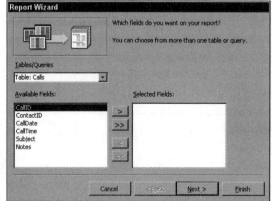

Figure 19-1:
The Report
Wizard
dialog box.

4. Click the Tables/Queries list box to select a database table to use.

For example, if you want to print a report that shows the results of each salesperson in your company, look for the database table that contains this type of information, such as Sales People or Sales Results.

5. Click the Available Fields list box and choose the fields that you want to print on your report.

The Available Fields list box lists all the fields used in the table or query that you select in the Tables/Queries list box. Be selective in choosing which fields to appear on the report — not every field has to appear on a report.

6. Click the single right arrow button, between the Available Fields and Selected Fields boxes.

Access displays the chosen field in the Selected Fields box. Repeat Steps 5 and 6 for each field that you want to use in your report.

7. Click Next.

Another Report Wizard dialog box, shown in Figure 19-2, appears and asks whether you want any grouping levels. A *grouping level* tells Access to organize your printed data according to a specific field. For example, if you want to organize the data in your report by state or province, choose the StateOrProvince field for your grouping level. With this grouping level, your report may group all the people in Alabama, Michigan, and Texas in separate parts of your report, letting you find someone in a specific state more easily.

Figure 19-2:
Grouping
levels help
organize
how Access
displays
your data.

8. **If you want to group the information, click the field that you want to group by, and then click the right arrow button.**

   Access shows you what your report will look like if you group a level. Grouping levels can help you organize your report by a specific field, such as date or last name. That way you can flip through the report and see only records that are based on a certain date or name.

9. **Click Next.**

   Another Report Wizard dialog box, shown in Figure 19-3, appears and asks what sort order you want for detail records. This is Access's confusing way of asking how you want it to sort the data on your report.

   For example, if you defined a grouping level in Step 8, Access can alphabetically sort names within each grouping level by first or last name.

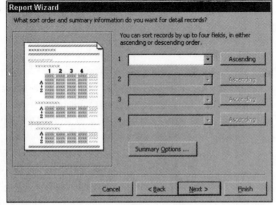

Figure 19-3:
Access
sorts your
data on a
report.

10. **Click the downward-pointing arrow of the 1 list box and choose a field that you want to sort by (if any). If you want to sort by more than one field, choose fields in the 2, 3, and 4 list boxes. Then click <u>N</u>ext.**

 Still another Report Wizard dialog box appears and asks, "How would you like to lay out your report?"

11. **Click an option under Layout and an option under Orientation to specify the design of your report.**

 Different layout options simply print your report in different ways, depending on what you like best. Each time you click a layout option, Access politely shows you what your report will look like, on the left side of the Report Wizard dialog box.

12. **Click <u>N</u>ext.**

 Another Report Wizard dialog box appears, asking you to specify a *style* — a definition of the fonts used to print out your report. Each time you click a style, Access shows you an example of your chosen style at the left of the Report Wizard dialog box.

13. **Click a style in the list box and then click <u>N</u>ext.**

 Another Report Wizard dialog box appears, asking, "What title do you want for your report?"

14. **Type a title for your report and then click <u>F</u>inish.**

 Your report title should be something descriptive, such as "Profits made in March" or "How much money we lost because of Bob's stupid mistake."

 Access displays your report on-screen.

15. **Choose <u>F</u>ile⇨<u>C</u>lose (or click the Close box of the report window).**

 Access displays the Database window again and automatically saves your report in the Reports section of the Database window. The next time you need to use that report, just double-click the report name.

Using a Report

After you create and save a report, you can add or delete as much data as you want. Then when you want to print that data, use the report that you already designed.

To use an existing report, open the database file containing your report and then follow these steps:

1. **Choose Window➪Database.**

2. **Click the Reports icon in the left panel.**

   A list of your available reports appears.

3. **Double-click the report name that you want to use.**

   Access displays your chosen report in a window. At this point, you can print the report by choosing File➪Print, or pressing Ctrl+P.

4. **Click the Close box (the X in the upper-right corner) to remove the window displaying your report.**

Deleting a Report

As you add, delete, and modify the data in your database, you may find that a particular report no longer serves its purpose because you no longer need the information it prints out or because you changed the design of your database. To keep your database window from overflowing with useless reports, delete the ones you don't need.

Deleting a report does not delete data. When you delete a report, you're just deleting the way you told Access to print your data.

After you delete a report, you can't retrieve it again, so make sure that you really don't need it anymore before you decide to delete it. To delete a report, follow these steps:

1. **Choose Window➪Database.**

2. **Click the Reports icon in the left panel.**

   A list of your available reports appears.

3. **Click the report that you want to delete.**

4. **Choose Edit➪Delete, press the Delete key, or click the Delete icon in the Database window toolbar.**

   A dialog box appears, asking whether you really want to delete your chosen report.

5. **Click Yes.**

   Your report disappears from the Database window.

Giving Your Access Reports a Facelift

Instead of using Access's rather feeble report-generating abilities, you can create better-looking reports if you combine the professional report-making capabilities of Access with the wonderful writing, formatting, and publishing features available in Word.

Of course, you can't work with your Access data in Word until you copy your work from Access into Word. To use Word to make your Access data look better, follow these steps:

1. **Choose <u>W</u>indow⇨Database.**

2. **Click the Tables icon in the left panel.**

3. **Double-click the database table containing the data that you want to copy into Word.**

   Access displays your database table and any data stored inside it.

4. **Choose <u>T</u>ools⇨Office <u>L</u>inks⇨<u>P</u>ublish It with Microsoft Word.**

   Word loads and displays your chosen Access database table in a Word document as a series of rows and columns.

5. **Make any changes you want to your Access data, or type additional text around the Access data.**

   For example, you can change the font and size of the type. (For more information about using Word, see Part II of this book.) At this point you can print or save your Word document.

When you work with an Access database table in a Word document, Microsoft Office XP simply copies the data from Access and pastes it into Word. Any changes you make to your data in Word won't affect data stored in Access, and vice versa.

Part VII

Making Web Pages with FrontPage

The 5th Wave   By Rich Tennant

"See? I created a little felon figure that runs around our Web site hiding behind banner ads. On the last page, our logo puts him in a nonlethal choke hold and brings him back to the home page."

In this part . . .

FrontPage is one of the most popular Web page designing programs in the world. Practically everyone is creating a Web page these days, whether for personal or business use, so you might want to create a Web page of your own to advertise your services or business, or just to advertise yourself for the whole world to read about.

Creating Web pages with FrontPage is simple and fast, so you can focus on typing and editing the actual Web page content without worrying about the underlying details that make the Web page actually appear on the Internet.

To help you get started making your own Web pages, this part of the book provides a gentle introduction to using and working with FrontPage. Best of all, FrontPage is a powerful Web designing program; as you get better at designing Web pages, you can keep using FrontPage to design everything from a simple one page Web site to a complicated Web site that dazzles your viewers with its sheer elegance and state-of-the-art design. (If you're doing what everybody is doing, why not do it better?)

Chapter 20

Designing a Web Page
with FrontPage

Microsoft FrontPage 2002 is designed for creating and editing Web pages — from creating frames to editing the HTML code that makes up your Web page.

FrontPage is available only in the Premium and Professional versions of Office XP. If you have a different edition of Office XP, you may have to buy FrontPage separately.

Creating New Web Pages

With FrontPage, you can create a single Web page or you can create a new *Web site* (which consists of two or more Web pages).

Before you can create any Web pages, you have to start the program. In case you forget how to load FrontPage, refer to Chapter 1 to refresh your memory.

To create one new Web page, follow these steps:

1. **Choose File⇨New⇨Page or Web. (You may skip this step if the New Page or Web pane is already on your screen.)**

   A New Page or Web pane appears, as shown in Figure 20-1, listing available Web page designs you can use.

2. **Click Blank Page under the New category to create a single blank Web page. Or click Page Templates under the New from Template category.**

If you click Blank Page, FrontPage displays a blank Web page on-screen, ready for you to start typing text or adding graphics. If you click Page Templates, a Page Templates dialog box appears, as shown in Figure 20-2.

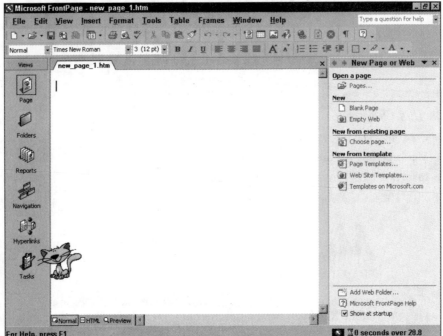

Figure 20-1:
The New
Page or
Web pane.

3. **Click the page template you want to use (such as Feedback Form or Bibliography) and then click OK.**

   FrontPage displays a Web page, ready for you to add your own text.

To create an entirely new Web site, follow these steps:

1. **Choose File⇨New⇨Page or Web.**

   A New Page or Web pane appears.

2. **Click Empty Web under the New category.**

   A Web Site Templates dialog box appears, as shown in Figure 20-3.

3. **Click the Browse button.**

   A New Web Location dialog box appears.

4. **Double-click the folder in which you want to store your Web pages; then click Open.**

   Your chosen folder opens.

5. **Click the Web site design you want to use (such as Customer Support Web) and then click OK.**

FrontPage displays your Web site on the screen, ready for you to modify any way you please.

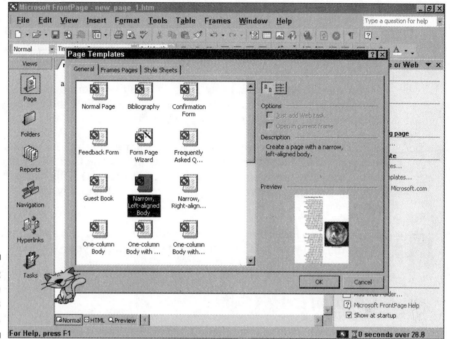

Figure 20-2:
The Page
Templates
dialog box.

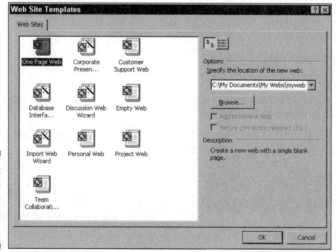

Figure 20-3:
The Web
Site
Templates
dialog box.

Playing with Text on a Web Page

Nearly every Web page must display text of some sort, whether the name of the company running the Web site or several paragraphs explaining the merits of a product. Fortunately, typing text onto a Web page is similar to typing text in a word processor. You just click where you want the text to appear; FrontPage then displays a cursor to show you where your text will appear when you start typing. As you type, FrontPage automatically wraps your words to the next line so your text appears as one continuous paragraph (such as the paragraph that you're looking at right now).

If you want to add a paragraph break (which displays a blank line between two lines of text, such as the top line of this paragraph and the bottom line of the previous paragraph), just press the Enter or Return key.

If you want to display the next line of text underneath the previous line without waiting for FrontPage to wrap your words to the next line, you can insert a line break by pressing Shift+Enter (or Shift+Return). This causes the text to appear directly underneath the previous line without any space between the two lines.

If you want to indent text, press the Tab key or press the spacebar several times to align your text as you want it to appear on your Web page.

Formatting text

Text by itself can look plain and unattractive. Take a few moments to spruce up the appearance of your information by formatting one or more lines of text.

To format text, follow these steps:

1. **Highlight the text that you want to modify.**

2. **Choose Format➪Font.**

   A Font dialog box appears.

3. **Choose the formatting that you want (font, underlining, font size, color, and so on) and then click OK.**

   If you click the Apply button, you can see the changes to your text without exiting the Font dialog box.

Adding color and borders to text

To emphasize your text, enclose it in a border or change the background and foreground colors.

To add a border around text, follow these steps:

1. **Click the text that you want to surround with a border.**

2. **Choose Format⇨Borders and Shading.**

   A Borders and Shading dialog box appears, as shown in Figure 20-4.

3. **Click Box for a border surrounding your text. (If you just want a border on the top, bottom, or sides of your text, click the top, bottom, left, or right border buttons in the Preview group.)**

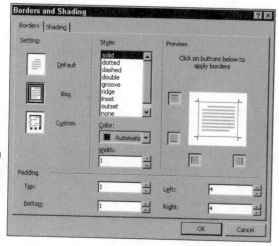

Figure 20-4:
The Borders
and Shading
dialog box.

4. **Click the Style list and choose a style, such as dotted or ridge.**

5. **Click the downward-pointing arrow in the Color list box and choose a color.**

6. **Click OK.**

Borders give the text more prominence on the page, but you may want to include color to make sure that people don't miss your text. FrontPage gives you the choice of changing the background and foreground color, so you can display shocking hot-pink text against a neon-green background (provided you *want* to hurt the eyes of anyone who looks at it).

To color your text, follow these steps:

1. **Click the text that you want to color.**

2. **Choose Format⇨Borders and Shading.**

   A Borders and Shading dialog box appears.

3. **Click the Shading tab.**

   The Shading tab appears.

4. **Click the downward-pointing arrow next to the <u>B</u>ackground Color list box and choose a color for your background.**

5. **Click the downward-pointing arrow next to the <u>F</u>oreground Color list box and choose a color for your text.**

6. **Click OK.**

Be careful when choosing colors for your background and text. Choosing a dark background color and dark text color can make your Web pages hard to read. For best results, use contrasting colors such as a light background color and dark color for text.

If you don't define the colors for your background and text, a viewer's browser may use its default colors for displaying your Web pages, which can make your Web pages appear slightly or drastically different from the way they look on your computer.

Using text styles

To spare you the struggles of formatting text yourself, FrontPage can do it for you by using text *styles* — settings with appropriate formatting built in. Text styles can have odd names such as Heading 1, Normal, and Heading 4. (To see which styles may be available for your Web page, click in the Style list box on the Formatting toolbar.)

To use a text style, follow these steps:

1. **Click the text that you want to format by using a text style.**

2. **Click the downward-pointing arrow next to the Style list box and choose a text style, such as Normal or Heading 3.**

   FrontPage automatically formats your text according to your chosen text style.

As an alternative, click the downward-pointing arrow next to the Style list box first, choose a text style, and then start typing. Whatever you type automatically appears in your chosen text style.

If you choose a style that makes your text look revolting, press Ctrl+Z or click the Undo button to reverse any changes you made.

You cannot apply more than one text style to a paragraph. You end a paragraph whenever you press Enter or Return. To see paragraph marks that show the end of your paragraphs, click the Show All button on the Standard toolbar. (It looks like a paragraph mark.)

Adding dynamic HTML effects

In the old days, Web pages looked pretty boring. To spice up Web pages and make them look fancier, programmers created something called *dynamic HTML* (or *DHTML* to its friends), which can make your text respond to the user by sliding across the screen or changing colors when the user clicks it.

Dynamic HTML effects may not work with all types and versions of browsers. For example, Internet Explorer 3.0 can't display dynamic HTML effects but version 4.0 (and later) of Internet Explorer can. Even so, not everyone uses the latest version of a browser; that means not everyone can see dynamic HTML effects on your Web page.

Despite such drawbacks, dynamic HTML effects can make your Web pages more animated and interesting. (Of course, you've got to have interesting *information* on your Web site or who's gonna look at those special effects?)

To add dynamic HTML effects, follow these steps:

1. **Click the text that you want to format.**

2. **Choose Format⇨Dynamic HTML Effects.**

   The DHTML Effects toolbar appears, as shown in Figure 20-5.

Figure 20-5: The DHTML Effects toolbar.

3. **Click the downward-pointing arrow next to the On list box.**

   A list of events appears, including Click, Double Click, Mouse Over, and Page Load.

4. **Choose an event (such as Click or Mouse Over).**

5. **Click the downward-pointing arrow next to the Apply list box.**

   A list of options appears in the Apply list box, such as Fly Out and Formatting.

6. **Choose the option you want from the Apply list box.**

   Depending on the event you chose in Step 4, the available options in Step 5 may vary.

7. **Click the Close box of the DHTML toolbar to make it go away.**

8. **Choose File⇨Preview in Browser.**

   FrontPage displays a dialog box that asks you to choose a browser and resolution.

9. **Click the browser and resolution you want to use, and then click Preview.**

   If you haven't saved your Web page yet, a dialog box reminds you to do so. Your browser appears, displaying your Web page for you to admire as sheer genius.

10. **Choose File⇨Close to get rid of the browser and return to FrontPage.**

You can always remove dynamic HTML effects from text by repeating Steps 1 and 2 and clicking the Remove Effects button on the DHTML Effects toolbar.

Putting Pretty Pictures on a Web Page

Besides text, the most important element of a Web page is graphics. Graphics can be decorative (such as a picture of your company's logo) or actual buttons that link to another Web page.

Graphics can make the difference between an inviting Web page and one that looks drab (or just plain revolting). Take some time to select (or create) and add some graphics to enhance your Web pages' appearance.

Although FrontPage displays a variety of graphic files, the two types of graphic files that Web pages can use are GIF and JPEG files. (JPEG files often have the JPG file extension.) If you want to use a graphic file that's stored in a different file format (such as PCX or BMP), you have to get a special program to convert that file into either a GIF or JPEG format before you can use it in your Web page.

Adding pictures to a Web page

FrontPage can get graphic images from two sources: *clip art* — predrawn cartoons that Microsoft forced some starving artist to draw for you to use — or other graphics files that you've stored on your computer.

Because clip art can't always offer the exact image you want, many people (especially those good at drawing) create their own images by using a painting or drawing program. People who can't draw have to resort to getting an image through a scanner, a digital camera, or the Internet.

To add a clip-art image to a Web page, follow these steps:

1. **Click the Web page where you want the clip-art image to appear.**

2. **Choose Insert⇨Picture⇨Clip Art.**

   The Insert Clip Art pane appears, as shown in Figure 20-6.

3. **Click in the Search Text box and type a description of the type of clip art you want to see, such as** *cat* **or** *Paris*.

4. **Click Search.**

   The Insert Clip Art pane displays thumbnail images of the clip-art images that match the word you typed in Step 3.

5. **Click the downward-pointing arrow that appears to the right of the image you want to use.**

   A drop-down menu appears.

6. **Click Insert.**

   FrontPage inserts your chosen image on your Web page. You may want to resize the image.

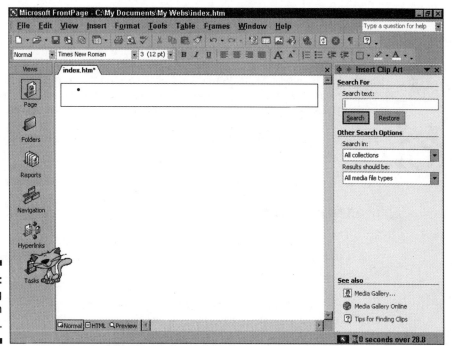

Figure 20-6:
Choosing clip art in FrontPage.

If you want to resize your picture, click the picture so FrontPage displays black handles around the edges of your picture. Then move the mouse pointer over a black handle, hold down the left mouse button, and drag the mouse to resize your picture.

Rather than use the clip-art images provided by Microsoft, you might want to use graphic files that you stored on your own, such as images captured through a scanner or digital camera. To display such a graphic file on a Web page, follow these steps:

1. **Click the Web page where you want the graphic file image to appear.**

2. **Choose Insert➪Picture➪From File.**

   The Picture dialog box appears.

   Web pages can display only images that are stored in the GIF or JPEG file format.

3. **Click the graphic file that you want to use and then click Insert.**

   FrontPage displays the image you chose on the Web page. You may have to move or resize the image to make it fit on the Web page.

Displaying a background image

To add a little color to your Web pages, you can choose to display a background image — a single graphic file displayed on your Web pages like the wallpaper image on your computer. Because a single graphic file is rarely large enough to fill an entire page, FrontPage tiles your chosen graphic file, where the single image of your graphic file is repeated over and over again.

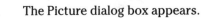

For best results, a background graphic image should not interfere with any text or graphics on your Web pages.

To display a background image for your Web page, follow these steps:

1. **Choose Format➪Background.**

   The Page Properties dialog box appears.

2. **Click the Background Picture check box so a check mark appears.**

3. **Click Browse.**

   A Select Background Picture dialog box appears.

4. **Click the graphic file that you want to use and click Open.**

   The Page Properties dialog box appears again.

5. Click OK.

FrontPage displays your Web page with your chosen image in the
background.

Using themes

As a shortcut to choosing a background image and using text styles, FrontPage
provides themes. A theme contains predefined background images, text, and
graphic styles for creating different types of Web pages. By using a theme,
you're essentially copying the design of an existing Web page. Then you just
have to modify the Web page for your own use.

To define a theme for your Web page, follow these steps:

1. Choose Format⇨Theme.

The Themes dialog box appears, as shown in Figure 20-7.

**2. Select a radio button to choose the theme for All Pages or Selected
Page(s).**

**3. Click the theme that you want to use, such as Citrus Punch or
Romanesque.**

FrontPage shows what your chosen theme looks like so that you can
approve it or change your mind right now.

4. Click OK.

FrontPage uses your chosen theme for your Web page. If you already formatted any text by using a text style, such as Heading 1, it may now look
different depending on the theme you chose.

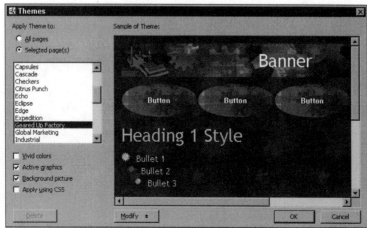

Figure 20-7:
Decorating
a Web page
by using the
Themes
dialog box.

Connecting Everything with Hyperlinks

The final step to making your Web pages useful, interesting, and ready for the Internet is adding hyperlinks. Both text and graphics can be hyperlinks. A hyperlink simply points to another Web page or Web site when the viewer clicks it.

To create hyperlinks, follow these steps:

1. **Click the graphic image (or highlight the text) that you want to turn into a hyperlink.**

2. **Choose Insert⇨Hyperlink, press Ctrl+K, or click the Hyperlink button on the Standard toolbar.**

   An Insert Hyperlink dialog box appears, as shown in Figure 20-8, offering options to connect your Web page to other Web pages.

3. **Click the Web page that you want the hyperlink to display or type the Web site address (such as `www.dummies.com`) in the Address text box.**

4. **Click OK.**

To edit or remove a hyperlink, follow these steps:

1. **Click the graphic or text hyperlink that you want to change.**

2. **Choose Insert⇨Hyperlink, press Ctrl+K, or click the Hyperlink button on the Standard toolbar to bring up the Edit Hyperlink dialog box.**

3. **Edit the text that appears in the Address text box (or delete the text that appears in the text box to remove the hyperlink).**

   The Address text box displays the address of another Web site or the name of a Web page.

4. **Click OK.**

   FrontPage removes or makes changes to your hyperlink.

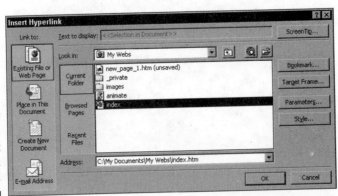

Figure 20-8: The Insert Hyperlink dialog box.

Previewing Your Web Pages

After creating, editing, and modifying your Web pages, you may find minor mistakes when you view the pages on the Internet. If so, you have to modify your Web pages and then post them back to the Internet again, which can be time-consuming, annoying, and boring. However, FrontPage provides two handy ways to preview your pages so you can head off the trouble of posting uncorrected Web pages on the Internet.

While previewing your Web pages, if you click a hyperlink that points towards another Web site, such as www.dummies.com, FrontPage tries to load your browser and connect to the Internet. Make sure that's what you want to happen.

No matter how pretty your Web pages may look on your computer screen, eventually you'll want to post them on a Web site for everyone to see. Depending on the specific Web site hosting service you use, the exact steps may differ, but in most cases, you'll just need a password and a specific directory name (such as /yourisp/homepages) for storing your Web pages on the Web hosting computer.

Previewing a single page

To find out how a single Web page looks, follow these steps:

1. **Click the Page icon on the Views Bar.**

   FrontPage displays the Folder List to the right of the Views Bar.

   If the Views Bar is hidden, choose View➪Views Bar to make it appear on your screen.

2. **Double-click the Web page that you want to preview.**

3. **Click the Preview tab that appears on the bottom of the Web page.**

   FrontPage shows you what your chosen Web page will look like over the Internet. You can also click hyperlinks to see whether they work.

4. **Click the Normal tab to return back to editing your Web page.**

Previewing your Web site in a browser

The trouble with previewing your Web pages with FrontPage is that you can't tell how your Web pages may look on a browser. As an alternative, FrontPage can load any browser from your hard disk and let you view your Web pages within your chosen browser. By using this method, you can see how your Web pages may look in different versions of Netscape Navigator or Internet Explorer.

To preview your Web pages in a browser, follow these steps:

1. **Choose File⇨Preview in Browser to bring up a Preview in Browser dialog box.**

2. **Click the browser that you want to use.**

3. **Click the option button of the screen resolution that you want to use, such as 800 x 600.**

4. **Click Preview.**

   Your chosen browser appears and displays your Web pages. You can also click the hyperlinks to make sure they work. (What a concept.)

5. **Click File⇨Close File.**

   FrontPage reappears, and your browser goes away.

For a fast way to preview your Web pages, click the Preview in Browser button on the Standard toolbar in Step 1. Preview displays your Web pages in your default browser right away.

Seeing HTML code

HTML code contains a lot of cryptic symbols that actually define how your Web pages will look on the Internet. FrontPage shields you from the complexities of editing HTML code; if you're really curious, you can view and edit your HTML code. However . . .

Make sure you know what you're doing if you decide to edit HTML code; typos and other errors can really mess up your Web pages. For more info on HTML, check out *HTML For Dummies,* Third Edition, by Ed Tittel, Natanya Pitts, and Stephen N. James (Hungry Minds, Inc.).

To view the HTML code that gives life to your Web pages, follow these steps:

1. **Click the Page icon on the Views Bar.**

   FrontPage displays the Folder List to the right of the Views Bar.

   (If the Views Bar is hidden, choose View⇨Views Bar first.)

2. **Double-click the Web page that you want to preview.**

   FrontPage displays your chosen Web page.

3. **Click the HTML tab at the bottom of the Web page.**

   FrontPage displays the cryptic HTML code that makes up your Web page, as shown in Figure 20-9.

4. **Click the Normal tab at the bottom of the Web page to return to an HTML-free view of your Web page.**

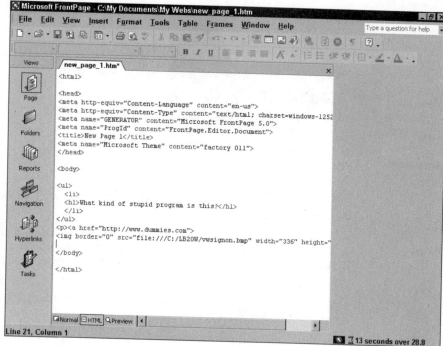

Figure 20-9:
Viewing
the HTML
code — the
guts of your
Web page.

Posting Your Web Pages

After you've designed your Web pages and previewed them so they look the way you want them to appear, the final step is to post your Web pages on the Internet so anyone in the whole world can see them.

To post Web pages on a Web hosting service (such as Geocities, at `geocities.yahoo.com/home`), you need a password (so only you can update your Web site) and a folder to store your Web page files. If this already sounds confusing to you, ask your friendly Web hosting service for help in posting your Web pages to the Internet.

FrontPage includes a command to make posting your Web pages to the Internet simple. Just be aware that not all Web hosting services support FrontPage's Web publishing commands, so check with your Web hosting service before trying the steps below.

To post your FrontPage Web pages, follow these steps:

1. Choose File➪Publish Web

A Publish Destination dialog box appears, as shown in Figure 20-10.

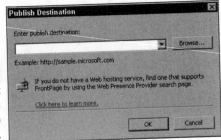

Figure 20-10:
You need to
specify the
Web site
domain
address that
displays
your Web
pages.

2. **Type the domain address, such as** www.dummies.com, **that stores your Web pages and click OK.**

   If you aren't connected to the Internet, a dialog box appears asking for your Internet connection name and password. When you're connected to the Internet, a dialog box appears asking you to type the name and password needed to access your Web-hosting service.

   If you don't know the name and password you need to type in Step 2, contact your Web hosting service for help.

3. **Type the name and password needed to access your Web hosting service and click OK.**

   FrontPage displays a dialog box showing you the Web pages the program is updating. When FrontPage finishes updating your Web pages, a dialog box appears to inform you that your Web pages have been posted.

4. **Click Done.**

After posting your Web pages, you may want to load your Web browser and check to make sure your Web pages appear and behave the way you expect them to look and act. To make sure your Web pages appear exactly the way you want, visit your Web site using different Web browsers and computers, such as a Macintosh running Netscape Navigator.

Chapter 21

Organizing Your Pages with Tables, Frames, and Lines

• •

In This Chapter

▶ Putting text in a table

▶ Constructing a frame

▶ Using framed pages

▶ Adding horizontal lines

• •

*Y*ou need only add text and graphics to a Web page to make it functional, but why stop there? To help you align those basic elements on a Web page, you can also use tables and frames. Tables can organize text and graphics in neat rows and columns. Frames can divide a Web page into two or more parts, with each part displaying its information independently of the other parts.

Organizing Text into Tables

Although you can type text anywhere on a Web page, trying to align where you want text to appear can be cumbersome at times. Sometimes the text appears exactly where you want it, and other times you have to keep hitting the spacebar or Tab key to align your text properly. But why torture yourself? Use a table to organize your text.

A table displays rows and columns, much like a spreadsheet, where you can type text. Because each chunk of text appears in its own row and column (called a *cell*), a table makes organizing your text easy.

Drawing a table

To give you as many options as possible, FrontPage provides three different ways to draw a table. You can choose the method you like best (or get confused by all three methods and not use any of them). To draw a table, follow these steps:

1. **Click where you want the table to appear on your Web page.**

2. **Click the Insert Table button on the Standard toolbar.**

   A drop-down menu appears, displaying blank cells.

3. **Drag the mouse across the drop-down menu to highlight the number of rows and columns you want.**

4. **Click the left mouse button.**

   FrontPage draws your table.

To try another method of drawing a table that gives you more flexibility, follow these steps:

1. **Click where you want the table to appear on your Web page.**

2. **Choose Table⇨Insert⇨Table.**

   The Insert Table dialog box appears, as shown in Figure 21-1.

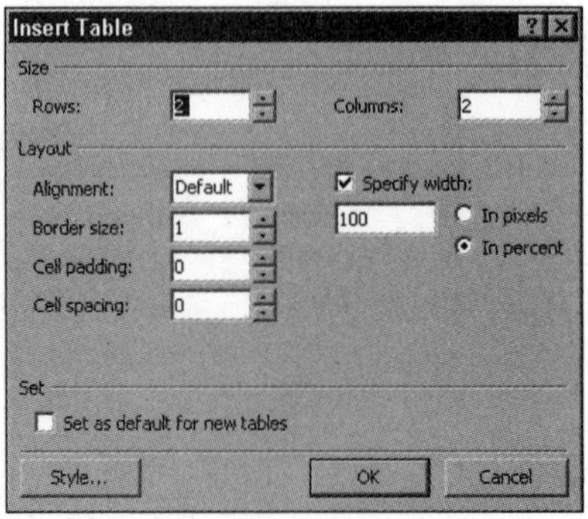

Figure 21-1:
Drawing a
table using
the Insert
Table dialog
box.

3. **Type the number of rows and columns you want.**

4. **Click OK.**

   FrontPage draws your table.

If you already have a lot of text typed on a page but want to organize it into a table, don't bother creating a new table and typing the text into that table. Instead, FrontPage can convert text into a table automatically. To convert text into a table, follow these steps:

1. **Divide the text that you want to display in a table by using paragraph marks or commas.**

   The method that you use to divide your text will determine what radio button you click in Step 4. For example, if you have a list of names that you want to appear in individual cells of your table, separate each name by a comma and then click the Commas radio button later in Step 4.

2. **Highlight the text that you want to display in a table.**

3. **Choose Table⇨Convert⇨Text to Table.**

   A Convert Text to Table dialog box appears.

4. **Click a radio button to choose how to separate text into cells, such as by Paragraphs or Commas and then click OK.**

   FrontPage displays your highlighted text in a table.

Adding (and deleting) rows and columns

After you draw your table, you may need to add or delete rows and columns. To add a row or column, follow these steps:

1. **Click the row or column of the table where you want to add another row or column.**

2. **Choose Table⇨Insert⇨Rows or Columns.**

   An Insert Rows or Columns dialog box appears.

3. **Click the Rows or Columns radio button.**

4. **Click the Number of Rows/Columns text box and then type how many rows or columns you want to add.**

5. **In the Location group, click a radio button to specify where to insert the new row or column (such as Right of Selection or Above Selection).**

6. **Click OK.**

   FrontPage politely inserts your rows or columns in the table.

Eventually you may decide you have too many rows or columns. If you want to delete a row or column, follow these steps:

1. **Click the row or column of the table that you want to delete.**

2. **Choose Table⇨Select⇨Row (or Column).**

   FrontPage highlights your chosen row or column.

3. **Choose Table⇨Delete Cells.**

   FrontPage wipes out your chosen row or column.

Changing the size of a table

Most likely FrontPage won't draw a table exactly the size you want. Fortunately, you can resize a table easily by following these steps:

1. **Move the mouse pointer over a table border (either the outside edges or the inside borders).**

   The mouse pointer turns into a double-pointing arrow.

2. **Hold down the left mouse button and drag the mouse.**

   FrontPage displays a dotted line to show you the new location of your table border.

3. **Release the left mouse button.**

Deleting a table

Tables can be handy, but after you draw one, you may decide that you don't need it after all. To completely obliterate a table and its contents, follow these steps:

1. **Click the table you want to delete.**

2. **Choose Table⇨Select⇨Table.**

   FrontPage highlights the entire table.

3. **Choose Table⇨Delete Cells.**

Framing Your Web Pages

In the old days, Web sites displayed only a single Web page on the entire screen. Unfortunately, this confused many people because whenever they clicked a hyperlink, the entire page disappeared and a new Web page took its place.

To provide a sense of continuity among all the Web pages in a Web site, programmers invented frames. *Frames* divide your Web page into two or more parts, where each part displays entirely different Web pages. Because frames often provide their own vertical scrollbars, users can scroll up or down within each frame without affecting the contents of the other frames. Many Web pages use one frame to display a list of hyperlink buttons and another to display the actual contents of the Web page, as shown in Figure 21-2.

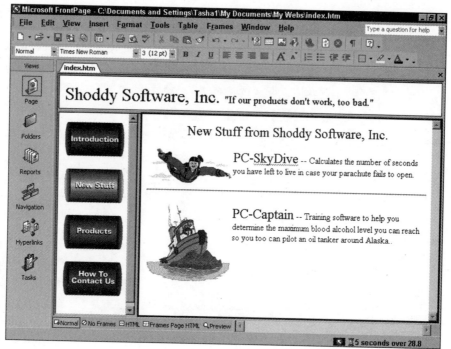

Figure 21-2:
Frames
organize
material on
a Web page.

Older versions of Netscape Navigator and Internet Explorer cannot display frames. In order to make sure your Web pages that everyone can view (including people who use obscure Web browsers such as Mosaic or Lynx), either avoid frames or create two versions of your Web pages: a framed version and a nonframed version.

Creating a framed Web page

To create a framed Web page, follow these steps:

1. **Choose File➪New➪Page or Web.**

   The New Page or Web pane appears.

2. **Click Page Templates under the New from Template category.**

   The Page Templates dialog box appears.

3. **Click the Frames Pages tab.**

   FrontPage displays a list of Web page templates that use frames, as shown in Figure 21-3.

4. **Click a frame page template that you want to use (such as Contents or Vertical Split) and click OK.**

   FrontPage creates an empty framed page, as shown in Figure 21-4.

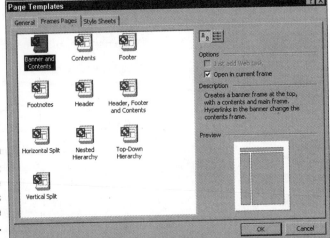

Figure 21-3:
FrontPage provides frame page templates.

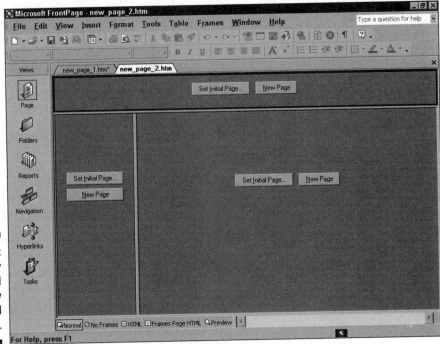

Figure 21-4:
An empty framed page ready for text and graphics.

Filling in a framed Web page

After you create an empty framed Web page, the next step is to fill the frame with information — either brand new information (which you have to type or insert on your own) or another existing Web page. To place brand new information into a frame, follow these steps:

1. **Click the <u>N</u>ew Page button inside the frame that you want to use.**

   FrontPage displays an empty frame.

2. **Start typing text or inserting graphics.**

   See Chapter 20 for more information on adding text and graphics to a Web page.

Rather than create new information inside a frame, you can tell FrontPage to display an existing Web page inside your frame. To define a Web page to appear in a frame, follow these steps:

1. **Click the Set <u>I</u>nitial Page button inside the frame that you want to use.**

   An Insert Hyperlink dialog box appears, as shown in Figure 21-5.

Figure 21-5:
The Insert Hyperlink dialog box helps you display an existing Web page inside a frame.

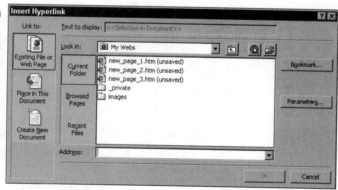

2. **Click the Web page that you want to use inside your frame.**

   You may need to switch folders or drives to find the Web page that you want to display.

3. **Click OK.**

   FrontPage displays your chosen Web page inside your frame.

Hyperlinking framed Web pages

When you save a framed Web page, FrontPage saves each frame as a separate file. So, you can create a hyperlink in one frame that opens a Web page inside another frame. To create a hyperlink between frames, follow these steps:

1. **Highlight text or click a picture that you want to use as a hyperlink.**

2. **Choose Insert⇨Hyperlink, or press Ctrl+K.**

   An Edit Hyperlink dialog box appears.

3. **Choose the Web page that you want to open from the list box.**

4. **Click the Target Frame button in the Edit Hyperlink dialog box.**

   A Target Frame dialog box appears, as shown in Figure 21-6.

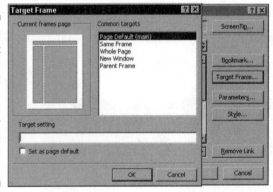

Figure 21-6:
The Target
Frame
dialog box
enables you
to pick a
frame for
your Web
page to
appear in.

5. **In the Current Frames Page box, click the frame that you want your Web page to appear in.**

   FrontPage highlights your chosen frame.

6. **Click OK to close the Target Frame dialog box and then click OK to close the Edit Hyperlink dialog box.**

   You may want to click the Preview tab at the bottom of the screen to test your hyperlink.

Changing a framed Web page's properties

After you create a framed page, you can modify it at any time. The simplest way to modify a frame is to change the properties of the frame, which enables you to modify the following:

✔ The frame's name

✔ The initial Web page that you want the frame to display

✔ The frame size

✔ The frame margins

✔ Whether the frame is resizable when viewed inside a browser

✔ Frame borders

✔ The frame spacing

✔ Whether the frame displays scrollbars

To modify the properties of a frame, follow these steps:

1. **Click the Normal tab at the bottom of the screen.**

2. **Click inside the frame you want to modify.**

3. **Choose Frames⇨Frame Properties.**

    A Frame Properties dialog box appears, as shown in Figure 21-7.

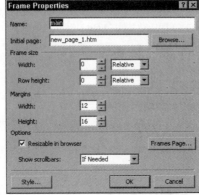

Figure 21-7:
The Frame
Properties
dialog box
gives you
options for
changing
the size and
appearance
of your
frame.

4. **Click the Name text box and type a new name for your frame, if you want.**

5. **Click the Initial Page text box and type the Web page that you want the frame to display.**

    If you click Browse, you can click the Web page that you want to display without having to type a thing.

6. **In the Frame Size group, click the Width or Row Height boxes and type a new frame width or height.**

7. **In the Margins group, click the Width or Height boxes and type a new margin width or height.**

8. **Click the Show scrollbars list box and choose an option, such as If Needed or Always.**

9. **Make sure a check mark appears in the Resizable in Browser check box, or clear the check box if you don't want the frames to be resizable when viewed in a browser.**

10. **Click the Frames Page button.**

    A Page Properties dialog box appears.

11. **Make sure a check mark appears in the Show Borders check box, or clear the check box if you don't want the frames to display borders.**

12. **Click the Frame Spacing box and type a number to define the width of your frame borders.**

13. **Click OK.**

Deleting a frame

Although you can keep splitting frames like amoebas multiplying, you may want to delete the extras if you have more than you need. To delete a frame, follow these steps:

1. **Click the Normal tab at the bottom of the screen.**

2. **Click inside the frame you want to delete.**

3. **Choose Frames➪Delete Frame.**

    FrontPage wipes out your chosen frame.

Viewing your frame as a full screen

Because frames divide your Web page in to smaller pieces, you may find that editing a frame can be difficult in such a small space. Fortunately, the clever programmers at Microsoft have already anticipated this problem and solved it by enabling you to view a single frame as a single Web page. That way, you can edit it in a full screen and when you finish, you can see how it looks as a frame. To view a frame as a full screen, follow these steps:

1. **Click the Normal tab at the bottom of the screen.**

2. **Click the frame that you want to view.**

3. **Choose Frames⇨Open Page in New Window.**

   FrontPage displays your frame as a window all by itself.

4. **Edit your Web page until your heart's content, and then choose File⇨ Close or press Ctrl+F4 to return to the frame view of your Web page.**

Using Horizontal Lines

As a final method for organizing information on your Web pages, consider using (ready for this?) horizontal lines. Although not exactly high-tech (a horizontal line simply breaks up your Web page), if you have great hordes of text and pictures to display, a simple line helps keep your visitors from being overwhelmed.

Creating a horizontal line

To add a horizontal line to a Web page, follow these steps:

1. **Click the Web page where you want the line to appear.**

2. **Choose Insert⇨Horizontal Line.**

   FrontPage displays a plain, boring, *useful* horizontal line across your Web page.

Moving a horizontal line

After you create a horizontal line, you may want to move it to a new location. To move a horizontal line, follow these steps:

1. **Click the horizontal line that you want to move.**

   FrontPage highlights your chosen horizontal line.

2. **Move the mouse pointer over the line, hold down the left mouse button, and drag the mouse.**

   FrontPage displays a gray line in the left margin of your Web page to show where the horizontal line will appear when you release the left mouse button.

3. **Release the left mouse button when you're happy with the horizontal line's new location.**

Deleting a horizontal line

If you get tired of looking at a horizontal line, you can delete it by following these steps:

1. **Click the horizontal line that you want to delete.**

   FrontPage highlights your chosen horizontal line.

2. **Press Delete.**

   Your horizontal line disappears into oblivion.

Part VIII
The Part of Tens

The 5th Wave   By Rich Tennant

KEVIN ACCIDENTALLY E-MAILS HIS OUTLINE FOR A MYSTERY NOVEL IN PLACE OF HIS RESUME.

Yes, we received your resume. Can you tell us more about the period you spent handcuffed in the hull of the Russian freighter?

In this part . . .

After spending your valuable time figuring out the many powers and puzzles of Microsoft Office XP, flip through this part of the book to find out the secret short-cuts and hints that can make any of the programs in Microsoft Office XP even easier and more effective for your personal or business use.

Just make sure that your family, co-workers, or boss don't catch you reading this part of the book. They may stop thinking that you're an Office XP super-guru and realize you're just an ordinary person relying on a really great book. (Why not? Many of the best gurus do.)

Then again, why not buy extra copies of this book and give them to your friends, coworkers, and boss so they'll be able to figure out how to use Office XP on their own and leave you with enough time to actually do some useful work?

Chapter 22

Ten Tips for Using Microsoft Office XP

Microsoft Office contains so many features and commands that you should take some time to browse the tips in this chapter. See how quickly you can turn yourself from a computer novice to an Office XP guru (as long as you keep a copy of this book with you at all times).

Customizing the Microsoft Office XP User Interface

Microsoft tried to create the easiest, most intuitive collection of programs in the world. Yet chances are good that the programs are still too complicated for most mere mortals to use and understand. So rather than suffer in silence, take a few moments to customize the Microsoft Office XP user interface.

Tearing off your toolbars

Toolbars usually appear at the top of the screen (if they appear at all). You may find two or more toolbars smashed together (which can look confusing). So feel free to tear your menus off and move them anywhere around the screen — including the side, bottom, or right in the middle of the screen instead.

To tear off a toolbar, follow these steps:

1. **Choose <u>V</u>iew➪<u>T</u>oolbars and then choose the menu that you want to display.**

   Your chosen toolbar appears on the screen.

2. **Move the mouse pointer over the toolbar handle.**

   The toolbar handle appears as a vertical line at the far left of the menu (as shown in Figure 22-1). The mouse pointer turns into a four-way pointing arrow when you move the mouse over the menu handle.

Figure 22-1:
To move a toolbar or menu, move the mouse pointer over the toolbar or menu handle.

Handles

3. **Hold down the left mouse button and drag the mouse to move the toolbar.**

   As you move the toolbar away from the top, it turns into a floating window. You can leave the menu as a floating window or move it to the side, top, or bottom of your screen.

4. **Release the mouse button when you're happy with the position of your toolbar.**

   To move a floating window, move the mouse pointer over the title bar of the floating toolbar until the mouse pointer turns into a four-way pointing arrow.

You can use the above steps to move the menu of any Microsoft Office XP program to the side, bottom, or in the middle of your screen as a floating menu bar, too.

Zooming to avoid eye strain

To cram as much text on-screen as possible, Microsoft Office XP displays everything in a tiny font size. If you'd rather not strain your eyes, you can zoom in on your screen, blowing up your text so that the letters are easier to see.

FrontPage and Outlook don't offer a Zoom feature.

To zoom in (expand) or zoom out (shrink) the appearance of text on-screen, follow these steps:

1. **Choose View⇨Zoom.**
2. **Choose a magnification (such as 200% or 25%) and then click OK.**

   Your document appears at the desired magnification for your viewing pleasure.

If you own a mouse with a wheel stuck between the two buttons (such as the Microsoft IntelliMouse), you have another way to zoom in and out. Just hold down the Ctrl key and roll the wheel back and forth.

Enlarging your buttons

The Microsoft Office XP toolbar buttons can be cryptic but hard to see. Rather than squint and ruin your eyesight, you can enlarge the buttons. To make your toolbar buttons larger, follow these steps:

1. **Choose Tools⇨Customize.**

   The Customize dialog box appears.

2. **Click the Options tab.**
3. **Select the Large Icons check box.**

   Microsoft Office XP displays your buttons to make them look as if radiation mutated them to three times their normal size.

4. **Click Close.**

If you get sick of seeing large buttons staring back at you while you work, just repeat the preceding steps and clear the check mark from the Large Icons check box. Voilá — the buttons return to their normal size.

When in doubt, click the right mouse button

When you want to rename, edit, or modify anything in Office XP, use the handy right mouse button pop-up menu. To use this pop-up menu, follow these steps:

1. **Place the mouse cursor over the item you want to edit.**

2. **Click the right mouse button.**

   The right mouse button pop-up menu appears.

3. **Click a command in the pop-up menu.**

Using the What's This? feature

Choosing commands from the Microsoft Office pull-down menus can be clumsy, slow, and annoying. To solve this problem, Microsoft put the most commonly used commands on toolbars that appear at the top of the screen.

Unfortunately, toolbars often display cryptic buttons that confuse even veteran Egyptian hieroglyphic experts. Rather than guess what these toolbar buttons do (or waste time experimenting), you can use the handy What's This? feature, which offers you a quick explanation of any toolbar button that confuses you.

To use the What's This? feature, follow these steps:

1. **Choose <u>H</u>elp⇨What's <u>T</u>his?**

   The mouse cursor turns into an arrow with a question mark next to it.

2. **Click a toolbar button that confuses you.**

   A window appears, briefly explaining what commands the button represents.

3. **Click anywhere to remove the explanation from the screen.**

If you want to use the What's This? Feature to examine another button on a toolbar, you have to repeat Steps 1 through 3.

Taking shortcuts with macros

Many people dream of the day they can give orders to a computer by talking to it; the current reality is that you still have to type on a keyboard if you hope to use your computer at all. Because most people would rather avoid typing, Microsoft Office offers a partial solution — *macros.*

Macros don't eliminate typing entirely, but they can reduce the number of keys you have to press to get something done. A *macro* is a mini-program that records your keystrokes as you type. After you record the keystrokes in a macro, whenever you need to use those exact same keystrokes again, you can tell Microsoft Office XP to "play back" your recorded keystrokes.

For example, suppose you find yourself typing the name of your company, The Mississippi Mudflat Corporation, over and over again. You can instead type it once and save it as a macro. Then, when you want the company name to appear in your document, Office XP can automatically type *The Mississippi Mudflat Corporation* for you.

You can create and run macros within Word, Excel, and PowerPoint.

Recording macros in Word

To record a macro in Word, follow these steps:

1. **Choose Tools➪Macro➪Record New Macro.**

   A Record Macro dialog box appears, as shown in Figure 22-2.

Figure 22-2:
The Record
Macro
dialog box is
where you
can name
your macro
and assign a
keystroke
for running
it later.

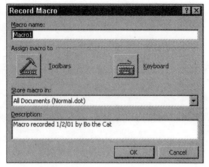

2. **Type a name for your macro in the Macro name box.**

3. **Click the Keyboard button.**

   A Customize Keyboard dialog box appears (as shown in Figure 22-3); it's where you assign a keystroke combination to your macro.

4. **Press the keystroke that you want to represent your macro (such as Alt+F12).**

   You can repeat this step to assign multiple keystrokes to the same macro if you want.

5. **Click the Assign button.**

6. **Click the Close button.**

   The mouse pointer turns into an arrow with an audiocassette icon; a Stop Recording toolbar appears (as shown in Figure 22-4), which you can use to pause or stop recording a macro.

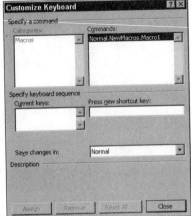

Figure 22-3:
The
Customize
Keyboard
dialog box.

Stop Recording

Pause Recording

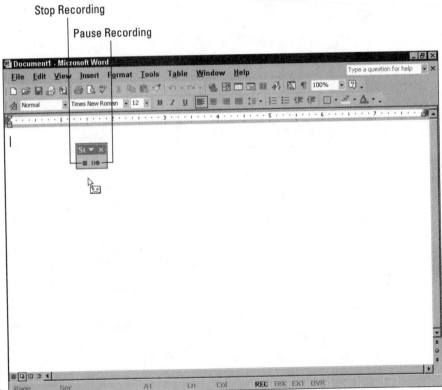

Figure 22-4:
The Stop
Recording
toolbar.

7. **Press the keystrokes that you want to record in your macro.**

If you click the Pause Recording button, you can temporarily stop the recording of your macro.

8. **Click the Stop Recording button when you finish recording the keystokes.**

To run your macro, press the keystroke combination that you chose in Step 4.

Recording macros in Excel

To record a macro in Excel, follow these steps:

1. **Choose Tools➪Macro➪Record New Macro.**

A Record Macro dialog box appears.

2. **Type a name for your macro in the Macro name box.**

3. **Click in the Shortcut Key box (the one that has Ctrl+ to the left) and type a letter.**

For example, if you want to replay your macro by pressing Ctrl+W, type **W** in the Shortcut Key box.

4. **Click OK.**

A Stop Recording toolbar appears.

5. **Press the keystrokes that you want to record in your macro.**

6. **Click the Stop Recording button when you finish recording the keystokes.**

To run a macro, press the keystroke combination that you chose in Step 3.

Recording macros in PowerPoint

To record a macro in PowerPoint, follow these steps:

1. **Choose Tools➪Macro➪Record New Macro.**

A Record Macro dialog box appears.

2. **Type a name for your macro in the Macro name box.**

3. **Click OK.**

A Stop Recording toolbar appears.

4. **Press the keystrokes that you want to record in your macro.**

5. **Click the Stop Recording button when you finish recording the keystokes.**

To run a macro in PowerPoint, follow these steps:

1. **Choose Tools⇨Macro⇨Macros (or press Alt+F8).**

   A macro dialog box appears.

2. **Click the name of the macro that you want to run.**

3. **Click Run.**

Protecting Your Microsoft Office XP Files

After you spend all your time learning how to use Microsoft Office XP, the last thing you want to happen is to lose all your precious data that you sweated to create in the first place. So take steps now to protect yourself in the event of disaster, and you won't be sorry later.

Watching out for macro viruses

Microsoft Office XP gives you two ways to create a macro. The simplest way, as explained in the previous section, is to record your keystrokes and then play them back when you need them. The harder way to create a macro is to use the Microsoft special macro programming language (called Visual Basic for Applications or *VBA*) to create more powerful and complicated macros.

Although the Microsoft macro programming language gives you the power to create macros of your own, it has also given mischievous programmers the opportunity to write computer viruses.

This new breed of computer viruses, dubbed *macro viruses*, can infect Word documents, Excel worksheets, PowerPoint presentations, and Access databases. When you give a copy of a document or worksheet that contains a virus to another person, you risk passing along the macro virus at the same time.

So to help prevent macro viruses from infecting and spreading through your Office XP files, Office XP offers a limited form of macro virus protection.

The most common macro viruses infect Word documents. The second most common macro viruses infect Excel worksheets; a handful of macro viruses attack PowerPoint or Access files. But make sure you buy an antivirus program and keep it updated regularly, just to protect yourself from any future macro viruses that might attack your computer in the future.

To turn on macro virus protection in Word, follow these steps:

1. **Choose File➪Save or Save As.**

    A Save As dialog box appears.

2. **Click in the Tools menu that appears in the upper right-hand corner of the Save As dialog box**

    A drop-down menu appears.

3. **Click Security Options.**

    A Security dialog box appears.

4. **Click Macro Security.**

    Another Security dialog box appears (as shown in Figure 22-5).

Figure 22-5:
The Security dialog box for changing the macro security setting for Word documents.

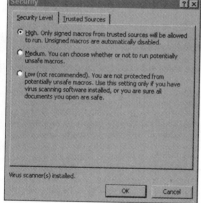

5. **Click the Security Level tab and click on the High, Medium, or Low radio button.**

    Unless you have a good reason for choosing a lower security level, you should always choose the High radio button.

    The High Security Level helps prevent macro viruses from infecting your files, but some macro viruses are clever enough to shut this feature off, so don't rely on Office XP's macro virus protection alone to keep your computer virus-free.

6. **Click OK twice.**

    The Save As dialog box appears again. Each time you save your document, Word uses your chosen security settings for this document.

7. **Click Save.**

If a macro virus has already infected your Word documents or Excel worksheets, turning on Office XP's macro virus protection won't remove the virus. That's why you should also get an antivirus program, such as McAfee's VirusScan (www.mcafee.com) or Symantec's Norton AntiVirus (symantec.com) that can detect and remove macro and other types of viruses.

Encrypting your files

In case you want to keep your Office XP documents private, you can use Office XP's built-in encryption program or buy an encryption program. Encryption scrambles your data so that no one else but you (and anyone else who steals or figures out your password) can read it.

To turn on Office XP's encryption protection in Word, Excel, or PowerPoint, follow these steps:

1. **Choose File⇨Save or Save As.**

   A Save As dialog box appears.

2. **Click in the Tools menu that appears in the upper right-hand corner of the Save As dialog box**

   A drop-down menu appears.

3. **Click Security Options. (Click General Options in Excel.)**

   A Security dialog box appears.

4. **Type a password in the Password to Open text box.**

   Your password appears as a series of asterisks to hide your password in case someone's peeking over your shoulder. (Quick! Turn around and look!)

   No matter what encryption program you use, just remember that if you pick a simple password, people may be able to guess your password, which makes encryption as effective as locking a bank vault but taping the combination to the front of the door.

5. **Click the Advanced button.**

   An Encryption Type dialog box appears.

6. **Click on the encryption method you want to use and click OK.**

   Office XP has three forms of built-in encryption: Weak Encryption (XOR), Office 97/2000 Compatible, and various versions of an encryption method dubbed RC4. If you choose RC4 encryption (which is the most secure of the three encryption methods), you can also click the up/down arrows in the Choose a key length text box. The higher the key number (such as 56), the more secure your document will be.

7. (Optional) Type a password in the Password to Modify text box.

You can choose two different passwords in Steps 4 and 7 if you want. That way you can have one password that lets you open but not change a file (the password you chose in Step 4) and a second password that lets you open and edit that same file.

8. Click OK.

A Confirm Password dialog box appears for each password you typed.

9. Retype each password and click OK.

The Save As dialog box appears again.

10. Click Save.

Office XP's encryption can stop most people from viewing your data, but determined thieves and spies will have little trouble opening Office XP encrypted files. For better protection, get a separate encryption program instead. Two popular encryption programs are Pretty Good Privacy (often called PGP and available from www.pgp.com) and GNU Privacy Guard (www.gnupg.org). Both of these programs allow you to encrypt individual files, entire folders, or complete hard drives so only you can access your data (unless you forget your password).

Shredding your files

Encryption is one way to protect your data. However, when you encrypt a file, you usually wind up with two separate files: the newly encrypted file and the original unencrypted file. If you erase the original unencrypted file, someone can undelete that file and see your documents while avoiding your encrypted files altogether.

The problem stems from the way computers delete files. When you tell your computer to delete a file, it actually plays a trick on you. Instead of physically erasing the file, the computer simply pretends the file doesn't exist. That's why someone can use a utility program, such as The Norton Utilities, and unerase a file that you may have erased several hours, days, weeks, or even months ago.

So if you want to delete a file, don't use the file deletion feature of Windows 98/95/Me/NT/2000. Instead, get a special file-shredding program instead. These file shredding programs not only delete a file, but they overwrite that file several times with random bits of data. That way, if someone tries to unerase that file at a later date, all they see is gibberish.

Two popular file shredding programs are Eraser (www.tolvanen.com/eraser) and East-Tec Eraser (www.east-tec.com/eraser).

If you accidentally delete a file by using a file shredding program, you can never retrieve that file again, so be careful!

Backing up your files

You should always keep extra copies of your files in case you accidentally mess up a file by mistake. If you happen to lose or delete a file by mistake, a backup copy of your files enables you to continue working even though your original file may be history.

The simplest way (which is also the easiest to forget) to make backup copies is to do it yourself by using the Windows Explorer to copy files from your hard drive to a floppy disk (or vice versa). Because this method requires conscious effort on your part, it's also the least likely method to rely on when disaster strikes.

As an alternative, get a backup program and a backup device such as a tape drive, Zip drive, rewritable CD, or similar mass storage device. If you can manage to get your backup program configured properly (good luck), the backup program can automatically back up your entire hard drive to your backup drive without any extra effort on your part.

As another way to back up files automatically, Word and Excel have a special backup feature that creates a backup copy of your files each time you save a file. Unfortunately, using the Word or Excel backup feature won't protect you in case your entire hard drive crashes, so you may still have to store your backup copies on a floppy disk and keep them separate from your computer.

To turn on this special backup feature in Word or Excel, follow these steps:

1. **Choose File⇨Save As.**

   The Save As dialog box appears.

2. **Click the Tools button.**

   A drop-down list appears.

3. **Click Save Options. (In Excel, click General Options.)**

   A Save dialog box appears.

4. **Select the Always Create Backup Copy check box.**

5. **Click OK.**

When you save a file with the backup feature turned on, your backup file has a name like Backup of. For example, if you saved a file called *Ransom note,* your backup copy would have a name of *Backup copy of Ransom note* and have a file extension of .WBK (for Word documents) or .XLK (for Excel worksheets).

Using Pocket Office

Laptop computers continue to drop in price and weight, yet increase in power. Some of the latest laptop computers weigh less than three pounds and have enough memory and processing power to run a full-blown copy of Microsoft Office XP.

But rather than lug a laptop computer around the country, many people are opting for smaller, cheaper, and lighter handheld computers that run a slightly different operating system called PocketPC.

PocketPC comes with a miniature version of Microsoft Office dubbed Pocket Office that includes Pocket Word, Pocket Excel, Pocket PowerPoint, and Pocket Access.

These pocket versions of Microsoft Office provide fewer features than the complete Microsoft Office XP suite. But Pocket Office can share data with your Microsoft Office XP programs, making it perfect for taking your data on the road and viewing or editing it on a handheld computer.

So if you travel frequently but dread breaking your back carrying a heavy and expensive laptop computer, consider buying a handheld PocketPC computer and using Pocket Office instead.

Using Smart Tags

Smart Tags are a new Office XP feature that provide shortcuts for sharing and transferring data between the various Office XP programs. Rather than force you to copy text from Word, load Outlook, and then paste the data into Outlook, a Smart Tag can do all that for you with a click of the mouse.

Smart Tags can automatically recognize certain text such as names, addresses, e-mail addresses, and telephone numbers. To tell Microsoft Office XP what type of text to recognize with Smart Tags (or to turn on/off Smart Tags completely), follow these steps:

1. **Choose Tools⇨AutoCorrect Options.**

   An AutoCorrect Options dialog box appears.

2. **Click on the Smart Tags tab.**

   A list of items that Smart Tags recognizes appears, as shown in Figure 22-6.

3. **Make sure a check mark appears in the Label text (or data) with Smart Tags check box.**

   You can turn Smart Tags off completely if you clear this check box.

4. **Click in any of the check boxes to turn on (or off) Smart Tags for certain items such as names or telephone numbers.**

   Depending on the Office XP program you're using, the available options for Smart Tags may vary.

5. **Click OK.**

   Your Office XP program is ready to start using Smart Tags with your data.

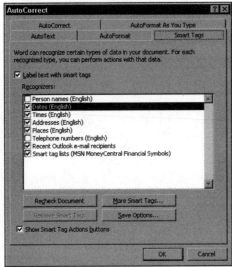

Figure 22-6:
The AutoCorrect dialog box is where you can modify Smart Tags or turn them off completely.

Once you've turned on Smart Tags and customized the type of data you want Smart Tags to identify, you can start using Smart Tags. To use Smart Tags, follow these steps:

1. **Type your text.**

   The moment Smart Tags recognizes certain text, Office XP highlights that data with a purple underline.

2. **Move the cursor or mouse pointer over the data identified by the purple underline.**

   A box appears hovering nearby your Smart Tag-identified text.

3. **Move the mouse pointer over the box.**

   A downward-pointing arrow appears.

4. **Click on the downward-pointing arrow.**

   A menu of different options appears.

5. **Click on an option.**

   Office XP immediately performs your chosen action, such as adding a name to your Outlook Contacts database.

Chapter 23

Ten Common Microsoft Office XP Shortcuts

*W*ith each reincarnation of Microsoft Office, Microsoft tries to make all the different Office programs look and work more and more alike. That way, after you learn how to use one Office program, you'll be able to master other ones fairly easily.

To help you master Microsoft Office XP, this chapter lists the common keystrokes (shortcuts) that every Office XP program uses. That way, you spend less time figuring out how to use each program's commands and more time actually doing some work.

Creating a New File (Ctrl+N)

Any time you want to create a new file in any Microsoft Office XP program, press Ctrl+N or click the New button on the Standard toolbar. Office XP cheerfully responds by creating an empty file that you can use to start creating anything your heart desires.

Pressing Ctrl+N in Microsoft Outlook can create anything from a new e-mail message to a contact or appointment, depending on what you happen to be doing at the time.

Opening an Existing File (Ctrl+O)

You often need to open an existing file in order to make changes to it. Whenever you want to open a file, press Ctrl+O or click the Open button on the Standard toolbar to see an Open dialog box, where you can choose the specific file you want to open.

By default, Microsoft Office XP looks for existing files in the My Documents folder, which is usually C:\My Documents. Rather than lump all your files in the My Documents folder, create separate subfolders within the My Documents folder, which prevents files that belong to different projects or programs from getting mixed up.

To create a new folder:

1. **Click the Start button on the Windows taskbar and then choose Programs⇨Windows Explorer (or Programs⇨Accessories⇨Windows Explorer if you're using Windows Me or Windows 2000).**

   The Windows Explorer program appears.

2. **Click the My Documents folder.**

3. **Choose File⇨New ⇨Folder.**

   Windows Explorer creates a new folder, unimaginatively called *New Folder*.

4. **Type a new name for your folder and press Enter.**

By default, Word, Excel, PowerPoint, and Access always look in the My Documents folder whenever you try to open an existing file. (FrontPage looks in the My Documents\My Webs folder by default.) To define a different folder for Word, Excel, PowerPoint, or Access to look in first:

1. **Start Word, Excel, PowerPoint, or Access.**

2. **Choose Tools⇨Options.**

   An Options dialog box appears.

3. **Follow the steps for the program you're using:**

   • **If you're using Access:** Click the General tab; click the Default Database Folder text box and then type a new directory name (such as C:\My Documents\Secrets).

- **If you're using Excel:** Click the General tab; click the Default file location text box and then type a new directory name (such as `C:\My Documents\Useless Work`).

- **If you're using PowerPoint:** Click the Save tab; click the Default file location text box; and then type a new directory name (such as `C:\My Documents\Useless Work`).

- **If you're using Word:** Click the File Locations tab; click Documents in the File Types box; click Modify; then click a folder.

4. **Click OK.**

   Regardless of which Office XP program you're using, you're done. (Ah, simplicity. What a concept.)

If you open or save a file in a different directory, the next time you choose the Open command, your Office XP program looks in the directory where you last opened or saved a file. So, if you save a file to a directory called `A:\Stuff`, then the next time you open a file, Office XP assumes that you want to look for a file stored in the `A:\Stuff` directory.

Saving Your Work (Ctrl+S)

Save your work often — every ten minutes is good. That way, if the power suddenly goes out, you won't lose all the work you did over the past five hours. Whenever you take a break or walk away from your computer, press Ctrl+S or click the Save button on the Standard toolbar to save your work. This advice is easy to remember after you lose an entire day's work because you forgot to save it to a disk.

Microsoft Word, Excel, and PowerPoint provide a special AutoRecover feature that automatically saves your work after a specified amount of time. To turn on the AutoRecover feature — and specify how often you want to save your work automatically — follow these steps:

1. **Choose Tools⇨Options.**

   The Options dialog box appears.

2. **Click the Save tab.**

3. **Click the Save AutoRecover info every check box.**

4. **Click the up or down arrow in the Minutes box to specify how often Word or PowerPoint should save your file.**

5. **Click OK.**

Access 2002 automatically saves your data whether you like it or not, so it doesn't offer an AutoRecover feature that you can change or disable.

Printing Your Work (Ctrl+P)

No matter how often magazines tout the myth of the paperless office, your printer is one of the most important parts of your entire computer system. Whenever you want to print your files, just press Ctrl+P to make the Print dialog box appear. Specify which pages you want to print and how many copies you want, and then click the OK button.

If you're in a hurry to print, just click the Print button on the Standard toolbar. Clicking the Print button automatically sends your entire file to the printer, so make sure that you really do want to print every single page of that document.

Cutting (Ctrl+X), Copying (Ctrl+C), and Pasting (Ctrl+V)

If you want to move data from one place to another, cut and paste the data. If you want your data to appear in the original place as well as another place, copy and paste the data. To cut or copy data to another place:

1. **Select the data that you want to cut or copy.**

2. **Press Ctrl+X or click the Cut button on the Standard toolbar to cut the data. Press Ctrl+C or click the Copy button on the Standard toolbar to copy the data.**

3. **Move the cursor to the location where you want the data to appear.**

4. **Press Ctrl+V or click the Paste button on the Standard toolbar.**

When you cut or copy anything from within any Microsoft Office XP program, the cut or copied object gets stored on the Windows Clipboard (which can only hold one item at a time) and the Office Clipboard, which can hold up to twenty-four items at a time. To view the Office Clipboard in Access, Excel, PowerPoint, or Word, choose Edit⇨Office Clipboard. The Windows Clipboard is used when copying or cutting data from an Office XP program to a non-Office XP program, such as WordPerfect or Quicken. Use the Office Clipboard to copy or cut data between two Office XP programs.

Finding a Word or Phrase (Ctrl+F)

Any time you want to look for a specific word or number, you can use the fabulous Find command by pressing Ctrl+F. When you use the Find command, Microsoft Office XP presents you with the Find dialog box, which gives you the following options:

- ✔ **Match case:** If you want to find *Bill* but don't want to waste time looking for *bill*.

- ✔ **Find whole words only:** If you want to find *cat* but not words like *catastrophic* and *catatonic*.

- ✔ **Use wildcards:** If you want to find parts of a sequence. For example, if you want to find all words that begin with *fail*, tell Microsoft Office XP to search for *fail**. (This option is only available in Word.)

- ✔ **Sounds like:** If you know what you want to find but don't know how to spell it, for example, searching for *elefant* when you really want *elephant*. (This option is only available in Word.)

- ✔ **Find all word forms:** If you want to find all uses of a word, such as *sing*, *singing*, and *sings*. (This option is only available in Word.)

Finding and Replacing a Word or Phrase (Ctrl+H)

The Find and Replace command lets you look for a word or number and replace it with a different word or number. For example, you may misspell your boss's name as *Frank the Jerk* when his real title should be *Frank the Imbecile.* Although you could manually search for *Frank the Jerk* and replace it with *Frank the Imbecile,* it's easier to leave such mindless, tedious, boring tasks to your computer and Microsoft Office XP.

The Find and Replace command lets you search for specific strings. Unlike the Find command, the Find and Replace command also automatically replaces any text or numbers it finds with a new string of text or numbers.

When you press Ctrl+H to use the Find and Replace command, the Find and Replace dialog box appears and offers two buttons: Replace and Replace All.

The Replace button lets you review every string that Microsoft Office XP finds, so you can make sure that you really *want* to replace the string. The Replace All button doesn't give you the chance to review each string found; if you click the Replace All button, you may find Microsoft Office XP replacing words that you didn't really want to replace, so be careful.

Checking Your Spelling (F7)

Unfortunately, poor spelling can make even the most brilliantly written paper look amateurish and conceal its stellar quality. To prevent the raucous laughter of people who misconstrue such flaws as moronic, check your spelling before you let anyone see your files.

To check your spelling in a Microsoft Office XP document, press F7 or click the Spell Check button on the Standard toolbar.

If you don't want Office XP to spell-check your entire file, highlight the text you want to spell-check and then press F7.

Using Undo (Ctrl+Z) and Redo (Ctrl+Y)

Microsoft Office XP is a forgiving chunk of software. If you make a mistake at any time, you can undo your last action by clicking the Undo button on the Standard toolbar or by pressing Ctrl+Z.

Not all actions can be undone. When you're about to do something that Microsoft Office XP can't undo, a dialog box pops up to warn you that your next action is irreversible.

If you made a mistake undoing an action, click the Redo button on the Standard toolbar or press Ctrl+Y to redo your last undone action.

If you click the down arrow next to the Undo or Redo buttons on the Standard toolbar, a drop-down list of your past actions appears. To undo or redo multiple actions, drag the mouse to highlight the actions you want and then click the left mouse button.

Index

• G •

Gallery tab (Office Assistant), selecting new animations, 33
General tab (New Office Document dialog box), 13
General Templates dialog box (File menu), 48–49
Go To command
  navigating documents using, 63–64
  navigating worksheets using, 134
Gradient tab (Background dialog box), 204
grammar, checking in Word, 76–81
Grammar dialog box (Word), 77–78
graphics
  adding to framed Web pages, 337
  adding to slides, 205–207
  adding to Web pages, 322–324
  adding to Word documents, 116–123
  copying and pasting, 27–30
  deleting from slides, 211
  deleting from Word documents, 74
  moving in Word documents, 122–123
  wrapping text around, in Word, 121–122
greater than (>) operator (Excel), 148
greater than or equal to (>=) operator (Excel), 148
green wavy line, meaning of (Word), 77
grouping levels (Access), 308

• H •

handouts (PowerPoint), printing, 197
Hang Manager, 41
Hanging Indent icon (Word ruler), 60
Header and Footer dialog box (View menu), 112–114
header text box (Word), 113
headers (Word), 69, 111–113
headings (PowerPoint), converting to subheadings, 193–194
heights, of rows, adjusting
  in Excel, 141
  in Word, 103–106
Help menu
  Detect and Repair command, 40
  hiding/displaying Office Assistance, 32–33
  Office on the Web option, 38–39
  reactivating Office Assistant, 34

help systems
  Answer Wizard, 36
  available on Internet, 38–39
  basic Help window, 35
  Office Assistant, 31–37
  What's This? command, 38
Help window, 35
hiding
  menu commands, options for, 20–21
  Office Assistant, 32–33
Highlight button (Formatting toolbar, Word), 58
horizontal lines, in Web pages, 341–342
horizontal scroll bar
  using in Excel, 133
  using in Word, 53–54
HTM/HTML files, 52
HTML code, viewing, 328–329
hyperlinks
  adding to framed Web pages, 338
  adding to slides, 219–221
  using in Web pages, 326

• I •

I-beam pointer, 5
icons
  identifying, using What's This? command, 38
  for indents on ruler (Word), 60
  for Office programs, names of, 16
  for tab settings on ruler (Word), 59
  used in book, meaning of, 6
images. *See* graphics
importing
  clip art, 117–118
  text from other programs, 51–52
Inbox folder (Outlook), 256–258
  Delete button, 263
Increase Decimal button (Formatting toolbar, Excel), 136–137
Increase Font Size button (Formatting toolbar, PowerPoint), 184
Increase Indent button (Formatting toolbar)
  Excel, 136–137
  PowerPoint, 184
  Word, 58, 94

• Q •

• R •

FOR DUMMIES®

The easy way to get more done and have more fun

PERSONAL FINANCE & BUSINESS

0-7645-2431-3

0-7645-5331-3

0-7645-5307-0

Also available:

Accounting For Dummies
(0-7645-5314-3)

Business Plans Kit For
Dummies
(0-7645-5365-8)

Managing For Dummies
(1-5688-4858-7)

Mutual Funds For Dummies
(0-7645-5329-1)

QuickBooks All-in-One Desk
Reference For Dummies
(0-7645-1963-8)

Resumes For Dummies
(0-7645-5471-9)

Small Business Kit For
Dummies
(0-7645-5093-4)

Starting an eBay Business
For Dummies
(0-7645-1547-0)

Taxes For Dummies 2003
(0-7645-5475-1)

HOME, GARDEN, FOOD & WINE

0-7645-5295-3

0-7645-5130-2

0-7645-5250-3

Also available:

Bartending For Dummies
(0-7645-5051-9)

Christmas Cooking For
Dummies
(0-7645-5407-7)

Cookies For Dummies
(0-7645-5390-9)

Diabetes Cookbook For
Dummies
(0-7645-5230-9)

Grilling For Dummies
(0-7645-5076-4)

Home Maintenance For
Dummies
(0-7645-5215-5)

Slow Cookers For Dummies
(0-7645-5240-6)

Wine For Dummies
(0-7645-5114-0)

FITNESS, SPORTS, HOBBIES & PETS

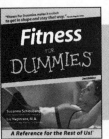

0-7645-5167-1

0-7645-5146-9

0-7645-5106-X

Also available:

Cats For Dummies
(0-7645-5275-9)

Chess For Dummies
(0-7645-5003-9)

Dog Training For Dummies
(0-7645-5286-4)

Labrador Retrievers For
Dummies
(0-7645-5281-3)

Martial Arts For Dummies
(0-7645-5358-5)

Piano For Dummies
(0-7645-5105-1)

Pilates For Dummies
(0-7645-5397-6)

Power Yoga For Dummies
(0-7645-5342-9)

Puppies For Dummies
(0-7645-5255-4)

Quilting For Dummies
(0-7645-5118-3)

Rock Guitar For Dummies
(0-7645-5356-9)

Weight Training For Dummies
(0-7645-5168-X)

Available wherever books are sold.
Go to www.dummies.com or call 1-877-762-2974 to order direct

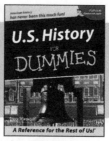

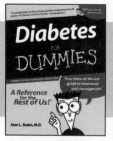

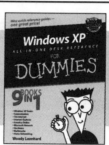

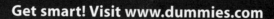

ATTICUS CLAW

Jennifer Gray is a barrister, so she knows how to spot a cat burglar when she sees one, especially when he's a large tabby with a chewed ear and a handkerchief round his neck that says Atticus Claw. Jennifer's other books include *Guinea Pigs Online*, a comedy series co-written with Amanda Swift and published by Quercus, and *Chicken Mission*, her new series for Faber. Jennifer lives in London and Scotland with her husband and four children, and, of course, Henry, a friendly but enigmatic cat.

By the same author

ATTICUS CLAW
Breaks the Law

ATTICUS CLAW
Settles a Score

ATTICUS CLAW
Lends a Paw

ATTICUS CLAW
Goes Ashore

ATTICUS CLAW
Learns to Draw

ATTICUS CLAW
on the Misty Moor

ATTICUS CLAW
Hears a Roar